THE
OREGON TRAIL

THE
OREGON TRAIL

AN ILLUSTRATED EDITION
OF FRANCIS PARKMAN'S WESTERN ADVENTURE

INTRODUCTION BY ANTHONY BRANDT

ZENITH
PRESS

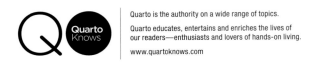

Quarto is the authority on a wide range of topics.

Quarto educates, entertains and enriches the lives of our readers—enthusiasts and lovers of hands-on living.

www.quartoknows.com

First published in 2015 by Zenith Press, an imprint of Quarto Publishing Group USA Inc., 400 First Avenue North, Suite 400, Minneapolis, MN 55401 USA. Telephone: (612) 344-8100 Fax: (612) 344-8692

quartoknows.com
Visit our blogs at quartoknows.com

Zenith Press titles are also available at discounts in bulk quantity for industrial or sales-promotional use. For details contact the Special Sales Manager at Quarto Publishing Group USA Inc., 400 First Avenue North, Suite 400, Minneapolis, MN 55401 USA.

10 9 8 7 6 5 4 3 2 1

ISBN: 978-0-7603-5024-9

Library of Congress Cataloging-in-Publication Data

Names: Parkman, Francis, 1823-1893, author.
Title: The Oregon Trail : an illustrated edition of Francis Parkman's western
   adventure / by Francis Parkman ; introduction by Anthony Brandt.
Description: Illustrated edition. | Minneapolis, Minnesota : Zenith Press,
   2016. | Includes index.
Identifiers: LCCN 2015040819 | ISBN 9780760350249 (plc w/ jkt)
Subjects: LCSH: West (U.S.)--Description and travel. | Indians of North
   America--West (U.S.) | Frontier and pioneer life--West (U.S.) | Oregon
   National Historic Trail. | California National Historic Trail. | West
   (U.S.)--History--To 1848. | Parkman, Francis, 1823-1893--Travel--West (U.S.)
Classification: LCC F592 .P284 2016 | DDC 917.8/0204--dc23
LC record available at http://lccn.loc.gov/2015040819

Zenith Press
Acquiring Editor: Erik Gilg
Project Manager: Madeleine Vasaly
Art Director: James Kegley

Whole Green Productions
Creative Director: Wendy Palitz
Editor: Anthony Brandt
Picture Research: Jennifer Berry
Project Manager: Mike Urban
Editorial Research: Sarah Richardson

Front cover and spine: N.C. Wyeth, Courtesy of the Wells Fargo History Museum, Phoenix, Arizona
Spine: Hagen & Pfau/Anzeiger des Westens/Library of Congress
Case: Henry Bryan Hall/Library of Congress; George Catlin/Paul Mellon Collection/National
   Gallery of Art, 1965.16.18
Endpapers: Charles W. Carter/Bridgeman Images
Facing title page: J.H. Colton/Library of Congress

Printed in China

CONTENTS

INTRODUCTION

BY ANTHONY BRANDT

Well traveled as it was, the Oregon Trail never became a comfortable or easy route to the West. Nobody ever graded it or smoothed it out, it had no signposts, and travelers commonly wandered off it and got lost. Eventually they could follow the ruts that the wagon wheels made in the dirt, but the ruts were not continuous. When they got into the mountains it was questionable whether they could take wagons over the passes or through the gorges, and ruts were no longer an issue. In the prairies, hired guides, who were usually ex-mountain men, led the way. In the mountains, they saved lives.

To venture along the 2,000-mile length of it, you took more than a ton of provisions, more if you had a big family. Among the unwise, it was common to take some of the stuff that people leaving home cannot imagine living without—like the bureau drawers your grandmother had originally brought with her from Boston. Abandoned furniture became one of the signs that let emigrants know they were still on the trail. That, and the graves. The first guidebooks recommended 200 pounds of flour per person, 100 pounds of bacon, and as much in the way of rice, beans, hardtack (ship's biscuits) as you could fit in. What else? Coffee, 75 pounds, salt and pepper, 25 pounds, sugar, dried fruit, cooking utensils, tools, clothes, bedding, pistols, rifles, and plenty of ammunition.

All these things, and courage.

The first such emigrant wagon train left Independence, Missouri, in 1841, but it was small—in the end, 34 survivors made it to California. By 1846, when young Francis Parkman set out on the trail, most emigrants were going to Oregon; California by then had an easier trail through the Southwest. Parkman had no interest in going to either place.

He was not an emigrant looking for fresh land, or out to make a new start in life, nor did he need to escape the law. He came from Boston, a scion of one of its most distinguished families. He had gone to Harvard, and he had spent summers in the Maine wilderness, exploring, hunting, camping, often by himself. He already had a fixed purpose in life—to write the history of the contest between the French and the English for control of North America. To do that, he believed, he needed to learn as much as possible about the Indian way of life. No such way of life existed any more in the East.

He went west, therefore, to find it, to find Indians as yet relatively uninfected by the western version of civilization and, if he could, to live with them for a while. Joining a wagon train was not the way to accomplish this goal, nor would it have been anything but suicidal to go alone. So, he and two friends ventured out in a party of their own, joined by a few Englishmen who traveled with them from time to time, on the Oregon Trail. It was both research and adventure for Parkman. Out of it came this American classic you hold in your hands, the first great literature about the West since the *Journals of Lewis and Clark*.

It was a courageous adventure indeed that Parkman undertook. You never knew, for one thing, how Indians were going to react to the presence of whites, and each tribe was different. For another, Parkman was frequently ill, coming down unexpectedly with something that was never diagnosed but would render him so weak he could barely mount a horse, that sometimes made him semi-blind for long periods of time, and that afflicted him all his life. But he achieved his goal, living for several weeks with a movable village of Oglala Sioux as it ventured into dangerous Snake Indian territory in the foothills of the Rockies in search of buffalo, whose fresh skins they needed to replace the old, worn-out ones they were using to cover their teepees. His description of these Indians and their lives forms the vivid heart of the book. Parkman joins buffalo hunts, lives in the lodge of one of the chiefs, watches children play their wild games, women do the everlasting work of cooking and cleaning, old men telling stories, and young men boasting of their exploits. He has with him a French half-breed, Reynal, married to a Sioux squaw, who speaks the language.

What is it, he asked the Sioux, that makes the thunder? "At last old Mene-Seela, or Red-Water, . . . looked up with his withered face, and said he had always known what the thunder was. It was a great black bird; and once he had seen it in a dream, swooping down from the Black Hills, with its loud-roaring wings, and when it flapped them over a lake, they struck lightning from the water."

One day, sitting among the chiefs, one picked up a large black and green cricket, known to the Sioux as "They who point out the buffalo."

"Tell me, my father, where must we go tomorrow to find the buffalo?" this chief asked the cricket. The cricket's long horns seemed to point west. Next day they went west—and found buffalo.

American pioneers circa 1850.

He describes watching a slim teenage boy riding a horse bareback, no stirrups, using a piece of the horse's mane as a rein, chasing a buffalo at full speed with his bow and arrows, and at full speed arming the bow and shooting arrow after arrow into the beast until it fell. They ate the best pieces of a buffalo they had killed immediately—and raw. They also ate pemmican, that universal concoction of tribes in the West: dried buffalo meat, berries, and fat. Parkman partook of it and pronounced it good. At one point, Parkman arranges a feast of dog for the village; dog was a delicacy for the Sioux, and they had hundreds of them around the camp.

Mene-Seela proved to be a great friend to whites. He told Parkman that "he considered the beaver and the whites the wisest people on earth; indeed, he was convinced they were the same." How so? Once as a young boy he had wormed his way into a beaver lodge by swimming underwater to the entrance, nearly suffocating in the dark tunnels. He fell

into a swoon, and then, when he began to revive, he dimly saw three forms before him, three people, entirely white, sitting at the edge of a black pool of water. When he reached daylight again, he made a hole in the lodge from above with his war club and seized three beaver when they emerged. These, he said, must have been the three white people he saw. He had never seen a white man before this happened.

So it goes on. Parkman describes the feats in battle—and the cruelties—of a chief named Kongra-Tonga, the weapons and magnificent dress of a warrior named White Shield. They are fierce, no question about it, but a bad dream can stop an Indian from joining a war party. They believe in their dreams as if they were real. They believe in fate. If an Indian feels himself doomed, he will take on a grizzly bear single-handed or ride into the midst of an enemy camp in order to get rid of his unfortunate life.

These Sioux were friendly and even felt honored by Parkman's stay with them, but he was always aware that much depended on his partnership with the Frenchman Reynal and Reynals's Sioux wife, and that much also depended on the gifts he scattered about during his stay. He also knew that if he had met a group of Sioux warriors while alone on the plains or wandered into their camp at night, they might just as easily have slaughtered him. Most of the emigrants on the Oregon Trail whom Indians killed were killed this way— not in attacks on the wagon trains, which after 1842 only grew more formidable, numbering over a thousand people most years, but as stragglers, or men who had foolishly ridden out alone or with one or two others, or who had forgotten their rifles.

Many emigrants died on the trail, but not this way. They died trying to ford swollen rivers; they died of disease and once in a while of starvation; they died in accidents with guns, which were common. They died of ignorance, not knowing the ways of the West, not knowing how to find water, growing careless or arrogant, losing the trail and never finding it again.

Parkman had little interest in the emigrants he met, looking down on them with patrician disdain, and we leave him here after his stay with the Oglala Sioux. His book is mistitled. Parkman only traveled on the Oregon Trail for a third of its distance, never got into the Rockies, and abandoned the route to turn south toward the Santa Fe Trail and make for home via the Arkansas River. Accordingly, we have truncated his text to make room for selections from the many accounts by emigrants of their experiences on the trail.

These accounts are just as vivid as Parkman's in many respects, yet quite different. Theirs were not expeditions of a few men but caravans numbering in the hundreds or a thousand or more. More than a thousand such caravans left Independence the spring of 1843. Nearly 900 made it to Oregon in October and November. This, too, was like a traveling village, but unlike the Sioux's, theirs had elected governments, rules, and work assignments. Some of them took herds of cattle. They took liquor to trade, contributing to the long drunk that eventually destroyed Indian culture. They took dreams: Richer land. Manifest Destiny. Trade with Asia. Better climate. A better life. They embodied

American restlessness, that urge to go west, dating to the early 1600s, when, even in Plymouth Colony, groups of colonists abandoned the community and made their way into the Connecticut River valley because the land there was better.

The emigrants were primarily middle class. You needed money to make the trip, at least $1,000 when $1,000 was a significant amount of money, enough to buy a house. You had to contribute to the paying of guides, you had to pay for horses if you took them, oxen to haul the wagons, provisions, equipment, the wagons themselves, and you had to take cash for getting started again in Oregon. Women generally were reluctant to go, but they knew if they stayed behind, they might never see their husbands again.

But the way was difficult. The mountains were especially hard, but even on the Great Plains the terrain was by no means easy. Land that looked flat from a distance was riddled with cliffs, steep ravines, creeks and rivers that had to be crossed, and plentiful mud. Huge thunderstorms rose up suddenly out of the west, yet the land was arid. Even though the trail followed the South Platte River to Fort Laramie, clean spring water was scarce. The main cause of death on the trail, after accidental shootings, was drowning. Forty-nine emigrants drowned at the crossing of the North Platte in 1849-50. The South Platte, a river that in the plains was described as "a mile wide and an inch deep," was treacherous enough when it had to be crossed: In 1850, nineteen people drowned at the crossing of the South Platte near Fort Laramie, close to its source.

The plains were treeless. Sometimes cottonwood trees grew in the river bottoms, but for long stretches there were no trees at all. When wood was unavailable, the emigrants used "buffalo chips" (dried buffalo dung) for fuel. Usually it was the children's job to gather it. Women managed the children, and their work on the trail and in the camp was, as the saying goes, never done. The women faced other problems, too. Lack of privacy was one. The prairie did not provide bathroom facilities. The voluminous skirts standard at the time harbored large numbers of mosquitoes. And how do you manage a family of restless young children in a covered wagon?

The plains had other dangers, like rattlesnakes, prickly pear cactus, gopher holes, wolves, and the Pawnee, whom everyone despised for their untrustworthiness and thievery. But the mountains, beautiful and majestic as they were, and a relief from the barrenness and aridity of the plains, were the real barrier the emigrants faced.

The route had been pioneered years before by a party going the other way, the American founders of John Jacob Astor's fur-trading settlement, Astoria, near the mouth of the Columbia River. When Astor's facilities were taken over by the British early in the War of 1812, the Americans were forced out and returned to civilization via the mountains, taking a more southerly route than Lewis and Clark to avoid hostile Indian tribes. They discovered South Pass, a broad, 35-mile-wide, windswept area south of the Wind

485

Indian Lodges of Buffalo skins & Cedar poles.

Diameter 18 feet; height 20ft.   Notice method of fastening covering on frame;

also arrangement for ventillation; the entrance as closed where occupants are out.

Shield with scalp in centre, on tripod in fore-ground.

Teepees constructed from cedar poles and buffalo skins at a Comanche camp in Indian Territory circa 1872.

River range of the Rockies and the lowest crossing on the Continental Divide. Before the railroads came, half a million emigrants would traverse South Pass. They got there by way of the Sweetwater River, a tributary of the North Platte, and then took a zigzag route through valleys to the north until they reached the Snake River, one of the West's wildest rivers, "the river of no return."

This was perhaps the toughest country they had experienced so far—300 miles of desolation, rocky and forbidding, running through what is now southern Idaho, an arid area of little game and thick with the sagebrush and artemisia that was such a hardship to drag wagons through. To call the terrain rocky doesn't quite cover it; the rocks were often razor-sharp obsidian, which cut the hooves of the oxen so badly the trail would at times be red with blood. Mosquitoes here were a hell of their own, covering every part of an animal except its eyes. The horses would whinny and moan all night long. Sleep was impossible.

The rivers were running west now, toward the emigrants' destination, but the Snake was impassible and the Columbia nearly so. In the mountains, emigrant trains would sometimes fall apart, as their various factions, which were inevitable in such large groups, grew increasingly hostile, or as provisions ran low, wagons broke down, and livestock became a drag on their owners. The forts along the way were not military forts; they were trading posts that sold provisions at exorbitant prices. In 1843 the wagon train reached Fort Hall, on the Snake, only to find that the first Fremont expedition had already reached it and bought up all the supplies. Starvation was always a possibility in the mountains.

The final obstacle on the trail was the rapids on the Columbia River. By this time winter was approaching, snow flurries were blowing, the emigrants were desperate to reach the Willamette Valley, the paradise they all sought. Most emigrants abandoned their wagons at the Columbia and chose to buy boats from the Hudson's Bay Company and brave the rapids, almost always with an Indian guide. These rapids were far rougher than anyone from the East had ever seen. People regularly died in them. Those who didn't buy boats built rafts out of pine logs, six or eight of them, twenty feet long, lashed together. Some families broke down their wagons into parts and tied them to their rafts.

Did they all make it? Emigrants had reached the limits of endurance by this time. They might be eating insects, berries, roots, acorns; they were certainly exhausted, and they must have wondered whether it had all been worth it. But most of them did make it. They were in Oregon at last, they had reached the promised land, found their fruitful valley. When news of their success got back to the East, more people would come each year, and each year after that. Oregon would fill up with Americans, as Texas had done a decade or so before, as the entire continent below Canada and above Mexico would in the end. It's an amazing story. Here we get a glimpse of the personal suffering, the courage, the endurance that it took to make the West what it became: American.

NOTE TO THE READER:
The text of the book has largely been left in the style, usage, vocabulary, and spellings that Francis Parkman and the other contributors employed in their original works. The book's introduction, captions, and other notations reflect contemporary style, usage, and spellings.

A bird's-eye view of St. Louis in the mid-1800s. Francis Parkman's journey embarked from this city in 1846.

THE FRONTIER

Last spring, 1846, was a busy season in the City of St. Louis. Not only were emigrants from every part of the country preparing for the journey to Oregon and California, but an unusual number of traders were making ready their wagons and outfits for Santa Fe. Many of the emigrants, especially those bound for California, were persons of wealth and standing. The hotels were crowded, and the gunsmiths and saddlers were kept constantly at work in providing arms and equipment for the different parties of travelers. Almost every day steamboats were leaving the levee and passing up the Missouri, crowded with passengers on their way to the frontier.

In one of these, the *Radnor*, since snagged and lost, my friend and relative, Quincy A. Shaw, and myself left St. Louis on the 28th of April, on a tour of curiosity and amusement to the Rocky Mountains. The boat was loaded until the water broke alternately over her guards. Her upper deck was covered with large weapons of a peculiar form, for the Santa Fe trade, and her hold was crammed with goods for the same destination. There were also the equipment and provisions of a party of Oregon emigrants, a band of mules and horses, piles of saddles and harness, and a multitude of nondescript articles, indispensable on the prairies. Almost hidden in this medley one might have seen a small French cart, of the sort very appropriately called a "mule-killer" beyond the frontiers, and not far distant a tent, together with a miscellaneous assortment of boxes and barrels. The whole equipage was far from prepossessing in its appearance; yet, such as it was, it was destined to a long and arduous journey, on which the persevering reader will accompany it.

The passengers on board the *Radnor* corresponded with her freight. In her cabin were Santa Fe traders, gamblers, speculators, and adventurers of various descriptions, and her steerage was crowded with Oregon emigrants, "mountain men," negroes, and a party of Kansas Indians, who had been on a visit to St. Louis.

Thus laden, the boat struggled upward for seven or eight days against the rapid current of the Missouri, grating upon snags, and hanging for two or three hours at a time upon sand-bars. We entered the mouth of the Missouri in a drizzling rain, but the weather soon became clear, and showed distinctly the broad and turbid river, with its eddies, its sand-bars, its ragged islands, and forest-covered shores. The Missouri is constantly changing its course; wearing away its banks on one side, while it forms new ones on the other. Its channel is shifting continually. Islands are formed, and then washed away; and while the old forests on one side are undermined and swept off, a young growth springs up from the new soil upon the other. With all these changes, the water is so charged with mud and sand that it is perfectly opaque, and in a few minutes deposits a sediment an inch thick in the bottom of a tumbler. The river was now high; but when we descended in the autumn it was fallen very low, and all the secrets of its treacherous shallows were exposed to view. It was frightful to see the dead and broken trees, thick-set as a military abatis, firmly imbedded in the sand, and all pointing down stream, ready to impale any unhappy steamboat that at high water should pass over that dangerous ground.

In five or six days we began to see signs of the great western movement that was then taking place. Parties of emigrants, with their tents and wagons, would be encamped on open spots near the bank, on their way to the common rendezvous at Independence. On a rainy day, near sunset, we reached the landing of this place, which is situated some miles from the river, on the extreme frontier of Missouri. The scene was characteristic, for here were represented at one view the most remarkable features of this wild and enterprising region. On the muddy shore stood some thirty or forty dark slavish-looking Spaniards, gazing stupidly out from beneath their broad hats. They were attached to one of the Santa Fe companies, whose wagons were crowded together on the banks above. In the midst of these, crouching over a smoldering fire, was a group of Indians, belonging to a remote Mexican tribe. One or two French hunters from the mountains with their long hair and buckskin dresses, were looking at the boat; and seated on a log close at hand were three men, with rifles lying across their knees. The foremost of these, a tall, strong figure, with a clear blue eye and an open, intelligent face, might very well represent that race of restless and intrepid pioneers whose axes and rifles have opened a path from the Alleghenies to the western prairies. He was on his way to Oregon, probably a more congenial field to him than any that now remained on this side the great plains.

Early on the next morning we reached Kansas, about five hundred miles from the mouth of the Missouri. Here we landed and leaving our equipment in charge of my good friend Colonel Chick, whose log-house was the substitute for a tavern, we set out in a wagon for Westport, where we hoped to procure mules and horses for the journey.

A pioneer family heading west in the Loup valley of Nebraska in 1886.

It was a remarkably fresh and beautiful May morning. The rich and luxuriant woods through which the miserable road conducted us were lighted by the bright sunshine and enlivened by a multitude of birds. We overtook on the way our late fellow-travelers, the Kansas Indians, who, adorned with all their finery, were proceeding homeward at a round pace; and whatever they might have seemed on board the boat, they made a very striking and picturesque feature in the forest landscape.

Westport was full of Indians, whose little shaggy ponies were tied by dozens along the houses and fences. Sacs and Foxes, with shaved heads and painted faces, Shawanoes and Delawares, fluttering in calico frocks, and turbans, Wyandottes dressed like white men, and a few wretched Kansas wrapped in old blankets, were strolling about the streets, or lounging in and out of the shops and houses.

As I stood at the door of the tavern, I saw a remarkable looking person coming up the street. He had a ruddy face, garnished with the stumps of a bristly red beard and mustache; on one side of his head was a round cap with a knob at the top, such as Scottish laborers sometimes wear; his coat was of a nondescript form, and made of a gray Scotch plaid, with the fringes hanging all about it; he wore pantaloons of coarse homespun, and hob-nailed shoes; and to complete his equipment, a little black pipe was stuck in one corner of his mouth. In this curious attire, I recognized Captain C. of the British army, who, with his brother, and Mr. R., an English gentleman, was bound on a hunting expedition across the continent. I had seen the captain and his companions at St. Louis. They had now been for some time at Westport, making preparations for their departure, and waiting for a re-enforcement, since they were too few in number to attempt it alone. They might, it is true, have joined some of the parties of emigrants who were on the point of setting out for Oregon and California; but they professed great disinclination to have any connection with the "Kentucky fellows."

The captain now urged it upon us, that we should join forces and proceed to the mountains in company. Feeling no greater partiality for the society of the emigrants than they did, we thought the arrangement an advantageous one, and consented to it. Our future fellow-travelers had installed themselves in a little log-house, where we found them all surrounded by saddles, harness, guns, pistols, telescopes, knives, and in short their complete appointments for the prairie. R., who professed a taste for natural history, sat at a table stuffing a woodpecker; the brother of the captain, who was an Irishman, was splicing a trail-rope on the floor, as he had been an amateur sailor. The captain pointed out, with much complacency, the different articles of their outfit. "You see," said he, "that we are all old travelers. I am convinced that no party ever went upon the prairie better provided." The hunter whom they had employed, a surly looking Canadian, named Sorel, and their muleteer, an American from St. Louis, were lounging about the building. In a little log stable close at hand were their horses and mules, selected by the captain, who was an excellent judge.

Magnet for Migrants

From *Ox-Team Days on the Oregon Trail*

BY EZRA MEEKER

With his wife and newborn son, Meeker headed west from Iowa in 1852 to settle a farm in Oregon. He became a prolific writer about the pioneer experience.

I vowed then and there that I did not like the Iowa climate, and the Oregon fever that had already seized me was heightened. The settlement of the northern boundary by treaty in 1846 had ended the dispute between the United States and Great Britain for ownership of the region north of the Columbia. As a consequence, American settlers were beginning to cross the Columbia in numbers, and stories were coming back of the wonderful climate, the rich soil, and the wealth of lumber. The Oregon Country of that day included the present states of Oregon and Washington, and parts of Idaho and Wyoming.

It was a special consideration for us that if we went to Oregon the government would give us 320 acres of land, whereas in Iowa we should have to purchase it…There were no preemption laws or beneficial homestead laws in force then.

Blacksmiths played a critical role in the westward migration.

The alliance entered into, we left them to complete their arrangements, while we pushed our own to all convenient speed. The emigrants for whom our friends professed such contempt were encamped on the prairie about eight or ten miles distant, to the number of a thousand or more, and new parties were constantly passing out from Independence to join them. They were in great confusion, holding meetings, passing resolutions, and drawing up regulations, but unable to unite in the choice of leaders to conduct them across the prairie. Being at leisure one day, I rode over to Independence. The town was crowded. A multitude of shops had sprung up to furnish the emigrants and Santa Fe traders with necessaries for their journey; and there was an incessant hammering and banging from a dozen blacksmiths' sheds, where the heavy wagons were being repaired, and the horses and oxen shod. The streets were thronged with men, horses, and mules. While I was in the town, a train of emigrant wagons from Illinois passed through, to join the camp on the prairie, and stopped in the principal street. A multitude of healthy children's faces were peeping out from under the covers of the wagons. Here and there a buxom damsel was seated on horseback, holding over her sunburnt face an old umbrella or a parasol, once gaudy enough but now miserably faded. The men, very sober-looking countrymen, stood about their oxen; and as I passed I noticed three old fellows, who, with their long whips in their hands, were zealously discussing the doctrine of regeneration. The emigrants, however, are not all of this stamp. Among them are some of the vilest outcasts in the country. I have often perplexed myself to divine the various motives that give impulse to this strange migration; but whatever they may be, whether an insane hope of a better condition in life, or a desire of shaking off restraints of law and society, or mere restlessness, certain it is that multitudes bitterly repent the journey, and after they have reached the land of promise are happy enough to escape from it.

In the course of seven or eight days we had brought our preparations near to a close. Meanwhile our friends had completed theirs, and becoming tired of Westport, they told us that they would set out in advance and wait at the crossing of the Kansas till we should come up. Accordingly R. and the muleteers went forward with the wagon and tent, while the captain and his brother, together with Sorel, and a trapper named Boisverd, who had joined them, followed with the band of horses. The commencement of the journey was ominous, for the captain was scarcely a mile from Westport, riding along in state at the head of his party, leading his intended buffalo horse by a rope, when a tremendous thunderstorm came on, and drenched them all to the skin. They hurried on to reach the place, about seven miles off, where R. was to have had the camp in readiness to receive them. But this prudent person, when he saw the storm approaching, had selected a sheltered glade in the woods, where he pitched his tent, and was sipping a comfortable cup of coffee, while the captain galloped for miles beyond through the rain to look for him. At length the storm cleared away, and the

Mormon emigrants wait in long lines to
cross the Missouri River in 1856. "Green
River Crossing," by W. H. Jackson.

sharp-eyed trapper succeeded in discovering his tent: R. had by this time finished his coffee, and was seated on a buffalo robe smoking his pipe. The captain was one of the most easy-tempered men in existence, so he bore his ill-luck with great composure, shared the dregs of the coffee with his brother, and lay down to sleep in his wet clothes.

We ourselves had our share of the deluge. We were leading a pair of mules to Kansas when the storm broke. Such sharp and incessant flashes of lightning, such stunning and continuous thunder, I have never known before. The woods were completely obscured by the diagonal sheets of rain that fell with a heavy roar, and rose in spray from the ground; and the streams rose so rapidly that we could hardly ford them. At length, looming through the rain, we saw the log-house of Colonel Chick, who received us with his usual bland hospitality; while his wife, who, though a little soured and stiffened by too frequent attendance on camp-meetings, was not behind him in hospitable feeling, supplied us with the means of repairing our drenched and bedraggled condition. The storm, clearing away at about sunset, opened a noble prospect from the porch of the colonel's house, which stands upon a high hill.

Returning on the next day to Westport, we received a message from the captain, who had ridden back to deliver it in person, but finding that we were in Kansas, had intrusted it with an acquaintance of his named Vogel, who kept a small grocery and liquor shop. Whisky by the way circulates more freely in Westport than is altogether safe in a place where every man carries a loaded pistol in his pocket. As we passed this establishment, we saw Vogel's broad German face and knavish-looking eyes thrust from his door. He said he had something to tell us, and invited us to take a dram. Neither his liquor nor his message was very palatable. The captain had returned to give us notice that R., who assumed the direction of his party, had determined upon another route from that agreed upon between us; and instead of taking the course of the traders, to pass northward by Fort Leavenworth, and follow the path marked out by the dragoons in their expedition of last summer. Suppressing our dissatisfaction as well as we could, we made up our minds to join them at Fort Leavenworth, where they were to wait for us.

Accordingly, our preparation being now complete, we attempted one fine morning to commence our journey. The first step was an unfortunate one. No sooner were our animals put in harness, than the shaft mule reared and plunged, burst ropes and straps, and nearly flung the cart into the Missouri. Finding her wholly uncontrollable, we exchanged her for another, with which we were furnished by our friend Mr. Boone of Westport, a grandson of Daniel Boone, the pioneer. This foretaste of prairie experience was very soon followed by another. Westport was scarcely out of sight, when we encountered a deep muddy gully, of a species that afterward became but too familiar to us; and here for the space of an hour or more the car stuck fast.

The Original Oregon Trailblazer

From *Oregon, or a Short History of a Long Journey from the Atlantic Ocean to the Region of the Pacific by Land*

By John Wyeth

More than a decade before Francis Parkman's travels, the Oregon Trail had an informal lobbyist, Boston educator Hall J. Kelley. Although Kelley failed to interest Congress in supporting the settlement of Oregon, he ignited the curiosity of enterprising New England businessman Nathaniel Wyeth (cousin of John Wyeth), who led an expedition establishing the route of the trail in 1832.

Mr. Hall J. Kelley's writing operated like a match applied to the combustible matter accumulated in the mind of the energetic Nathaniel J. Wyeth. Mr. Wyeth had listened with peculiar delight to all the flattering accounts from the Western regions. Mr. Wyeth, leader of the Band of the Oregon adventurers, after having inspired twenty-one persons with his own high hopes and expectations (among whom was his own brother, Dr. Jacob Wyeth, and a gun-smith, a blacksmith, two carpenters, and two fishermen, the rest being farmers and laborers, brought up to no particular trade) was ready, with his companions, to start off to the Pacific Ocean, the first of March, to go from Boston to the mouth of the Columbia River by land.

The company were uniform in their dress. Each one wore a coarse woollen jacket and pantaloons, a striped cotton shirt, and cowhide boots; every man had a musket, most of them rifles, all of them bayonets in a broad belt, together with a large clasped knife for eating and common purposes. The Captain and one or two more added pistols; but every one had in his belt a small axe. This uniformity had a pleasing effect, which, together with their curious wagons, was noticed with commendation in the Baltimore newspapers, as a striking contrast with the family emigrants of husband, wife, and children, who have for thirty years and more passed on to the Ohio, Kentucky, and other territories. The whole bore an aspect of energy, good contrivance, and competent means. I forgot to mention that we carried tents, camp-kettles, and the common utensils for cooking victuals, as our plan was to live like soldiers, and to avoid, as much as possible, inns and taverns.

The real and avowed object of this hardy-looking enterprise was to go to the river Columbia, otherwise called the river Oregon, or river of the West, which empties by a very wide mouth into the Pacific Ocean, and there and thereabouts commence a fur trade by trafficking with the Indians, as well as beaver and other hunting by ourselves.

American quail, a common sight on the Great Plains.

Breaking the Ice

Both Shaw and myself were tolerably inured to the vicissitudes of traveling. We had experienced them under various forms, and a birch canoe was as familiar to us as a steamboat. The restlessness, the love of wilds and hatred of cities, natural perhaps in early years to every unperverted son of Adam, was not our only motive for undertaking the present journey. My companion hoped to shake off the effects of a disorder that had impaired a constitution originally hardy and robust; and I was anxious to pursue some inquiries relative to the character and usages of the remote Indian nations, being already familiar with many of the border tribes.

Emerging from the mud-hole where we last took leave of the reader, we pursued our way for some time along the narrow track, in the checkeredsunshine and shadow of the woods, till at length, issuing forth into the broad light, we left behind us the farthest outskirts of that great forest, that once spread unbroken from the western plains to the shore of the Atlantic. Looking over an intervening belt of shrubbery, we saw the green, oceanlike expanse of prairie, stretching swell over swell to the horizon.

It was a mild, calm spring day; a day when one is more disposed to musing and reverie than to action, and the softest part of his nature is apt to gain the ascendency. I rode in advance of the party, as we passed through the shrubbery, and as a nook of green grass offered a strong temptation, I dismounted and lay down there. All the trees and saplings were in flower, or budding into fresh leaf; the red clusters of the maple-blossoms and the rich flowers of the Indian apple were there in profusion; and I was half inclined to regret leaving behind the land of gardens for the rude and stern scenes of the prairie and the mountains.

Meanwhile the party came in sight from out of the bushes. Foremost rode Henry Chatillon, our guide and hunter, a fine athletic figure, mounted on a hardy gray Wyandotte pony. He wore a white blanket-coat, a broad hat of felt, moccasins, and pantaloons of deerskin, ornamented along the seams with rows of long fringes. His knife was stuck in his belt; his bullet-pouch and powder-horn hung at his side, and his rifle lay before him, resting against the high pommel of his saddle, which, like all his equipment, had seen hard service, and was much the worse for wear. Shaw followed close, mounted on a little sorrel horse, and leading a larger animal by a rope. His outfit, which resembled mine, had been provided with a view to use rather than ornament. It consisted of a plain, black Spanish saddle, with holsters of heavy pistols, a blanket rolled up behind it, and the trail-rope attached to his horse's neck hanging coiled in front. He carried a double-barreled smooth-bore, while I boasted a rifle of some fifteen pounds' weight. At that time our attire, though far from elegant, bore some marks of civilization, and offered a very favorable contrast to the inimitable shabbiness of our appearance on the return journey. A red flannel shirt, belted around the waist like a frock, then constituted our upper garment; moccasins had supplanted our failing boots; and the remaining essential portion of our attire consisted of an extraordinary article, manufactured by a squaw out of smoked buckskin. Our muleteer, Delorier, brought up the rear with his cart, waddling ankle-deep in the mud, alternately puffing at his pipe, and ejaculating in his prairie patois: "Sacré enfant de garce!" as one of the mules would seem to recoil before some abyss of unusual profundity. The cart was of the kind that one may see by scores around the market-place in Montreal, and had a white covering to protect the articles within. These were our provisions and a tent, with ammunition, blankets, and presents for the Indians.

We were in all four men with eight animals; for besides the spare horses led by Shaw and myself, an additional mule was driven along with us as a reserve in case of accident.

After this summing up of our forces, it may not be amiss to glance at the characters of the two men who accompanied us.

Delorier was a Canadian, with all the characteristics of the true Jean Baptiste. Neither fatigue, exposure, nor hard labor could ever impair his cheerfulness and gayety, or his obsequious politeness to his bourgeois; and when night came he would sit down by the fire, smoke his pipe, and tell stories with the utmost contentment. In fact, the prairie was his congenial element. Henry Chatillon was of a different stamp. When we were at St. Louis, several gentlemen of the Fur Company had kindly offered to procure for us a hunter and guide suited for our purposes, and on coming one afternoon to the office, we found there a tall and exceedingly well-dressed man with a face so open and frank that it attracted our notice at once. We were surprised at being told that it was he who wished to guide us to the mountains. He was born in a little French town near St. Louis, and from the age of fifteen years had been

constantly in the neighborhood of the Rocky Mountains, employed for the most part by the Company to supply their forts with buffalo meat. As a hunter he had but one rival in the whole region, a man named Cimoneau, with whom, to the honor of both of them, he was on terms of the closest friendship. He had arrived at St. Louis the day before, from the mountains, where he had remained for four years; and he now only asked to go and spend a day with his mother before setting out on another expedition. His age was about thirty; he was six feet high, and very powerfully and gracefully molded. The prairies had been his school; he could neither read nor write, but he had a natural refinement and delicacy of mind such as is rarely found, even in women. His manly face was a perfect mirror of uprightness, simplicity, and kindness of heart; he had, moreover, a keen perception of character and a tact that would preserve him from flagrant error in any society. Henry had not the restless energy of an Anglo-American. He was content to take things as he found them; and his chief fault arose from an excess of easy generosity, impelling him to give away too profusely ever to thrive in the world. Yet it was commonly remarked of him, that whatever he might choose to do with what belonged to himself, the property of others was always safe in his hands. His bravery was as much celebrated in the mountains as his skill in hunting; but it is characteristic of him that in a country where the rifle is the chief arbiter between man and man, Henry was very seldom involved in quarrels. Once or twice, indeed, his quiet good-nature had been mistaken and presumed upon, but the consequences of the error were so formidable that no one was ever known to repeat it. No better evidence of the intrepidity of his temper could be wished than the common report that he had killed more than thirty grizzly bears. He was a proof of what unaided nature will sometimes do. I have never, in the city or in the wilderness, met a better man than my noble and true-hearted friend, Henry Chatillon.

We were soon free of the woods and bushes, and fairly upon the broad prairie. Now and then a Shawanoe passed us, riding his little shaggy pony at a "lope"; his calico shirt, his gaudy sash, and the gay handkerchief bound around his snaky hair fluttering in the wind. At noon we stopped to rest not far from a little creek replete with frogs and young turtles. There had been an Indian encampment at the place, and the framework of their lodges still remained, enabling us very easily to gain a shelter from the sun, by merely spreading one or two blankets over them. Thus shaded, we sat upon our saddles, and Shaw for the first time lighted his favorite Indian pipe; while Delorier was squatted over a hot bed of coals, shading his eyes with one hand, and holding a little stick in the other, with which he regulated the hissing contents of the frying-pan. The horses were turned to feed among the scattered bushes of a low oozy meadow. A drowsy springlike sultriness pervaded the air, and the voices of ten thousand young frogs and insects, just awakened into life, rose in varied chorus from the creek and the meadows.

Scarcely were we seated when a visitor approached. This was an old Kansas Indian; a man of distinction, if one might judge from his dress. His head was shaved and painted red, and from the tuft of hair remaining on the crown dangled several eagles' feathers, and the tails of two or three rattlesnakes. His cheeks, too, were daubed with vermilion; his ears were adorned with green glass pendants; a collar of grizzly bears' claws surrounded his neck, and several large necklaces of wampum hung on his breast. Having shaken us by the hand with a cordial grunt of salutation, the old man, dropping his red blanket from his shoulders, sat down cross-legged on the ground. In the absence of liquor we offered him a cup of sweetened water, at which he ejaculated "Good!" and was beginning to tell us how great a man he was, and how many Pawnees he had killed, when suddenly a motley concourse appeared wading across the creek toward us. They filed past in rapid succession, men, women, and children; some were on horseback, some on foot, but all were alike squalid and wretched. Old squaws, mounted astride of shaggy, meager little ponies, with perhaps one or two snake-eyed children seated behind them, clinging to their tattered blankets; tall lank young men on foot, with bows and arrows in their hands; and girls whose native ugliness not all the charms of glass beads and scarlet cloth could disguise, made up the procession; although here and there was a man who, like our visitor, seemed to hold some rank in this respectable community. They were the dregs of the Kansas nation, who, while their betters were gone to hunt buffalo, had left the village on a begging expedition to Westport.

When this ragamuffin horde had passed, we caught our horses, saddled, harnessed, and resumed our journey. Fording the creek, the low roofs of a number of rude buildings appeared, rising from a cluster of groves and woods on the left; and riding up through a long lane, amid a profusion of wild roses and early spring flowers, we found the log-church and school-houses belonging to the Methodist Shawanoe Mission. The Indians were on the point of gathering to a religious meeting. Some scores of them, tall men in half-civilized dress, were seated on wooden benches under the trees; while their horses were tied to the sheds and fences. Their chief, Parks, a remarkably large and athletic man, was just arrived from Westport, where he owns a trading establishment. Beside this, he has a fine farm and a considerable number of slaves. Indeed the Shawanoes have made greater progress in agriculture than any other tribe on the Missouri frontier; and both in appearance and in character form a marked contrast to our late acquaintance, the Kansas.

A few hours' ride brought us to the banks of the river Kansas. Traversing the woods that lined it, and plowing through the deep sand, we encamped not far from the bank, at the Lower Delaware crossing. Our tent was erected for the first time on a meadow close to the woods, and the camp preparations being complete we began to think of supper. An old Delaware woman, of some three hundred pounds' weight, sat in the porch of a little log-house close to the water, and a very pretty half-breed girl was engaged, under her superintendence, in feeding a large flock of turkeys that were fluttering and gobbling about the door. But no offers of money, or even of tobacco, could induce her to part with one of her favorites; so I took my rifle, to see if the woods or the river could furnish us

The Things We Carried

By Narcissa Whitman

Narcissa Whitman and her husband, Marcus Whitman, were Protestant missionaries who traveled west with a trapper's expedition in 1836. Leaving St. Louis in April, they arrived in Fort Vancouver on the Columbia River in September. Narcissa Whitman is known as the first white woman to cross the continent. Her diaries and letters are filled with vivid details of their daily life. This diary entry was written shortly after they began their journey.

I had made for me, in Brother Augustus' shoe store, in Rushville, a pair of gentlemen's boots, and from him we supplied ourselves with what shoes we wanted. We have each of us a life-preserver, so that if we fall into the water we shall not drown. They are made of India-rubber cloth, air-tight, and when filled with air and placed under the arm will prevent one from sinking. Each of us takes a plate, knife and fork, and a tin cup. Husband has got me an excellent sidesaddle, and a very easy horse. He made me a present of a mule to ride, the other day, so I do not know which I shall like best—I have not tried the latter . . .

anything. A multitude of quails were plaintively whistling in the woods and meadows; but nothing appropriate to the rifle was to be seen, except three buzzards, seated on the spectral limbs of an old dead sycamore, that thrust itself out over the river from the dense sunny wall of fresh foliage. Their ugly heads were drawn down between their shoulders, and they seemed to luxuriate in the soft sunshine that was pouring from the west. As they offered no epicurean temptations, I refrained from disturbing their enjoyment; but contented myself with admiring the calm beauty of the sunset, for the river, eddying swiftly in deep purple shadows between the impending woods, formed a wild but tranquillizing scene.

When I returned to the camp I found Shaw and an old Indian seated on the ground in close conference, passing the pipe between them. The old man was explaining that he loved the whites, and had an especial partiality for tobacco. Delorier was arranging upon the ground our service of tin cups and plates; and as other viands were not to be had, he set before us a repast of biscuit and bacon, and a large pot of coffee. Unsheathing our knives, we attacked it, disposed of the greater part, and tossed the residue to the Indian. Meanwhile our horses, now hobbled for the first time, stood among the trees, with their fore-legs tied together, in great disgust and astonishment. They seemed by no means to relish this foretaste of what was before them. Mine, in particular, had conceived a moral aversion to the prairie life. One of them, christened Hendrick, an animal whose strength and hardihood were his only merits, and who yielded to nothing but the cogent arguments of the whip, looked toward us with an indignant countenance, as if

This stereo image shows a Pawnee Indian camp in the Platte River valley.

202.—*Camp of Pawnee Indians on the Platte Valley.*

"Our Camp," an oil painting from the mid-1800s, by Alfred Jacob Miller.

he meditated avenging his wrongs with a kick. The other, Pontiac, a good horse, though of plebeian lineage, stood with his head drooping and his mane hanging about his eyes, with the grieved and sulky air of a lubberly boy sent off to school. Poor Pontiac! his forebodings were but too just; for when I last heard from him, he was under the lash of an Ogallalla brave, on a war party against the Crows.

As it grew dark, and the voices of the whip-poor-wills succeeded the whistle of the quails, we removed our saddles to the tent, to serve as pillows, spread our blankets upon the ground, and prepared to bivouac for the first time that season. Each man selected the place in the tent which he was to occupy for the journey. To Delorier, however, was assigned the cart, into which he could creep in wet weather, and find a much better shelter than his bourgeois enjoyed in the tent.

The river Kansas at this point forms the boundary line between the country of the Shawanoes and that of the Delawares. We crossed it on the following day, rafting over our horses and equipage with much difficulty, and unloading our cart in order to make our way up the steep ascent on the farther bank. It was a Sunday morning; warm, tranquil and bright; and a perfect stillness reigned over the rough inclosures and neglected fields of the Delawares, except the ceaseless hum and chirruping of myriads of insects. Now and then, an Indian rode past on his way to the meeting-house, or through the dilapidated entrance of some shattered log-house an old woman might be discerned, enjoying all the luxury of idleness. There was no village bell, for the Delawares have none; and yet upon that forlorn and rude settlement was the same spirit of Sabbath repose and tranquillity as in some little New England village among the mountains of New Hampshire or the Vermont woods.

Having at present no leisure for such reflections, we pursued our journey. A military road led from this point to Fort Leavenworth, and for many miles the farms and cabins of the Delawares were scattered at short intervals on either hand. The little rude structures of logs, erected usually on the borders of a tract of woods, made a picturesque feature in the landscape. But the scenery needed no foreign aid. Nature had done enough for it; and the alteration of rich green prairies and groves that stood in clusters or lined the banks of the numerous little streams, had all the softened and polished beauty of a region that has been for centuries under the hand of man. At that early season, too, it was in the height of its freshness and luxuriance. The woods were flushed with the red buds of the maple; there were frequent flowering shrubs unknown in the East; and the green swells of the prairies were thickly studded with blossoms.

Encamping near a spring by the side of a hill, we resumed our journey in the morning, and early in the afternoon had arrived within a few miles of Fort Leavenworth. The road crossed a stream densely bordered with trees, and running in the bottom of a deep woody hollow. We were about to descend into it, when a wild and confused procession appeared, passing through the water below, and coming up the steep ascent toward us. We stopped to let them pass. They were Delawares, just returned from a hunting expedition. All, both men and women, were mounted on horseback, and drove along with them a considerable number of pack mules, laden with the furs they had taken, together with the buffalo robes, kettles, and other articles of their traveling equipment, which as well as their clothing and their weapons, had a worn and dingy aspect, as if they had seen hard service of late. At the rear of the party was an old man, who, as he came up, stopped his horse to speak to us. He rode a little tough shaggy pony, with mane and tail well knotted with burrs, and a rusty Spanish bit in its mouth, to which, by way of reins, was attached a string of raw hide. His saddle, robbed probably from a Mexican, had no covering, being merely a tree of the Spanish form, with a piece of grizzly bear's skin laid over it, a pair of rude wooden stirrups attached, and in the absence of girth, a thong of hide passing around the horse's belly. The rider's dark features and keen snaky eyes were unequivocally Indian. He wore a buckskin frock, which, like his fringed leggings, was well polished and blackened by grease and long service; and an old handkerchief was tied around his head. Resting on the saddle before him lay his rifle; a weapon in the use of which the Delawares are skillful; though from its weight, the distant prairie Indians are too lazy to carry it.

"Who's your chief?" he immediately inquired.

Henry Chatillon pointed to us. The old Delaware fixed his eyes intently upon us for a moment, and then sententiously remarked:

"No good! Too young!" With this flattering comment he left us, and rode after his people.

This tribe, the Delawares, once the peaceful allies of William Penn, the tributaries of the conquering Iroquois, are now the most adventurous and dreaded warriors upon the prairies. They make war upon remote tribes the very names of which were unknown to their fathers in their ancient seats in Pennsylvania; and they push these new quarrels with true Indian rancor, sending out their little war parties as far as the Rocky Mountains, and into the Mexican territories. Their neighbors and former confederates, the Shawanoes, who are tolerable farmers, are in a prosperous condition; but the Delawares dwindle every year, from the number of men lost in their warlike expeditions.

Soon after leaving this party, we saw, stretching on the right, the forests that follow the course of the Missouri, and the deep woody channel through which at this point it runs. At a distance in front were the white barracks of Fort Leavenworth, just visible through the trees upon an eminence above a bend of the river. A wide green meadow, as level as a lake, lay between us and the Missouri, and upon this, close to a line of trees that bordered a little brook, stood the tent of the captain and his companions, with their horses feeding around it, but they themselves were invisible. Wright, their muleteer, was there, seated on the tongue of the wagon, repairing his harness. Boisverd stood cleaning his rifle at the door of the tent, and Sorel lounged idly about. On closer examination, however, we discovered the captain's brother, Jack, sitting in the tent, at his old occupation of splicing trail-ropes. He welcomed us in his broad Irish brogue, and said that his brother was fishing in the river, and R. gone to the garrison. They returned before sunset. Meanwhile we erected our own tent not far off, and after supper a council was held, in which it was resolved to remain one day at Fort Leavenworth, and on the next to bid a final adieu to the frontier: or in the phraseology of the region, to "jump off." Our deliberations were conducted by the ruddy light from a distant swell of the prairie, where the long dry grass of last summer was on fire.

OPPOSITE:
Carolina parrots, now extinct, were often spotted in the Missouri River valley during Parkman's time.

The American Parrot

From *Narrative of a Journey Across the Rocky Mountains to the Columbia River*

By John Kirk Townsend

Colorful parrots, now extinct, caught John Kirk Townsend's eye as they approached the town of Boonville on the west side of the Missouri River, halfway between St. Louis and what is now Kansas City.

We entered the town of Boonville early in the afternoon, and too, lodgings in a very clean, and respectably kept hotel. I was much pleased with Boonville, It is the prettiest town I have seen in Missouri; situated on the bank of the river, on an elevated and beautiful spot, and overlooks a large extent of lovely country. The town contains two good hotels, several furnished stores, and five hundred inhabitants. It was laid out thirty years ago by the celebrated western pioneer, whose name it bears.

We saw here vast numbers of the beautiful parrot of this country, (the *Psittacus carolinensis*). They flew around us in flocks, keeping a constant and loud screaming, as though they would chide us for invading their territory; and the splendid green and red of their plumage glancing in the sunshine, as they whirled and circled within a few feet of us, had a most magnificent appearance. They seem entirely unsuspicious of danger, and after being fired at, only huddle closer together, as if to obtain protection from each other, they curve down their necks, and look at them fluttering on the ground, as though perfectly at a loss to account for so unusual an occurrence. It is the most inglorious sort of shooting; down right, cold-blooded murder.

FORT LEAVENWORTH

O n the next morning we rode to Fort Leavenworth. Colonel, now General, Kearny, to whom I had had the honor of an introduction when at St. Louis, was just arrived, and received us at his headquarters with the high-bred courtesy habitual to him. Fort Leavenworth is in fact no fort, being without defensive works, except two block-houses. No rumors of war had as yet disturbed its tranquillity. In the square grassy area, surrounded by barracks and the quarters of the officers, the men were passing and repassing, or lounging among the trees; although not many weeks afterward it presented a different scene; for here the very off-scourings of the frontier were congregated, to be marshaled for the expedition against Santa Fe.

Passing through the garrison, we rode toward the Kickapoo village, five or six miles beyond. The path, a rather dubious and uncertain one, led us along the ridge of high bluffs that bordered the Missouri; and by looking to the right or to the left, we could enjoy a strange contrast of opposite scenery. On the left stretched the prairie, rising into swells and undulations, thickly sprinkled with groves, or gracefully expanding into wide grassy basins of miles in extent; while its curvatures, swelling against the horizon, were often surmounted by lines of sunny woods; a scene to which the freshness of the season and the peculiar mellowness of the atmosphere gave additional softness. Below us, on the right, was a tract of ragged and broken woods. We could look down on the summits of the trees, some living and some dead; some erect, others leaning at every angle, and others still piled in masses together by the passage of a hurricane. Beyond their extreme verge, the turbid waters of the Missouri were discernible through the boughs, rolling powerfully along at the foot of the woody declivities of its farther bank.

N. C. Wyeth's depiction of Parkman's entourage with Henry Chatillon on the lead horse.

The path soon after led inland; and as we crossed an open meadow we saw a cluster of buildings on a rising ground before us, with a crowd of people surrounding them. They were the storehouse, cottage, and stables of the Kickapoo trader's establishment. Just at that moment, as it chanced, he was beset with half the Indians of the settlement. They had tied their wretched, neglected little ponies by dozens along the fences and outhouses, and were either lounging about the place, or crowding into the trading house. Here were faces of various colors; red, green, white, and black, curiously intermingled and disposed over the visage in a variety of patterns. Calico shirts, red and blue blankets, brass ear-rings, wampum necklaces, appeared in profusion. The trader was a blue-eyed open-faced man who neither in his manners nor his appearance betrayed any of the roughness of the frontier; though just at present he was obliged to keep a lynx eye on his suspicious customers, who, men and women, were climbing on his counter and seating themselves among his boxes and bales.

The village itself was not far off, and sufficiently illustrated the condition of its unfortunate and self-abandoned occupants. Fancy to yourself a little swift stream, working its devious way down a woody valley; sometimes wholly hidden under logs and fallen trees, sometimes issuing forth and spreading into a broad, clear pool; and on its banks in little nooks cleared away among the trees, miniature log-houses in utter ruin and neglect. A labyrinth of narrow, obstructed paths connected these habitations. Sometimes we met a stray calf, a pig or a pony, belonging to some of the villagers, who usually lay in the sun in front of their dwellings, and looked on us with cold, suspicious eyes as we approached. Farther on, in place of the log-huts of the Kickapoos, we found the pukwi lodges of their neighbors, the Pottawattamies, whose condition seemed no better than theirs.

Growing tired at last, and exhausted by the excessive heat and sultriness of the day, we returned to our friend, the trader. By this time the crowd around him had dispersed,

The Arkansas River, which Parkman followed on his journey home, near Dardanelles, Arkansas. Photographed in 1909.

W. H. Jackson's drawing of the Arkansas River in the late 1850s. On the banks are a tent, covered wagons, and livestock.

and left him at leisure. He invited us to his cottage, a little white-and-green building, in the style of the old French settlements; and ushered us into a neat, well-furnished room. The blinds were closed, and the heat and glare of the sun excluded; the room was as cool as a cavern. It was neatly carpeted too and furnished in a manner that we hardly expected on the frontier. The sofas, chairs, tables, and a well-filled bookcase would not have disgraced an Eastern city; though there were one or two little tokens that indicated the rather questionable civilization of the region. A pistol, loaded and capped, lay on the mantelpiece; and through the glass of the bookcase, peeping above the works of John Milton glittered the handle of a very mischievous-looking knife.

Our host went out, and returned with iced water, glasses, and a bottle of excellent claret; a refreshment most welcome in the extreme heat of the day; and soon after appeared a merry, laughing woman, who must have been, a year of two before, a very rich and luxuriant specimen of Creole beauty. She came to say that lunch was ready in the next room. Our hostess evidently lived on the sunny side of life, and troubled herself with none of its cares. She sat down and entertained us while we were at table with anecdotes of fishing parties, frolics, and the officers at the fort. Taking leave at length of the hospitable trader and his friend, we rode back to the garrison.

Shaw passed on to the camp, while I remained to call upon Colonel Kearny. I found him still at table. There sat our friend the captain, in the same remarkable habiliments in which we saw him at Westport; the black pipe, however, being for the present laid aside. He dangled his little cap in his hand and talked of steeple-chases, touching occasionally upon his anticipated exploits in buffalo-hunting. There, too, was R., somewhat more elegantly attired. For the last time we tasted the luxuries of civilization, and drank adieus to it in wine good enough to make us almost regret the leave-taking. Then, mounting, we rode together to the camp, where everything was in readiness for departure on the morrow.

Jumping Off

Our transatlantic companions were well equipped for the journey. They had a wagon drawn by six mules, and crammed with provisions for six months, besides ammunition enough for a regiment; spare rifles and fowling-pieces, ropes and harness; personal baggage, and a miscellaneous assortment of articles, which produced infinite embarrassment on the journey. They had also decorated their persons with telescopes and portable compasses, and carried English double-barreled rifles of sixteen to the pound caliber, slung to their saddles in dragoon fashion.

By sunrise on the 23d of May we had breakfasted; the tents were leveled, the animals saddled and harnessed, and all was prepared. "Avance donc! get up!" cried Delorier from his seat in front of the cart. Wright, our friend's muleteer, after some swearing and lashing, got his insubordinate train in motion, and then the whole party filed from the ground. Thus we bade a long adieu to bed and board, and the principles of Blackstone's Commentaries. The day was a most auspicious one; and yet Shaw and I felt certain misgivings, which in the sequel proved but too well founded. We had just learned that though R. had taken it upon him to adopt this course without consulting us, not a single man in the party was acquainted with it; and the absurdity of our friend's high-handed measure very soon became manifest. His plan was to strike the trail of several companies of dragoons, who last summer had made an expedition under Colonel Kearny to Fort Laramie, and by this means to reach the grand trail of the Oregon emigrants up the Platte.

We rode for an hour or two when a familiar cluster of buildings appeared on a little hill. "Hallo!" shouted the Kickapoo trader from over his fence. "Where are you going?" A few rather emphatic exclamations might have been heard among us, when we found that we had gone miles out of our way, and were not advanced an inch toward the Rocky Mountains. So we turned in the direction the trader indicated, and with the sun for a

"American Progress," a color lithograph showing an allegorical female figure representing America leading pioneers westward.

guide, began to trace a "bee line" across the prairies. We struggled through copses and lines of wood; we waded brooks and pools of water; we traversed prairies as green as an emerald, expanding before us for mile after mile; wider and more wild than the wastes Mazeppa rode over:

> "Man nor brute,
> Nor dint of hoof, nor print of foot,
> Lay in the wild luxuriant soil;
> No sign of travel; none of toil;
> The very air was mute."

Riding in advance, we passed over one of these great plains; we looked back and saw the line of scattered horsemen stretching for a mile or more; and far in the rear against the horizon, the white wagons creeping slowly along. "Here we are at last!" shouted the captain. And in truth we had struck upon the traces of a large body of horse. We turned joyfully and followed this new course, with tempers somewhat improved; and toward sunset encamped on a high swell of the prairie, at the foot of which a lazy stream soaked along through clumps of rank grass. It was getting dark. We turned the horses loose to feed. "Drive down the tent-pickets hard," said Henry Chatillon, "it is going to blow." We did so, and secured the tent as well as we could; for the sky had changed totally, and a fresh damp smell in the wind warned us that a stormy night was likely to succeed the hot clear day. The prairie also wore a new aspect, and its vast swells had grown black and

Wolves were a pervasive problem on the trail, as they preyed on livestock and were a constant threat to small children.

An extreme

solicitude

tormented him,

lest some of his

favorites should

escape . . . He cast

an anxious eye

toward three

wolves who were

sneaking along

over the dreary

surface of the plain,

as if he dreaded

some hostile

demonstration

on their part.

somber under the shadow of the clouds. The thunder soon began to growl at a distance. Picketing and hobbling the horses among the rich grass at the foot of the slope, where we encamped, we gained a shelter just as the rain began to fall; and sat at the opening of the tent, watching the proceedings of the captain. In defiance of the rain he was stalking among the horses, wrapped in an old Scotch plaid. An extreme solicitude tormented him, lest some of his favorites should escape, or some accident should befall them; and he cast an anxious eye toward three wolves who were sneaking along over the dreary surface of the plain, as if he dreaded some hostile demonstration on their part.

On the next morning we had gone but a mile or two, when we came to an extensive belt of woods, through the midst of which ran a stream, wide, deep, and of an appearance particularly muddy and treacherous. Delorier was in advance with his cart; he jerked his pipe from his mouth, lashed his mules, and poured forth a volley of Canadian ejaculations. In plunged the cart, but midway it stuck fast. Delorier leaped out knee-deep in water, and by dint of *sacres* and a vigorous application of the whip, he urged the mules out of the slough. Then approached the long team and heavy wagon of our friends; but it paused on the brink.

"Now my advice is—" began the captain, who had been anxiously contemplating the muddy gulf.

"Drive on!" cried R.

But Wright, the muleteer, apparently had not as yet decided the point in his own mind; and he sat still in his seat on one of the shaft-mules, whistling in a low contemplative strain to himself.

"My advice is," resumed the captain, "that we unload; for I'll bet any man five pounds that if we try to go through, we shall stick fast."

"By the powers, we shall stick fast!" echoed Jack, the captain's brother, shaking his large head with an air of firm conviction.

"Drive on! drive on!" cried R. petulantly.

"Well," observed the captain, turning to us as we sat looking on, much edified by this by-play among our confederates, "I can only give my advice and if people won't be reasonable, why, they won't; that's all!"

Meanwhile Wright had apparently made up his mind; for he suddenly began to shout forth a volley of oaths and curses, that, compared with the French imprecations of Delorier, sounded like the roaring of heavy cannon after the popping and sputtering of a bunch of Chinese crackers. At the same time he discharged a shower of blows upon his mules, who hastily dived into the mud and drew the wagon lumbering after them. For a moment the issue was dubious. Wright writhed about in his saddle, and swore and lashed like a madman; but who can count on a team of half-broken mules? At the most critical point, when all should have been harmony and combined effort, the perverse brutes fell into lamentable disorder, and huddled together in confusion on the far-ther bank. There was the wagon up to the hub in mud, and visibly settling every instant. There was nothing for it but to unload; then to dig away the mud from before the wheels with a spade, and lay a causeway of bushes and branches. This agreeable labor accom-plished, the wagon at last emerged; but if I mention that some interruption of this sort occurred at least four or five times a day for a fortnight, the reader will understand that our progress toward the Platte was not without its obstacles.

We traveled six or seven miles farther, and "nooned" near a brook. On the point of resuming our journey, when the horses were all driven down to water, my homesick charger, Pontiac, made a sudden leap across, and set off at a round trot for the settle-ments. I mounted my remaining horse, and started in pursuit. Making a circuit, I headed the runaway, hoping to drive him back to camp; but he instantly broke into a gallop, made a wide tour on the prairie, and got past me again. I tried this plan repeatedly, with the same result; Pontiac was evidently disgusted with the prairie; so I abandoned it, and tried another, trotting along gently behind him, in hopes that I might quietly get near enough to seize the trail-rope which was fastened to his neck, and dragged about a dozen feet behind him. The chase grew interesting. For mile after mile I followed the rascal, with the utmost care not to alarm him, and gradually got nearer, until at length old Hendrick's nose was fairly brushed by the whisking tail of the unsuspecting Pontiac. Without drawing rein, I slid softly to the ground; but my long heavy rifle encumbered me, and the low sound it made in striking the horn of the saddle startled him; he pricked up his ears, and sprang off at a run. "My friend," thought I, remounting, "do that again, and I will shoot you!"

Fort Leavenworth was about forty miles distant, and thither I determined to follow him. I made up my mind to spend a solitary and supperless night, and then set out again in the morning. One hope, however, remained. The creek where the wagon had stuck was just before us; Pontiac might be thirsty with his run, and stop there to drink. I kept as near to him as possible, taking every precaution not to alarm him again; and the result proved as I had hoped: for he walked deliberately among the trees, and stooped down to the water. I alighted, dragged old Hendrick through the mud, and with a feeling of infinite satisfaction picked up the slimy trail-rope and twisted it three times round my hand. "Now let me see you get away again!" I thought, as I remounted. But Pontiac was exceedingly reluctant to turn back; Hendrick, too, who had evidently flattered himself with vain hopes, showed the utmost repugnance, and grumbled in a manner peculiar to himself at being compelled to face about. A smart cut of the whip restored his cheerful-ness; and dragging the recovered truant behind, I set out in search of the camp. An hour or two elapsed, when, near sunset, I saw the tents, standing on a rich swell of the prairie, beyond a line of woods, while the bands of horses were feeding in a low meadow close at hand. There sat Jack C., cross-legged, in the sun, splicing a trail-rope, and the rest were

These three Piegan Blackfoot Indian chiefs on the plains near a watering hole were photographed by Edward S. Curtis in the early 1900s.

lying on the grass, smoking and telling stories. That night we enjoyed a serenade from the wolves, more lively than any with which they had yet favored us; and in the morning one of the musicians appeared, not many rods from the tents, quietly seated among the horses, looking at us with a pair of large gray eyes; but perceiving a rifle leveled at him, he leaped up and made off in hot haste.

I pass by the following day or two of our journey, for nothing occurred worthy of record. Should any one of my readers ever be impelled to visit the prairies, and should he choose the route of the Platte (the best, perhaps, that can be adopted), I can assure him that he need not think to enter at once upon the paradise of his imagination. A dreary preliminary, protracted crossing of the threshold awaits him before he finds himself fairly upon the verge of the "great American desert," those barren wastes, the haunts of the buffalo and the Indian, where the very shadow of civilization lies a hundred leagues behind him. The intervening country, the wide and fertile belt that extends for several hundred miles beyond the extreme

frontier, will probably answer tolerably well to his preconceived ideas of the prairie; for this it is from which picturesque tourists, painters, poets, and novelists, who have seldom penetrated farther, have derived their conceptions of the whole region. If he has a painter's eye, he may find his period of probation not wholly void of interest. The scenery, though tame, is graceful and pleasing. Here are level plains, too wide for the eye to measure green undulations, like motionless swells of the ocean; abundance of streams, followed through all their windings by lines of woods and scattered groves. But let him be as enthusiastic as he may, he will find enough to damp his ardor. His wagons will stick in the mud; his horses will break loose; harness will give way, and axle-trees prove unsound. His bed will be a soft one, consisting often of black mud, of the richest consistency. As for food, he must content himself with biscuit and salt provisions; for strange as it may seem, this tract of country produces very little game. As he advances, indeed, he will see, moldering in the grass by his path, the vast antlers of the elk, and farther on, the whitened skulls of the buffalo, once swarming over this now deserted region. Perhaps, like us, he may journey for a fortnight, and see not so much as the hoof-print of a deer; in the spring, not even a prairie hen is to be had.

Yet, to compensate him for this unlooked-for deficiency of game, he will find himself beset with "varmints" innumerable. The wolves will entertain him with a concerto at night, and skulk around him by day, just beyond rifle shot; his horse will step into badger-holes; from every marsh and mud puddle will arise the bellowing, croaking, and trilling of legions of frogs, infinitely various in color, shape and dimensions. A profusion of snakes will glide away from under his horse's feet, or quietly visit him in his tent at night; while the pertinacious humming of unnumbered mosquitoes will banish sleep from his eyelids. When thirsty with a long ride in the scorching sun over some boundless reach of prairie, he comes at length to a pool of water, and alights to drink, he discovers a troop of young tadpoles sporting in the bottom of his cup. Add to this, that all the morning the hot sun beats upon him with sultry, penetrating heat, and that, with provoking regularity, at about four o'clock in the afternoon, a thunderstorm rises and drenches him to the skin. Such being the charms of this favored region, the reader will easily conceive the extent of our gratification at learning that for a week we had been journeying on the wrong track! How this agreeable discovery was made I will presently explain.

One day, after a protracted morning's ride, we stopped to rest at noon upon the open prairie. No trees were in sight; but close at hand, a little dribbling brook was twisting from side to side through a hollow; now forming holes of stagnant water, and now gliding over the mud in a scarcely perceptible current, among a growth of sickly bushes, and great clumps of tall rank grass. The day was excessively hot and oppressive. The horses and mules were rolling on the prairie to refresh themselves, or feeding among the bushes in the hollow. We had dined;

Packing Food

BY EZRA MEEKER

Buck's skill in camp work and his lack of ability to handle the team naturally settled the division of the work between us. It was he who selected the outfit to go into the wagon, while I fitted up the wagon and bought the team. We had butter packed in the center of the flour, which was in double sacks; eggs packed in corn meal or flour, enough to last us nearly five hundred miles; fruit in abundance, and dried pumpkins; a little jerked beef, not too salty. Last though not least, there was a demijohn of brandy "for medicinal purposes only," as Buck said, with a merry twinkle of the eye . . .

We baked the bread in a tin reflector instead of the heavy Dutch oven so much in use on the plains.

The butter in part melted and mingled with the flour, yet it did not matter much, as the "shortcake" that resulted made us almost glad the mishap had occurred. Besides, did we not have plenty of fresh butter, from the milk of our own cows, churned every day in the can by the jostling of the wagon?

Ezra Meeker in 1923, sitting in an old wagon rut in the Sweetwater Valley in Wyoming.

FOLLOWING SPREAD:
An emigrant family circa 1870, living in their wagons, bound for Oregon.

and Delorier, puffing at his pipe, knelt on the grass, scrubbing our service of tin plate. Shaw lay in the shade, under the cart, to rest for a while, before the word should be given to "catch up." Henry Chatillon, before lying down, was looking about for signs of snakes, the only living things that he feared, and uttering various ejaculations of disgust, at finding several suspicious-looking holes close to the cart. I sat leaning against the wheel in a scanty strip of shade, making a pair of hobbles to replace those which my contumacious steed Pontiac had broken the night before. The camp of our friends, a rod or two distant, presented the same scene of lazy tranquillity.

"Hallo!" cried Henry, looking up from his inspection of the snake-holes, "here comes the old captain!"

The captain approached, and stood for a moment contemplating us in silence.

"I say, Parkman," he began, "look at Shaw there, asleep under the cart, with the tar dripping off the hub of the wheel on his shoulder!"

At this Shaw got up, with his eyes half opened, and feeling the part indicated, he found his hand glued fast to his red flannel shirt.

"He'll look well when he gets among the squaws, won't he?" observed the captain, with a grin.

He then crawled under the cart, and began to tell stories of which his stock was inexhaustible. Yet every moment he would glance nervously at the horses. At last he jumped up in great excitement. "See that horse! There—that fellow just walking over the hill! By Jove; he's off. It's your big horse, Shaw; no it isn't, it's Jack's! Jack! Jack! hallo, Jack!" Jack thus invoked, jumped up and stared vacantly at us.

"Go and catch your horse, if you don't want to lose him!" roared the captain.

Jack instantly set off at a run through the grass, his broad pantaloons flapping about his feet. The captain gazed anxiously till he saw that the horse was caught; then he sat down, with a countenance of thoughtfulness and care.

"I tell you what it is," he said, "this will never do at all. We shall lose every horse in the band someday or other, and then a pretty plight we should be in! Now I am convinced that the only way for us is to have every man in the camp stand horse-guard in rotation whenever we stop. Supposing a hundred Pawnees should jump up out of that ravine, all yelling and flapping their buffalo robes, in the way they do? Why, in two minutes not a hoof would be in sight." We reminded the captain that a hundred Pawnees would probably demolish the horse-guard, if he were to resist their depredations.

"At any rate," pursued the captain, evading the point, "our whole system is wrong; I'm convinced of it; it is totally unmilitary. Why, the way we travel, strung out over the prairie for a mile, an enemy might attack the foremost men, and cut them off before the rest could come up."

"We are not in an enemy's country, yet," said Shaw; "when we are, we'll travel together."

"Then," said the captain, "we might be attacked in camp. We've no sentinels; we camp in disorder; no precautions at all to guard against surprise. My own convictions are that we ought to camp in a hollow square, with the fires in the center; and have sentinels, and a regular password appointed for every night. Besides, there should be vedettes, riding in advance, to find a place for the camp and give warning of an enemy. These are my convictions. I don't want to dictate to any man. I give advice to the best of my judgment, that's all; and then let people do as they please."

We intimated that perhaps it would be as well to postpone such burdensome precautions until there should be some actual need of them; but he shook his head dubiously. The captain's sense of military propriety had been severely shocked by what he considered the irregular proceedings of the party; and this was not the first time he had expressed himself upon the subject. But his convictions seldom produced any practical results. In the present case, he contented himself, as usual, with enlarging on the importance of his suggestions, and wondering that they were not adopted. But his plan of sending out vedettes seemed particularly dear to him; and as no one else was disposed to second his views on this point, he took it into his head to ride forward that afternoon, himself.

"Come, Parkman," said he, "will you go with me?"

We set out together, and rode a mile or two in advance. The captain, in the course of twenty years' service in the British army, had seen something of life; one extensive side of it, at least, he had enjoyed the best opportunities for studying; and being naturally a pleasant fellow, he was a very entertaining companion. He cracked jokes and told stories for an hour or two; until, looking back, we saw the prairie behind us stretching away to the horizon, without a horseman or a wagon in sight.

"Now," said the captain, "I think the vedettes had better stop till the main body comes up."

I was of the same opinion. There was a thick growth of woods just before us, with a stream running through them. Having crossed this, we found on the other side a fine level meadow, half encircled by the trees; and fastening our horses to some bushes, we sat down on the grass; while, with an old stump of a tree for a target, I began to display the superiority of the renowned rifle of the back woods over the foreign innovation borne by the captain. At length voices could be heard in the distance behind the trees.

"There they come!" said the captain: "let's go see how they get through the creek."

We mounted and rode to the bank of the stream, where the trail crossed it. It ran in a deep hollow, full of trees; as we looked down, we saw a confused crowd of horsemen riding through the water; and among the dingy habiliment of our party glittered the uniforms of four dragoons.

Shaw came whipping his horse up the back, in advance of the rest, with a somewhat indignant countenance. The first word he spoke was a blessing fervently invoked on the head of R., who was riding, with a crest-fallen air, in the rear. Thanks to the ingenious

In "Storm Waiting for the Caravan," 1830s-era pioneers wait in a driving rainstorm for the rest of the wagon train to catch up.

devices of the gentleman, we had missed the track entirely, and wandered, not toward the Platte, but to the village of the Iowa Indians. This we learned from the dragoons, who had lately deserted from Fort Leavenworth. They told us that our best plan now was to keep to the northward until we should strike the trail formed by several parties of Oregon emigrants, who had that season set out from St. Joseph's in Missouri.

In extremely bad temper, we encamped on this ill-starred spot; while the deserters, whose case admitted of no delay rode rapidly forward. On the day following, striking the St. Joseph's trail, we turned our horses' heads toward Fort Laramie, then about seven hundred miles to the westward.

THE BIG BLUE

The great medley of Oregon and California emigrants, at their camps around Independence, had heard reports that several additional parties were on the point of setting out from St. Joseph's farther to the northward. The prevailing impression was that these were Mormons, twenty-three hundred in number; and a great alarm was excited in consequence. The people of Illinois and Missouri, who composed by far the greater part of the emigrants, have never been on the best terms with the "Latter Day Saints"; and it is notorious throughout the country how much blood has been spilt in their feuds, even far within the limits of the settlements. No one could predict what would be the result, when large armed bodies of these fanatics should encounter the most impetuous and reckless of their old enemies on the broad prairie, far beyond the reach of law or military force. The women and children at Independence raised a great outcry; the men themselves were seriously alarmed; and, as I learned, they sent to Colonel Kearny, requesting an escort of dragoons as far as the Platte. This was refused; and as the sequel proved, there was no occasion for it. The St. Joseph's emigrants were as good Christians and as zealous Mormon-haters as the rest; and the very few families of the "Saints" who passed out this season by the route of the

"Perilous Ferriage of the Missouri," an 1849 drawing by Joseph Goldsborough Bruff, suggests the hazards of river crossings.

Platte remained behind until the great tide of emigration had gone by; standing in quite as much awe of the "gentiles" as the latter did of them.

We were now, as I before mentioned, upon this St. Joseph's trail. It was evident, by the traces, that large parties were a few days in advance of us; and as we too supposed them to be Mormons, we had some apprehension of interruption.

The journey was somewhat monotonous. One day we rode on for hours, without seeing a tree or a bush: before, behind, and on the other side, stretched the vast expanse, rolling in a succession of graceful swells, covered with the unbroken carpet of fresh green grass. Here and there a crow, a raven or a turkey buzzard, relieved the uniformity.

"What shall we do to-night for wood and water?" we began to ask of each other; for the sun was within an hour of setting. At length a dark green speck appeared, far off on the right; it was the top of a tree, peering over a swell of the prairie; and leaving the trail, we made all haste toward it. It proved to be the vanguard of a cluster of bushes and low trees, that surrounded some pools of water in an extensive hollow; so we encamped on the rising ground near it.

Shaw and I were sitting in the tent, when Delorier thrust his brown face and old felt hat into the opening, and dilating his eyes to their utmost extent, announced supper. There were the tin cups and the iron spoons, arranged in military order on the grass, and the coffee-pot predominant in the midst. The meal was soon dispatched; but Henry Chatillon still sat cross-legged, dallying with the remnant of his coffee, the beverage in universal use upon the prairie, and an especial favorite with him. He preferred it in its virgin flavor, unimpaired by sugar or cream; and on the present occasion it met his entire approval, being exceedingly strong, or, as he expressed it, "right black."

It was a rich and gorgeous sunset—an American sunset; and the ruddy glow of the sky was reflected from some extensive pools of water among the shadowy copses in the meadow below.

"I must have a bath to-night," said Shaw. "How is it, Delorier? Any chance for a swim down here?"

"Ah! I cannot tell; just as you please, monsieur," replied Delorier, shrugging his shoulders, perplexed by his ignorance of English, and extremely anxious to conform in all respects to the opinion and wishes of his bourgeois.

"Look at his moccasion," said I. "It has evidently been lately immersed in a profound abyss of black mud."

"Come," said Shaw; "at any rate we can see for ourselves."

We set out together; and as we approached the bushes, which were at some distance, we found the ground becoming rather treacherous. We could only get along by stepping upon large clumps of tall rank grass, with fathomless gulfs between, like innumerable

Justice on the Trail

By Ezra Meeker

It is true that no general organization for law and order was effected on the western side of the river. But the American instinct for fair play and a hearing for everybody prevailed, so that while there was no mob law, the law of self-preservation asserted itself, and the counsels of the level-headed older men prevailed. When an occasion called for action, a "high court" was convened, and woe betide the man that would undertake to defy its mandates after its deliberations were made public!

…From necessity, murder was punishable with death. The penalty for stealing was whipping, which, when inflicted by one of those long ox lashes in the hands of an expert, would bring the blood from the victim's back at every stroke. Minor offenses, or differences generally were arbitrated. Each party would abide by the decision as if it had come from a court of law. Lawlessness was not common on the plains.

little quaking islands in an ocean of mud, where a false step would have involved our boots in a catastrophe like that which had befallen Delorier's moccasins. The thing looked desperate; we separated, so as to search in different directions, Shaw going off to the right, while I kept straight forward. At last I came to the edge of the bushes: they were young waterwillows, covered with their caterpillar-like blossoms, but intervening between them and the last grass clump was a black and deep slough, over which, by a vigorous exertion, I contrived to jump. Then I shouldered my way through the willows, tramping them down by main force, till I came to a wide stream of water, three inches deep, languidly creeping along over a bottom of sleek mud. My arrival produced a great commotion. A huge green bull-frog uttered an indignant croak, and jumped off the bank with a loud splash: his webbed feet twinkled above the surface, as he jerked them energetically upward, and I could see him ensconcing himself in the unresisting slime at the bottom, whence several large air bubbles struggled lazily to the top. Some little spotted frogs instantly followed the patriarch's example; and then three turtles, not larger than a dollar, tumbled themselves off a broad "lily pad," where they had been reposing. At the same time a snake, gayly striped with black and yellow, glided out from the bank, and writhed across to the other side; and a small stagnant pool into which my foot had inadvertently pushed a stone was instantly alive with a congregation of black tadpoles.

"Any chance for a bath, where you are?" called out Shaw, from a distance.

The answer was not encouraging. I retreated through the willows, and rejoining my companion, we proceeded to push our researches in company. Not far on the right, a

The Missouri plains were flush with bird life, such as this brown thrasher in pursuit of a spider.

rising ground, covered with trees and bushes, seemed to sink down abruptly to the water, and give hope of better success; so toward this we directed our steps. When we reached the place we found it no easy matter to get along between the hill and the water, impeded as we were by a growth of stiff, obstinate young birch-trees, laced together by grapevines. In the twilight, we now and then, to support ourselves, snatched at the touch-me-not stem of some ancient sweet-brier. Shaw, who was in advance, suddenly uttered a somewhat emphatic monosyllable; and looking up I saw him with one hand grasping a sapling, and one foot immersed in the water, from which he had forgotten to withdraw it, his whole attention being engaged in contemplating the movements of a water-snake, about five feet long, curiously checkered with black and green, who was deliberately swimming across the pool. There being no stick or stone at hand to pelt him with, we looked at him for a time in silent disgust; and then pushed forward. Our perseverence was at last rewarded; for several rods farther on, we emerged upon a little level grassy nook among the brushwood, and by an extraordinary dispensation of fortune, the weeds and floating sticks, which elsewhere covered the pool, seemed to have drawn apart, and left a few yards of clear water just in front of this favored spot. We sounded it with a stick; it was four feet deep; we lifted a specimen in our cupped hands; it seemed reasonably transparent, so we decided that the time for action was arrived. But our ablutions were suddenly interrupted by ten thousand punctures, like poisoned needles, and the humming of myriads of over-grown mosquitoes, rising in all directions from their native mud and slime and swarming to the feast. We were fain to beat a retreat with all possible speed.

A 1932 drawing of pronghorn antelope on the Great Plains by William Herbert Dunton.

We made toward the tents, much refreshed by the bath which the heat of the weather, joined to our prejudices, had rendered very desirable.

"What's the matter with the captain? Look at him!" said Shaw. The captain stood alone on the prairie, swinging his hat violently around his head, and lifting first one foot and then the other, without moving from the spot. First he looked down to the ground with an air of supreme abhorrence; then he gazed upward with a perplexed and indignant countenance, as if trying to trace the flight of an unseen enemy. We called to know what was the matter; but he replied only by execrations directed against some unknown object. We approached, when our ears were saluted by a droning sound, as if twenty bee-hives had been overturned at once. The air above was full of large black insects, in a state of great commotion, and multitudes were flying about just above the tops of the grass blades.

"Don't be afraid," called the captain, observing us recoil. "The brutes won't sting."

At this I knocked one down with my hat, and discovered him to be no other than a "dorbug"; and looking closer, we found the ground thickly perforated with their holes.

We took a hasty leave of this flourishing colony, and walking up the rising ground to the tents, found Delorier's fire still glowing brightly. We sat down around it, and Shaw began to expatiate on the admirable facilities for bathing that we had discovered, and

Migratory locusts travel in large swarms and can decimate entire fields.

recommended the captain by all means to go down there before breakfast in the morning. The captain was in the act of remarking that he couldn't have believed it possible, when he suddenly interrupted himself, and clapped his hand to his cheek, exclaiming that "those infernal humbugs were at him again." In fact, we began to hear sounds as if bullets were humming over our heads. In a moment something rapped me sharply on the forehead, then upon the neck, and immediately I felt an indefinite number of sharp wiry claws in active motion, as if their owner were bent on pushing his explorations farther. I seized him, and dropped him into the fire. Our party speedily broke up, and we adjourned to our respective tents, where, closing the opening fast, we hoped to be exempt from invasion. But all precaution was fruitless. The dorbugs hummed through the tent, and marched over our faces until day-light; when, opening our blankets, we found several dozen clinging there with the utmost tenacity. The first object that met our eyes in the morning was Delorier, who seemed to be apostrophizing his frying-pan, which he held by the handle at arm's length. It appeared that he had left it at night by the fire; and the bottom was now covered with dorbugs, firmly imbedded. Multitudes beside, curiously parched and shriveled, lay scattered among the ashes.

The horses and mules were turned loose to feed. We had just taken our seats at breakfast, or rather reclined in the classic mode, when an exclamation from Henry Chatillon, and a shout of alarm from the captain, gave warning of some casualty, and looking up, we saw the whole band of animals, twenty-three in number, filing off for the settlements, the incorrigible Pontiac at their head, jumping along with hobbled feet, at a gait much more rapid than graceful. Three or four of us ran to cut them off, dashing as best we might through the tall grass, which was glittering with myriads of dewdrops. After a race of a mile or more, Shaw caught a horse. Tying the trail-rope by way of bridle round the animal's jaw, and leaping upon his back, he got in advance of the remaining fugitives, while we, soon bringing them together, drove them in a crowd up to the tents, where each man caught and saddled his own. Then we heard lamentations and curses; for half the horses had broke their hobbles, and many were seriously galled by attempting to run in fetters.

It was late that morning before we were on the march; and early in the afternoon we were compelled to encamp, for a thunder-gust came up and suddenly enveloped us in whirling sheets of rain. With much ado, we pitched our tents amid the tempest, and all night long the thunder bellowed and growled over our heads. In the morning, light peaceful showers succeeded the cataracts of rain, that had been drenching us through the canvas of our tents. About noon, when there were some treacherous indications of fair weather, we got in motion again.

Not a breath of air stirred over the free and open prairie; the clouds were like light piles of cotton; and where the blue sky was visible, it wore a hazy and languid aspect. The sun beat down upon us with a sultry penetrating heat almost insupportable, and as our party crept slowly along over the interminable level, the horses hung their heads as they waded fetlock deep through the mud, and the men slouched into the easiest position upon the saddle. At last, toward evening, the old familiar black heads of thunderclouds rose fast above the horizon, and the same deep muttering of distant thunder that had become the ordinary accompaniment of our afternoon's journey began to roll hoarsely over the prairie. Only a few minutes elapsed before the whole sky was densely shrouded, and the prairie and some clusters of woods in front assumed a purple hue beneath the inky shadows. Suddenly from the densest fold of the cloud the flash leaped out, quivering again and again down to the edge of the prairie; and at the same instant came the sharp burst and the long rolling peal of the thunder. A cool wind, filled with the smell of rain, just then overtook us, leveling the tall grass by the side of the path.

"Come on; we must ride for it!" shouted Shaw, rushing past at full speed, his led horse snorting at his side. The whole party broke into full gallop, and made for the trees in front. Passing these, we found beyond them a meadow which they half inclosed. We rode pell-mell upon the ground, leaped from horseback, tore off our saddles; and in a moment each man was kneeling at his horse's feet. The hobbles were adjusted, and the animals turned loose; then, as the wagons came wheeling rapidly to the spot, we seized upon the tent-poles, and just as the storm broke, we were prepared to receive it. It came upon us almost with the darkness of night; the trees, which were close at hand, were completely shrouded by the roaring torrents of rain.

We were sitting in the tent, when Delorier, with his broad felt hat hanging about his ears, and his shoulders glistening with rain, thrust in his head.

"Voulez-vous du souper, tout de suite? I can make a fire, sous la charette—I b'lieve so—I try."

"Never mind supper, man; come in out of the rain."

Delorier accordingly crouched in the entrance, for modesty would not permit him to intrude farther.

Our tent was none of the best defense against such a cataract. The rain could not enter bodily, but it beat through the canvas in a fine drizzle, that wetted us just as effectively. We sat upon our saddles with faces of the utmost surliness, while the water dropped from the vizors of our caps, and trickled down our cheeks. My india-rubber cloak conducted twenty little rapid streamlets to the ground; and Shaw's blanket-coat was saturated like a sponge. But what most concerned us was the sight of several puddles of water rapidly accumulating; one in particular, that was gathering around the tent-pole, threatened to overspread the whole area within the tent, holding forth but an indifferent promise of a comfortable night's rest. Toward sunset, however, the storm ceased as suddenly as it began. A bright streak of clear red sky appeared above the western verge

How One Sleeps on the Prairie

BY NARCISSA WHITMAN

Since we have been here, we have made our tent. It is made of bedticking, in a conical form, large enough for us all to sleep under—viz.: Mr. Spalding and wife, Dr. Whitman and wife, Mr. Gray, Richard Takk-ah-too-ah-tis, and John Altz; quite a little family—raised with a centerpole and fastened down with pegs, covering a large circle. Here we shall live, eat, and sleep for the summer to come, at least—perhaps longer. Mary, you inquired concerning my beds and bedding. I will tell you. We five spread our India-rubber cloth on the ground, then our blankets, and encamp for the night. We take plenty of Mackinaw blankets, which answer for our bed and bedding, and when we journey place them over our saddles and ride on them. I wish you could see our outfit.

of the prairie, the horizontal rays of the sinking sun streamed through it and glittered in a thousand prismatic colors upon the dripping groves and the prostrate grass. The pools in the tent dwindled and sunk into the saturated soil.

But all our hopes were delusive. Scarcely had night set in, when the tumult broke forth anew. The thunder here is not like the tame thunder of the Atlantic coast. Bursting with a terrific crash directly above our heads, it roared over the boundless waste of prairie, seeming to roll around the whole circle of the firmament with a peculiar and awful reverberation. The lightning flashed all night, playing with its livid glare upon the neighboring trees, revealing the vast expanse of the plain, and then leaving us shut in as by a palpable wall of darkness.

It did not disturb us much. Now and then a peal awakened us, and made us conscious

"Westward the Course of Empire Takes Its Way," a color lithograph by artist F. F. Palmer, 1868.

of the electric battle that was raging, and of the floods that dashed upon the stanch canvas over our heads. We lay upon india-rubber cloths, placed between our blankets and the soil. For a while they excluded the water to admiration; but when at length it accumulated and began to run over the edges, they served equally well to retain it, so that toward the end of the night we were unconsciously reposing in small pools of rain.

On finally awaking in the morning the prospect was not a cheerful one. The rain no longer poured in torrents; but it pattered with a quiet pertinacity upon the strained and saturated canvas. We disengaged ourselves from our blankets, every fiber of which glistened with little beadlike drops of water, and looked out in vain hope of discovering some token of fair weather. The clouds, in lead-colored volumes, rested upon the dismal verge of the prairie, or hung sluggishly overhead, while the earth wore an aspect no more attractive than the heavens, exhibiting nothing but pools of water, grass beaten down, and mud well trampled by our mules and horses. Our companions' tent, with an air of forlorn and passive misery, and their wagons in like manner, drenched and woe-begone, stood not far off. The captain was just returning from his morning's inspection of the horses. He stalked through the mist and rain, with his plaid around his shoulders; his little pipe projecting from beneath his mustache, and his brother Jack at his heels.

"Good-morning, captain."

"Good-morning to your honors," said the captain, affecting the Hibernian accent; but at that instant, as he stooped to enter the tent, he tripped upon the cords at the entrance, and pitched forward against the guns which were strapped around the pole in the center.

"You are nice men, you are!" said he, after an ejaculation not necessary to be recorded, "to set a man-trap before your door every morning to catch your visitors."

Then he sat down upon Henry Chatillon's saddle. We tossed a piece of buffalo robe to Jack, who was looking about in some embarrassment. He spread it on the ground, and took his seat, with a stolid countenance, at his brother's side.

"Exhilarating weather, captain!"

"Oh, delightful, delightful!" replied the captain. "I knew it would be so; so much for starting yesterday at noon! I knew how it would turn out; and I said so at the time."

"You said just the contrary to us. We were in no hurry, and only moved because you insisted on it."

"Gentlemen," said the captain, taking his pipe from his mouth with an air of extreme gravity, "it was no plan of mine. There is a man among us who is determined to have everything his own way. You may express your opinion; but don't expect him to listen. You may be as reasonable as you like: oh, it all goes for nothing! That man is resolved to rule the roost and he'll set his face against any plan that he didn't think of himself."

The captain puffed for a while at his pipe, as if meditating upon his grievances; then he began again:

"For twenty years I have been in the British army; and in all that time I never had half so much dissension, and quarreling, and nonsense, as since I have been on this cursed prairie. He's the most uncomfortable man I ever met."

"Yes," said Jack; "and don't you know, Bill, how he drank up all the coffee last night, and put the rest by for himself till the morning!"

"He pretends to know everything," resumed the captain; "nobody must give orders but he! It's, oh! we must do this; and, oh! we must do that; and the tent must be pitched here, and the horses must be picketed there; for nobody knows as well as he does."

We were a little surprised at this disclosure of domestic dissensions among our allies, for though we knew of their existence, we were not aware of their extent. The persecuted captain seeming wholly at a loss as to the course of conduct that he should pursue, we recommended him to adopt prompt and energetic measures; but all his military experience had failed to teach him the indispensable lesson to be "hard," when the emergency requires it.

"For twenty years," he repeated, "I have been in the British army, and in that time I have been intimately acquainted with some two hundred officers, young and old, and I never yet quarreled with any man. Oh, 'anything for a quiet life!' that's my maxim."

We intimated that the prairie was hardly the place to enjoy a quiet life, but that, in the present circumstances, the best thing he could do toward securing his wished-for tranquillity, was immediately to put a period to the nuisance that disturbed it. But again the captain's easy good-nature recoiled from the task. The somewhat vigorous measures necessary to gain the desired result were utterly repugnant to him; he preferred to pocket his grievances, still retaining the privilege of grumbling about them. "Oh, anything for a quiet life!" he said again, circling back to his favorite maxim.

But to glance at the previous history of our transatlantic confederates. The captain had sold his commission, and was living in bachelor ease and dignity in his paternal halls, near Dublin. He hunted, fished, rode steeple-chases, ran races, and talked of his former exploits. He was surrounded with the trophies of his rod and gun; the walls were plentifully garnished, he told us, with moose-horns and deer-horns, bear-skins, and fox-tails; for the captain's double-barreled rifle had seen service in Canada and Jamaica; he had killed salmon in Nova Scotia, and trout, by his own account, in all the streams of the three kingdoms. But in an evil hour a seductive stranger came from London; no less a person than R., who, among other multitudinous wanderings, had once been upon the western prairies, and naturally enough was anxious to visit them again. The captain's imagination was inflamed by the pictures of a hunter's paradise that his guest held forth; he conceived an ambition to add to his other trophies the horns of a buffalo, and the claws of a grizzly bear; so he and R. struck a league to travel in company. Jack followed his brother, as a matter of course.

Two weeks on board the Atlantic steamer brought them to Boston; in two weeks more of hard traveling they reached St. Louis, from which a ride of six days carried them to the frontier; and here we found them, in full tide of preparation for their journey.

We had been throughout on terms of intimacy with the captain, but R., the motive power of our companions' branch of the expedition, was scarcely known to us. His voice, indeed, might be heard incessantly; but at camp he remained chiefly within the tent, and on the road he either rode by himself, or else remained in close conversation with

"Three Island Crossing," a watercolor by W. H. Jackson. A wagon train makes a circuitous river crossing in Idaho circa 1880.

W.H. JACKSON.

his friend Wright, the muleteer. As the captain left the tent that morning, I observed R. standing by the fire, and having nothing else to do, I determined to ascertain, if possible, what manner of man he was. He had a book under his arm, but just at present he was engrossed in actively superintending the operations of Sorel, the hunter, who was cooking some corn-bread over the coals for breakfast. R. was a well-formed and rather good-looking man, some thirty years old; considerably younger than the captain. He wore a beard and mustache of the oakum complexion, and his attire was altogether more elegant than one ordinarily sees on the prairie. He wore his cap on one side of his head; his checked shirt, open in front, was in very neat order, considering the circumstances, and his blue pantaloons, of the John Bull cut, might once have figured in Bond Street.

"Turn over that cake, man! turn it over, quick! Don't you see it burning?"

"It ain't half done," growled Sorel, in the amiable tone of a whipped bull-dog.

"It is. Turn it over, I tell you!"

Sorel, a strong, sullen-looking Canadian, who from having spent his life among the wildest and most remote of the Indian tribes, had imbibed much of their dark, vindictive spirit, looked ferociously up, as if he longed to leap upon his bourgeois and throttle him; but he obeyed the order, coming from so experienced an artist.

"It was a good idea of yours," said I, seating myself on the tongue of a wagon, "to bring Indian meal with you."

"Yes, yes" said R. "It's good bread for the prairie—good bread for the prairie. I tell you that's burning again."

Here he stooped, and unsheathing the silver-mounted hunting-knife in his belt, began to perform the part of cook himself; at the same time requesting me to hold for a moment the book under his arm, which interfered with these important functions. I opened it; it was "Macaulay's Lays"; and I made some remark, expressing my admiration of the work.

"Yes, yes; a pretty good thing. Macaulay can do better than that though. I know him very well. I have traveled with him. Where was it we first met—at Damascus? No, no; it was in Italy."

"So," said I, "you have been over the same ground with your countryman, the author of 'Eothen'? There has been some discussion in America as to who he is. I have heard Milne's name mentioned."

"Milne's? Oh, no, no, no; not at all. It was Kinglake; Kinglake's the man. I know him very well; that is, I have seen him."

Here Jack C., who stood by, interposed a remark (a thing not common with him), observing that he thought the weather would become fair before twelve o'clock.

"It's going to rain all day," said R., "and clear up in the middle of the night."

Just then the clouds began to dissipate in a very unequivocal manner; but Jack, not caring to defend his point against so authoritative a declaration, walked away whistling, and we resumed our conversation.

"Borrow, the author of 'The Bible in Spain,' I presume you know him too?"

"Oh, certainly; I know all those men. By the way, they told me that one of your American writers, Judge Story, had died lately. I edited some of his works in London; not without faults, though."

Here followed an erudite commentary on certain points of law, in which he particularly animadverted on the errors into which he considered that the judge had been betrayed. At length, having touched successively on an infinite variety of topics, I found that I had the happiness of discovering a man equally competent to enlighten me upon them all, equally an authority on matters of science or literature, philosophy or fashion. The part I bore in the conversation was by no means a prominent one; it was only necessary to set him going, and when he had run long enough upon one topic, to divert him to another and lead him on to pour out his heaps of treasure in succession.

"What has that fellow been saying to you?" said Shaw, as I returned to the tent. "I have heard nothing but his talking for the last half-hour."

R. had none of the peculiar traits of the ordinary "British snob"; his absurdities were all his own, belonging to no particular nation or clime. He was possessed with an active devil that had driven him over land and sea, to no great purpose, as it seemed; for although he had the usual complement of eyes and ears, the avenues between these organs and his brain appeared remarkably narrow and untrodden. His energy was much more conspicuous than his wisdom; but his predominant characteristic was a magnanimous ambition to exercise on all occasions an awful rule and supremacy, and this propensity equally displayed itself, as the reader will have observed, whether the matter in question was the baking of a hoe-cake or a point of international law. When such diverse elements as he and the easy-tempered captain came in contact, no wonder some commotion ensued; R. rode roughshod, from morning till night, over his military ally.

At noon the sky was clear and we set out, trailing through mud and slime six inches deep. That night we were spared the customary infliction of the shower bath.

On the next afternoon we were moving slowly along, not far from a patch of woods which lay on the right. Jack C. rode a little in advance;

The livelong day he had not spoke; when suddenly he faced about, pointed to the woods, and roared out to his brother:

"O Bill! here's a cow!"

The captain instantly galloped forward, and he and Jack made a vain attempt to capture the prize; but the cow, with a well-grounded distrust of their intentions, took refuge among the trees. R. joined them, and they soon drove her out. We watched as they galloped around her, trying in vain to noose her with their trail-ropes. At length they resorted to milder measures, and the cow was driven along with the party. Soon after the

Ezra Meeker, with his oxcart and dog, in 1910.

A River of Life

By Ezra Meeker

During the ox-team days a mighty army of pioneers went west. In the year that we crossed (1852), when the migration was at its height, this army made an unbroken column fully five hundred miles long. We knew by the inscribed dates on Independence Rock and elsewhere that there were wagons three hundred miles ahead of us, and the throng continued crossing the river for more than a month after we had crossed it.

…The animals driven over the plains during these years were legion. Besides those that labored under the yoke, in harness, and under saddle, there was a vast herd of loose stock. A conservative estimate would be not less than six animals to the wagon, and surely there were three loose animals to each one in the teams. Sixteen hundred wagons passed us while we waited for Oliver to recover. With these teams must have been nearly ten thousand beasts of burden and thirty thousand head of loose stock.

Is it any wonder that the old trail was worn so deep that even now in places it looks like a great canal? At one point near Split Rock, Wyoming, I found the road cut so deep in the solid sandstone that the kingbolt of my wagon dragged on the high center.

The pioneer army was a moving mass of human beings and dumb brutes, at times mixed in inextricable confusion, a hundred feet wide or more. Sometimes two columns of wagons, traveling on parallel lines and near each other, would serve as a barrier to prevent loose stock from crossing; but usually there would be a confused mass of cows, young cattle, horses, and men afoot moving along the outskirts. Here and there would be the drivers of loose stock, some on foot and some on horseback; a young girl, maybe, riding astride and with a young child behind her, going here and there after an intractable cow, while the mother could be seen in the confusion lending a helping hand. As in a thronged city street, no one seemed to pay much attention, if any, to others, all being bent only on accomplishing the task in hand.

usual thunderstorm came up, the wind blowing with such fury that the streams of rain flew almost horizontally along the prairie, roaring like a cataract. The horses turned tail to the storm, while we drew our heads between our shoulders, and crouched forward, so as to make our backs serve as a pent-house for the rest of our persons. Meanwhile the cow, taking advantage of the tumult, ran off, to the great discomfiture of the captain, who seemed to consider her as his own especial prize. In defiance of the storm, he pulled his cap tight over his brows, jerked a huge buffalo pistol from his holster, and set out at full speed after her. This was the last we saw of them for some time, but at length we heard the captain's shout, and saw him looming through the tempest, with his cocked pistol held aloft, and a countenance of anxiety and excitement. The cow trotted before him, but exhibited evident signs of an intention to run off again, and the captain was roaring to us to head her. But the rain had got in behind our coat collars, and was traveling over our necks in numerous little streamlets, and being afraid to move our heads, for fear of admitting more, we sat stiff and immovable, looking at the captain askance, and laughing at his frantic movements. At last the cow made a sudden plunge and ran off; the captain spurred his horse, and galloped after, with evident designs of mischief. In a moment we heard the faint report, deadened by the rain, and then the conqueror and his victim reappeared, the latter shot through the body, and quite helpless. Not long after the storm moderated and we advanced again. The cow walked painfully along under the charge of Jack, to whom the captain had committed her. We were approaching a long line of trees, that followed a stream stretching across our path, when we beheld the vedette galloping toward us, much excited, but with a broad grin on his face.

"Let that cow drop behind!" he shouted to us; "here's her owners!" And in fact, as we approached the line of trees, a large white object, like a tent, was visible behind them. On approaching, however, we found, instead of the expected Mormon camp, nothing but the lonely prairie, and a large white rock standing by the path. The cow therefore resumed her place in our procession. She walked on until we encamped, when R. firmly approaching with his enormous English double-barreled rifle, calmly and deliberately took aim at her heart, and discharged into it first one bullet and then the other. She was then butchered on the most approved principles of woodcraft, and furnished a very welcome item to our somewhat limited bill of fare.

I n a day or two more we reached the river called the "Big Blue." By titles equally elegant, almost all the streams of this region are designated. We had struggled through ditches and little brooks all that morning; but on traversing the dense woods that lined the banks of the Blue, we found more formidable difficulties awaited us, for the stream, swollen by the rains, was wide, deep, and rapid.

No sooner were we on the spot than R. had flung off his clothes, and was swimming across, or splashing through the shallows, with the end of a rope between his teeth.

> ...When he saw that the men would not do as he told them, he wisely accommodated himself to circumstances, and with the utmost vehemence ordered them to do precisely that which they were at the time engaged upon...

"Crossing the Platte," an illustration in an 1859 issue of *Harper's Weekly*.

We all looked on in admiration, wondering what might be the design of this energetic preparation; but soon we heard him shouting: "Give that rope a turn round that stump! You, Sorel: do you hear? Look sharp now, Boisverd! Come over to this side, some of you, and help me!" The men to whom these orders were directed paid not the least attention to them, though they were poured out without pause or intermission. Henry Chatillon directed the work, and it proceeded quietly and rapidly. R.'s sharp brattling voice might have been heard incessantly; and he was leaping about with the utmost activity, multiplying himself, after the manner of great commanders, as if his universal presence and supervision were of the last necessity. His commands were rather amusingly inconsistent; for when he saw that the men would not do as he told them, he wisely accommodated himself to circumstances, and with the utmost vehemence ordered them to do precisely that which they were at the time engaged upon, no doubt recollecting the story of Mahomet and the refractory mountain. Shaw smiled significantly; R. observed it, and, approaching with a countenance of lofty indignation, began to vapor a little, but was instantly reduced to silence.

The raft was at length complete. We piled our goods upon it, with the exception of our guns, which each man chose to retain in his own keeping. Sorel, Boisverd, Wright and Delorier took their stations at the four corners, to hold it together, and swim across with it; and in a moment more, all our earthly possessions were floating on the turbid waters of the Big Blue. We sat on the bank, anxiously watching the result, until we saw the raft safe landed in a little cove far down on the opposite bank. The empty wagons were easily passed across; and then each man mounting a horse, we rode through the stream, the stray animals following of their own accord.

"Indian Encampment on the Prairie,"
by Edmund Montague Morris.

THE PLATTE
AND
THE DESERT

We were now arrived at the close of our solitary journeyings along the St. Joseph's trail. On the evening of the 23rd of May we encamped near its junction with the old legitimate trail of the Oregon emigrants. We had ridden long that afternoon, trying in vain to find wood and water, until at length we saw the sunset sky reflected from a pool encircled by bushes and a rock or two. The water lay in the bottom of a hollow, the smooth prairie gracefully rising in oceanlike swells on every side. We pitched our tents by it; not however before the keen eye of Henry Chatillon had discerned some unusual object upon the faintly-defined outline of the distant swell. But in the moist, hazy atmosphere of the evening, nothing could be clearly distinguished. As we lay around the fire after supper, a low and distant sound, strange enough amid the loneliness of the prairie, reached our ears—peals of laughter, and the faint voices of men and women. For eight days we had not encountered a human being, and this warning of their vicinity had an effect extremely wild and impressive.

About dark a sallow-faced fellow descended the hill on horseback, and splashing through the pool rode up to the tents. He was enveloped in a huge cloak, and his broad felt hat was weeping about his ears with the drizzling moisture of the evening. Another followed, a stout, square-built, intelligent-looking man, who announced himself as leader of an emigrant party encamped a mile in advance of us. About twenty wagons, he said, were with him; the rest of his party were on the other side of the Big Blue, waiting for a woman who was in the pains of child-birth, and quarreling meanwhile among themselves.

These were the first emigrants that we had overtaken, although we had found abundant and melancholy traces of their progress throughout the whole course of the journey. Sometimes we passed the grave of one who had sickened and died on the way. The earth was usually torn up, and covered thickly with wolf-tracks. Some had escaped this violation. One morning a piece of plank, standing upright on the summit of a grassy hill, attracted our notice, and riding up to it we found the following words very roughly traced upon it, apparently by a red-hot piece of iron:

MARY ELLIS DIED MAY 7TH, 1845.
Aged two months.

Such tokens were of common occurrence.

We were late in breaking up our camp on the following morning, and scarcely had we ridden a mile when we saw, far in advance of us, drawn against the horizon, a line of objects stretching at regular intervals along the level edge of the prairie. An intervening swell soon hid them from sight, until, ascending it a quarter of an hour after, we saw close before us the emigrant caravan, with its heavy white wagons creeping on in their slow procession, and a large drove of cattle following behind. Half a dozen yellow-visaged Missourians, mounted on horseback, were cursing and shouting among them; their lank angular proportions enveloped in brown homespun, evidently cut and adjusted by the hands of a domestic female tailor. As we approached, they greeted us with the polished salutation: "How are ye, boys? Are ye for Oregon or California?"

As we pushed rapidly past the wagons, children's faces were thrust out from the white coverings to look at us; while the care-worn, thin-featured matron, or the buxom girl, seated in front, suspended the knitting on which most of them were engaged to stare at us with wondering curiosity. By the side of each wagon stalked the proprietor, urging on his patient oxen, who shouldered heavily along, inch by inch, on their interminable journey. It was easy to see that fear and dissension prevailed among them; some of the men—but these, with one exception, were bachelors—looked wistfully upon us as we rode lightly and swiftly past, and then impatiently at their own lumbering wagons and heavy-gaited oxen. Others were unwilling to advance at all until the party they had left

Deaths on the Trail

From the diary of Mrs. Cecilia McMillen Adams

Cecelia Adams crossed the plains in 1852 and recorded the frequency of deaths along the way. An estimated five thousand were thought to die from cholera on the trip.

June 14: Passed seven new-made graves

June 16: Passed eleven new graves

June 17: Passed six new graves

June 18: We have passed twenty-one new graves today

June 19: Passed thirteen graves today

June 20: Passed ten graves

June 21: No report

June 22: Passed seven graves. If we should go by the camping grounds, we should see five times as many graves as we do.

The Old Platte Bridge in the 1860s, a wooden conveyance over the North Platte River at Fort Caspar near present-day Casper, Wyoming.

behind should have rejoined them. Many were murmuring against the leader they had chosen, and wished to depose him; and this discontent was fermented by some ambitious spirits, who had hopes of succeeding in his place. The women were divided between regrets for the homes they had left and apprehension of the deserts and the savages before them.

We soon left them far behind, and fondly hoped that we had taken a final leave; but unluckily our companions' wagon stuck so long in a deep muddy ditch that, before it was extricated, the van of the emigrant caravan appeared again, descending a ridge close at hand. Wagon after wagon plunged through the mud; and as it was nearly noon, and the place promised shade and water, we saw with much gratification that they were resolved to encamp. Soon the wagons were wheeled into a circle; the cattle were grazing over the meadow, and the men with sour, sullen faces, were looking about for wood and water. They seemed to meet with but indifferent success. As we left the ground, I saw a tall slouching fellow with the nasal accent of "down east," contemplating the contents of his tin cup, which he had just filled with water.

"Look here, you," he said; "it's chock full of animals!"

The cup, as he held it out, exhibited in fact an extraordinary variety and profusion of animal and vegetable life.

Riding up the little hill and looking back on the meadow, we could easily see that all was not right in the camp of the emigrants. The men were crowded together, and an angry discussion seemed to be going forward. R. was missing from his wonted place in the line, and the captain told us that he had remained behind to get his horse shod by a blacksmith who was attached to the emigrant party. Something whispered in our ears that mischief was on foot; we kept on, however, and coming soon to a stream of tolerable water, we stopped to rest and dine. Still the absentee lingered behind. At last, at the distance of a mile, he and his horse suddenly appeared, sharply defined against the sky on the summit of a hill; and close behind, a huge white object rose slowly into view.

"What is that blockhead bringing with him now?"

A moment dispelled the mystery. Slowly and solemnly one behind the other, four long trains of oxen and four emigrant wagons rolled over the crest of the declivity and gravely descended, while R. rode in state in the van. It seems that, during the process of shoeing the horse, the smothered dissensions among the emigrants suddenly broke into open rupture. Some insisted on pushing forward, some on remaining where they were, and some on going back. Kearsley, their captain, threw up his command in disgust. "And now, boys," said he, "if any of you are for going ahead, just you come along with me."

Four wagons, with ten men, one woman, and one small child, made up the force of the "go-ahead" faction, and R., with his usual proclivity toward mischief, invited them to join our party. Fear of the Indians—for I can conceive of no other motive—must have induced him to court so burdensome an alliance. As may well be conceived, these repeated instances of high-handed dealing sufficiently exasperated us. In this case, indeed, the men who joined us were all that could be desired; rude indeed in manner, but frank, manly, and intelligent. To tell them we could not travel with them was of course out of the question. I merely reminded Kearsley that if his oxen could not keep up with our mules he must expect to be left behind, as we could not consent to be further delayed on the journey; but he immediately replied, that his oxen "SHOULD keep up; and if they couldn't, why he allowed that he'd find out how to make 'em!"

Having availed myself of what satisfaction could be derived from giving R. to understand my opinion of his conduct, I returned to our side of the camp.

On the next day, as it chanced, our English companions broke the axle-tree of their wagon, and down came the whole cumbrous machine lumbering into the bed of a brook! Here was a day's work cut out for us. Meanwhile, our emigrant associates kept on their way, and so vigorously did they urge forward their powerful oxen that, with the broken axle-tree and other calamities, it was full a week before we overtook them; when at length we discovered them, one afternoon, crawling quietly along the sandy brink of the Platte. But meanwhile various incidents occurred to ourselves.

It was probable that at this stage of our journey the Pawnees would attempt to rob us. We began therefore to stand guard in turn, dividing the night into three watches, and appointing two men for each. Delorier and I held guard together. We did not march with military precision to and fro before the tents; our discipline was by no means so stringent and rigid. We wrapped ourselves in our blankets, and sat down by the fire; and Delorier, combining his culinary functions with his duties as sentinel, employed himself in boiling the head of an antelope for our morning's repast. Yet we were models of vigilance in comparison with some of the party; for the ordinary practice of the guard was to establish himself in the most comfortable posture he could; lay his rifle on the ground, and enveloping his nose in the blanket, meditate on his mistress, or whatever subject best pleased him. This is all well enough when among Indians who do not habitually proceed further in their hostility than robbing travelers of their horses and mules, though a Pawnee's forebearance is not always to be trusted; but in certain regions farther to the west, the guard must beware how he exposes his person to the light of the fire, lest perchance some keen-eyed skulking marksman should let fly a bullet or an arrow from amid the darkness.

Among various tales that circulated around our camp fire was a rather curious one, told by Boisverd, and not inappropriate here. Boisverd was trapping with several companions on the skirts of the Blackfoot country. The man on guard, well knowing that it behooved him to put forth his utmost precaution, kept aloof from the firelight, and sat watching intently on all sides. At length he was aware of a dark, crouching figure, stealing noiselessly into the circle of the light. He hastily cocked his rifle, but the sharp click of the lock caught the ear of Blackfoot, whose senses were all on the alert. Raising his arrow, already fitted to the string, he shot in the direction of the sound. So sure was his aim that he drove it through the throat of the unfortunate guard, and then, with a loud yell, bounded from the camp.

As I looked at the partner of my watch, puffing and blowing over his fire, it occurred to me that he might not prove the most efficient auxiliary in time of trouble.

"Delorier," said I, "would you run away if the Pawnees should fire at us?"

"Ah! oui, oui, monsieur!" he replied very decisively.

I did not doubt the fact, but was a little surprised at the frankness of the confession. At this instant a most whimsical variety of voices—barks, howls, yelps, and whines—all mingled as it were together, sounded from the prairie, not far off, as if a whole conclave of wolves of every age and sex were assembled there. Delorier looked up from his work with a laugh, and began to imitate this curious medley of sounds with a most ludicrous accuracy. At this they were repeated with redoubled emphasis, the musician being apparently indignant at the successful efforts of a rival. They all proceeded from the throat of one little wolf, not larger than a spaniel, seated by himself at some distance. He was of the species called the prairie wolf; a grim-visaged, but harmless little brute,

An encampment of Piegan
Indians, with grazing horses and
ever-present packs of dogs.

whose worst propensity is creeping among horses and gnawing the ropes of raw hide by which they are picketed around the camp. But other beasts roam the prairies, far more formidable in aspect and in character. These are the large white and gray wolves, whose deep howl we heard at intervals from far and near.

At last I fell into a doze, and, awakening from it, found Delorier fast asleep. Scandalized by this breach of discipline, I was about to stimulate his vigilance by stirring him with the stock of my rifle; but compassion prevailing, I determined to let him sleep awhile, and then to arouse him, and administer a suitable reproof for such a forgetfulness of duty. Now and then I walked the rounds among the silent horses, to see that all was right. The night was chill, damp, and dark, the dank grass bending under the icy dewdrops. At the distance of a rod or two the tents were invisible, and nothing could be seen but the obscure figures of the horses, deeply breathing, and restlessly starting as they slept, or still slowly champing the grass. Far off, beyond the black outline of the prairie, there was a ruddy light, gradually increasing, like the glow of a conflagration; until at length the broad disk of the moon, blood-red, and vastly magnified by the vapors, rose slowly upon the darkness, flecked by one or two little clouds, and as the light poured over the gloomy plain, a fierce and stern howl, close at hand, seemed to greet it as an unwelcome intruder. There was something impressive and awful in the place and the hour; for I and the beasts were all that had consciousness for many a league around.

Some days elapsed, and brought us near the Platte. Two men on horseback approached us one morning, and we watched them with the curiosity and interest that, upon the solitude of the plains, such an encounter always excites. They were evidently whites, from their mode of riding, though, contrary to the usage of that region, neither of them carried a rifle.

"Fools!" remarked Henry Chatillon, "to ride that way on the prairie; Pawnee find them—then they catch it!"

Pawnee *had* found them, and they had come very near "catching it"; indeed, nothing saved them from trouble but the approach of our party. Shaw and I knew one of them; a man named Turner, whom we had seen at Westport. He and his companion belonged to an emigrant party encamped a few miles in advance, and had returned to look for some stray oxen, leaving their rifles, with characteristic rashness or ignorance behind them. Their neglect had nearly cost them dear; for just before we came up, half a dozen Indians approached, and seeing them apparently defenseless, one of the rascals seized the bridle of Turner's fine horse, and ordered him to dismount. Turner was wholly unarmed; but the other jerked a little revolving pistol out of his pocket, at which the Pawnee recoiled; and just then some of our men appearing in the distance, the whole party whipped their rugged little horses, and made off. In no way daunted, Turner foolishly persisted in going forward.

Long after leaving him, and late this afternoon, we came suddenly upon the great Pawnee trail, leading from their villages on the Platte to their war and hunting grounds to the southward. Here every summer pass the motley concourse; thousands of savages, men, women, and children, horses and mules, laden with their weapons and implements, and an innumerable multitude of unruly wolfish dogs, who have not acquired the civilized accomplishment of barking, but howl like their wild cousins of the prairie.

The permanent winter villages of the Pawnees stand on the lower Platte, but throughout the summer the greater part of the inhabitants are wandering over the plains, a treacherous cowardly banditti, who by a thousand acts of pillage and murder have deserved summary chastisement at the hands of government. Last year a Dakota warrior performed a signal exploit at one of these villages. He approached it alone in the middle of a dark night, and clambering up the outside of one of the lodges which are in the form of a half-sphere, he looked in at the round hole made at the top for the escape of smoke. The dusky light from the smoldering embers showed him the forms of the sleeping inmates; and dropping lightly through the opening, he unsheathed his knife, and stirring the fire coolly selected his victims. One by one he stabbed and scalped them, when a child suddenly awoke and screamed. He rushed from the lodge, yelled a Sioux war-cry, shouted his name in triumph and defiance, and in a moment had darted out upon the dark prairie, leaving the whole village behind him in a tumult, with the howling and baying of dogs, the screams of women and the yells of the enraged warriors.

A Pawnee Indian shield, showing the thunderbird on high, creator of the mighty storms on the Great Plains.

Our friend Kearsley, as we learned on rejoining him, signalized himself by a less bloody achievement. He and his men were good woodsmen, and well skilled in the use of the rifle, but found themselves wholly out of their element on the prairie. None of them had ever seen a buffalo, and they had very vague conceptions of his nature and appearance. On the day after they reached the Platte, looking toward a distant swell, they beheld a multitude of little black specks in motion upon its surface.

"Take your rifles, boys," said Kearsley, "and we'll have fresh meat for supper." This inducement was quite sufficient. The ten men left their wagons and set out in hot haste, some on horseback and some on foot, in pursuit of the supposed buffalo. Meanwhile a high grassy ridge shut the game from view; but mounting it after half an hour's running and riding, they found themselves suddenly confronted by about thirty mounted Pawnees! The amazement and consternation were mutual. Having nothing but their bows and arrows, the Indians thought their hour was come, and the fate that they were no doubt conscious of richly deserving about to overtake them. So they began, one and all, to shout forth the most cordial salutations of friendship, running up with extreme earnestness to shake hands with the Missourians, who were as much rejoiced as they were to escape the expected conflict.

A low undulating line of sand-hills bounded the horizon before us. That day we rode ten consecutive hours, and it was dusk before we entered the hollows and gorges of these gloomy little hills. At length we gained the summit, and the long expected valley of the Platte lay before us. We all drew rein, and, gathering in a knot on the crest of the hill, sat joyfully looking down upon the prospect. It was right welcome; strange too, and striking to the imagination, and yet it had not one picturesque or beautiful feature; nor had it any of the features of grandeur, other than its vast extent, its solitude, and its wilderness. For league after league a plain as level as a frozen lake was outspread beneath us; here and there the Platte, divided into a dozen threadlike sluices, was traversing it, and an occasional clump of wood, rising in the midst like a shadowy island, relieved the monotony of the waste. No living thing was moving throughout the vast landscape, except the lizards that darted over the sand and through the rank grass and prickly-pear just at our feet.

We had passed the more toilsome and monotonous part of the journey; but four hundred miles still intervened between us and Fort Laramie; and to reach that point

This calumet, a sacred feathered pipe, was used in the Hako ceremony by the Pawnee Indian tribe.

cost us the travel of three additional weeks. During the whole of this time we were passing up the center of a long narrow sandy plain, reaching like an outstretched belt nearly to the Rocky Mountains. Two lines of sand-hills, broken often into the wildest and most fantastic forms, flanked the valley at the distance of a mile or two on the right and left; while beyond them lay a barren, trackless waste—The Great American Desert—extending for hundreds of miles to the Arkansas on the one side, and the Missouri on the other. Before us and behind us, the level monotony of the plain was unbroken as far as the eye could reach. Sometimes it glared in the sun, an expanse of hot, bare sand; sometimes it was veiled by long coarse grass. Huge skulls and whitening bones of buffalo were scattered everywhere; the ground was tracked by myriads of them, and often covered with the circular indentations where the bulls had wallowed in the hot weather. From every gorge and ravine, opening from the hills, descended deep, well-worn paths, where the buffalo issue twice a day in regular procession down to drink in the Platte. The river itself runs through the midst, a thin sheet of rapid, turbid water, half a mile wide, and scarce two feet deep. Its low banks for the most part without a bush or a tree, are of loose sand, with which the stream is so charged that it grates on the teeth in drinking. The naked landscape is, of itself, dreary and monotonous enough, and yet the wild beasts and wild men that frequent the valley of the Platte make it a scene of interest and excitement to the traveler. Of those who have journeyed there, scarce one, perhaps, fails to look back with fond regret to his horse and his rifle.

Early in the morning after we reached the Platte, a long procession of squalid savages approached our camp. Each was on foot, leading his horse by a rope of bull-hide. His attire consisted merely of a scanty cincture and an old buffalo robe, tattered and begrimed by use, which hung over his shoulders. His head was close shaven, except a ridge of hair reaching over the crown from the center of the forehead, very much like the long bristles on the back of a hyena, and he carried his bow and arrows in his hand, while his meager little horse was laden with dried buffalo meat, the produce of his hunting. Such were the first specimens that we met—and very indifferent ones they were—of the genuine savages of the plains.

They were the Pawnees whom Kearsley had encountered the day before, and belonged to a large hunting party known to be ranging the prairie in the vicinity. They strode rapidly past, within a furlong of our tents, not pausing or looking toward us, after the manner of Indians when meditating mischief or conscious of ill-desert. I went out and met them; and had an amicable conference with the chief, presenting him with half a pound of tobacco, at which unmerited bounty he expressed much gratification. These fellows, or some of their companions, had committed a dastardly outrage upon an emigrant party in advance of us. Two men, out on horseback at a distance, were seized by them, but lashing their horses, they broke loose and fled. At this the Pawnees raised

Prairie dogs, native to the grasslands of North America, lived in extensive colonies.

Storms of Dust and Rains

By Ezra Meeker

The steady flow of wind rushing through the South Pass would hurl the dust and sand like fine hail… Sometimes we had trying storms that would wet us to the skin in no time. One such I remember well, being caught in it while out on watch. The cattle traveled so fast that it was difficult to keep up with them. I could do nothing but follow, as it would have been impossible to turn them…

Anyhow, in an incredibly short time there was not a dry thread left to my name. My boots were as full of water as if I had been wading over boot-top depth, and the water ran through my hat as though it were a sieve. I was almost blinded in the fury of the wind and water. Many tents were leveled by this storm. One of our neighboring trains suffered great loss by the sheets of water on the ground floating away camp equipage, ox yokes, and all loose articles; and they narrowly escaped having a wagon engulfed in the raging torrent that came so unexpectedly upon them.

the yell and shot at them, transfixing the hindermost through the back with several arrows, while his companion galloped away and brought in the news to his party. The panic-stricken emigrants remained for several days in camp, not daring even to send out in quest of the dead body. The reader will recollect Turner, the man whose narrow escape was mentioned not long since. We heard that the men, whom the entreaties of his wife induced to go in search of him, found him leisurely driving along his recovered oxen, and whistling in utter contempt of the Pawnee nation. His party was encamped within two miles of us; but we passed them that morning, while the men were driving in the oxen, and the women packing their domestic utensils and their numerous offspring in the spacious patriarchal wagons. As we looked back we saw their caravan dragging its slow length along the plain; wearily toiling on its way, to found new empires in the West.

Our New England climate is mild and equable compared with that of the Platte. This very morning, for instance, was close and sultry, the sun rising with a faint oppressive heat; when suddenly darkness gathered in the west, and a furious blast of sleet and hail drove full in our faces, icy cold, and urged with such demoniac vehemence that it felt like a storm of needles. It was curious to see the horses; they faced about in extreme displeasure, holding their tails like whipped dogs, and shivering as the angry gusts, howling louder than a concert of wolves, swept over us. Wright's long train of mules came sweeping round before the storm like a flight of brown snowbirds driven by a winter tempest. Thus we all remained stationary for some minutes, crouching close to our horses' necks, much too surly to speak, though once the captain looked up from between the collars of his coat, his face blood-red, and the muscles of his mouth contracted by the cold into a most ludicrous grin of agony. He grumbled something that sounded like a curse, directed as we believed, against the unhappy hour when he had first thought of leaving home. The thing was too good to last long; and the instant the puffs of wind subsided we erected our tents, and remained in camp for the rest of a gloomy and lowering day. The emigrants also encamped near at hand. We, being first on the ground, had appropriated all the wood within reach; so that our fire alone blazed cheerfully. Around it soon gathered a group of uncouth figures, shivering in the drizzling rain. Conspicuous among them were two or three of the half-savage men who spend their reckless lives in trapping among the Rocky Mountains, or in trading for the Fur Company in the Indian villages. They were all of Canadian extraction; their hard, weather-beaten faces and bushy mustaches looked out from beneath the hoods of their white capotes with a bad and brutish expression, as if their owner might be the willing agent of any villainy. And such in fact is the character of many of these men.

On the day following we overtook Kearsley's wagons, and thenceforward, for a week or two, we were fellow-travelers. One good effect, at least, resulted from the alliance; it materially diminished the serious fatigue of standing guard; for the party being now more numerous, there were longer intervals between each man's turns of duty.

THE BUFFALO

"Buffalo on the Plains," an oil painting. Albert Bierstadt, late 1800s.

F our days on the Platte, and yet no buffalo! Last year's signs of them were provokingly abundant; and wood being extremely scarce, we found an admirable substitute in bois de vache, which burns exactly like peat, producing no unpleasant effects. The wagons one morning had left the camp; Shaw and I were already on horseback, but Henry Chatillon still sat cross-legged by the dead embers of the fire, playing pensively with the lock of his rifle, while his sturdy Wyandotte pony stood quietly behind him, looking over his head. At last he got up, patted the neck of the pony (whom, from an exaggerated appreciation of his merits, he had christened "Five Hundred Dollar"), and then mounted with a melancholy air.

"What is it, Henry?"

"Ah, I feel lonesome; I never been here before; but I see away yonder over the buttes, and down there on the prairie, black—all black with buffalo!"

In the afternoon he and I left the party in search of an antelope; until at the distance of a mile or two on the right, the tall white wagons and the little black specks of horsemen were just visible, so slowly advancing that they seemed motionless; and far on the left rose the broken line of scorched, desolate sand-hills. The vast plain waved with tall rank grass that swept our horses' bellies; it swayed to and fro in billows with the light breeze, and far and near antelope and wolves were moving through it, the hairy backs of the latter alternately appearing and disappearing as they bounded awkwardly along; while the antelope, with the simple curiosity peculiar to them, would often approach as closely, their little horns and white throats just visible above the grass tops, as they gazed eagerly at us with their round black eyes.

An 1874 *Harper's Weekly* cover illustration, "Slaughtered for the Hide," showing the skinning of a buffalo.

I dismounted, and amused myself with firing at the wolves. Henry attentively scrutinized the surrounding landscape; at length he gave a shout, and called on me to mount again, pointing in the direction of the sand-hills. A mile and a half from us, two minute black specks slowly traversed the face of one of the bare glaring declivities, and disappeared behind the summit. "Let us go!" cried Henry, belaboring the sides of Five Hundred Dollar; and I following in his wake, we galloped rapidly through the rank grass toward the base of the hills.

From one of their openings descended a deep ravine, widening as it issued on the prairie. We entered it, and galloping up, in a moment were surrounded by the bleak sand-hills. Half of their steep sides were bare; the rest were scantily clothed with clumps of grass, and various uncouth plants, conspicuous among which appeared the

Full a quarter of a mile distant, a long procession of buffalo were walking, in Indian file, with the utmost gravity and deliberation; then more appeared, clambering from a hollow not far off, and ascending, one behind the other, the grassy slope of another hill . . .

reptile-like prickly-pear. They were gashed with numberless ravines; and as the sky had suddenly darkened, and a cold gusty wind arisen, the strange shrubs and the dreary hills looked doubly wild and desolate. But Henry's face was all eagerness. He tore off a little hair from the piece of buffalo robe under his saddle, and threw it up, to show the course of the wind. It blew directly before us. The game were therefore to windward, and it was necessary to make our best speed to get around them.

We scrambled from this ravine, and galloping away through the hollows, soon found another, winding like a snake among the hills, and so deep that it completely concealed us. We rode up the bottom of it, glancing through the shrubbery at its edge, till Henry abruptly jerked his rein, and slid out of his saddle. Full a quarter of a mile distant, on the outline of the farthest hill, a long procession of buffalo were walking, in Indian file, with the utmost gravity and deliberation; then more appeared, clambering from a hollow not far off, and ascending, one behind the other, the grassy slope of another hill; then a shaggy head and a pair of short broken horns appeared issuing out of a ravine close at hand, and with a slow, stately step, one by one, the enormous brutes came into view, taking their way across the valley, wholly unconscious of an enemy. In a moment Henry was worming his way, lying flat on the ground, through grass and prickly-pears, toward his unsuspecting victims. He had with him both my rifle and his own. He was soon out of sight, and still the buffalo kept issuing into the valley. For a long time all was silent. I sat holding his horse, and wondering what he was about, when suddenly, in rapid succession, came the sharp reports of the two rifles, and the whole line of buffalo, quickening their pace into a clumsy trot, gradually disappeared over the ridge of the hill. Henry rose to his feet, and stood looking after them.

"You have missed them," said I.

"Yes," said Henry; "let us go." He descended into the ravine, loaded the rifles, and mounted his horse.

We rode up the hill after the buffalo. The herd was out of sight when we reached the top, but lying on the grass not far off, was one quite lifeless, and another violently struggling in the death agony.

"You see I miss him!" remarked Henry. He had fired from a distance of more than a hundred and fifty yards, and both balls had passed through the lungs—the true mark in shooting buffalo.

The darkness increased, and a driving storm came on. Tying our horses to the horns of the victims, Henry began the bloody work of dissection, slashing away with the science of a connoisseur, while I vainly endeavored to imitate him. Old Hendrick recoiled with horror and indignation when I endeavored to tie the meat to the strings of raw hide, always carried for this purpose, dangling at the back of the saddle. After some difficulty we overcame his scruples; and heavily burdened with the more eligible portions of the buffalo, we set out on our return. Scarcely had we emerged from the labyrinth of gorges and ravines, and issued upon the open prairie, when the pricking sleet came driving, gust upon gust, directly in our faces. It was strangely dark, though wanting still an hour of sunset. The freezing storm soon penetrated to the skin, but the uneasy trot of our heavy-gaited horses kept us warm enough, as we forced them unwillingly in the teeth of the sleet and rain, by the powerful suasion of our Indian whips. The prairie in this place was hard and level. A flourishing colony of prairie dogs had burrowed into it in every direction, and the little mounds of fresh earth around their holes were about as numerous as the hills in a cornfield; but not a yelp was to be heard; not the nose of a single citizen was visible; all had retired to the depths of their burrows, and we envied them their dry and comfortable habitations. An hour's hard riding showed us our tent dimly looming through the storm, one side puffed out by the force of the wind, and the other collapsed in proportion, while the disconsolate horses stood shivering close around, and the wind kept up a dismal whistling in the boughs of three old half-dead trees above. Shaw, like a patriarch, sat on his saddle in the entrance, with a pipe in his mouth, and his arms folded, contemplating, with cool satisfaction, the piles of meat that we flung on the ground before him. A dark and dreary night succeeded; but the sun rose with heat so sultry and languid that the captain excused himself on that account from waylaying an old buffalo bull, who with stupid gravity was walking over the prairie to drink at the river. So much for the climate of the Platte!

But it was not the weather alone that had produced this sudden abatement of the sportsmanlike zeal which the captain had always professed. He had been out on the afternoon before, together with several members of his party; but their hunting was attended with no other result than the loss of one of their best horses, severely injured by Sorel, in vainly chasing a wounded bull. The captain, whose ideas of hard riding were all derived from transatlantic sources, expressed the utmost amazement at the feats of Sorel, who went leaping ravines, and dashing at full speed up and down the sides of precipitous hills, lashing his horse with the recklessness of a Rocky Mountain rider. Unfortunately for the poor animal he was the property of R., against whom Sorel entertained an unbounded aversion. The captain himself, it seemed, had also attempted to "run" a buffalo, but though a good and practiced horseman, he had soon given over the attempt, being astonished and utterly disgusted at the nature of the ground he was required to ride over.

Nothing unusual occurred on that day; but on the following morning Henry Chatillon, looking over the oceanlike expanse, saw near the foot of the distant hills something that looked like a band of buffalo. He was not sure, he said, but at all events, if they were buffalo, there was a fine chance for a race. Shaw and I at once determined to try the speed of our horses.

"Come, captain; we'll see which can ride hardest, a Yankee or an Irishman."

But the captain maintained a grave and austere countenance. He mounted his led horse, however, though very slowly; and we set out at a trot. The game appeared about three miles distant. As we proceeded the captain made various remarks of doubt and indecision; and at length declared he would have nothing to do with such a breakneck business; protesting that he had ridden plenty of steeple-chases in his day, but he never knew what riding was till he found himself behind a band of buffalo day before yesterday. "I am convinced," said the captain, "that, 'running' is out of the question. Take my advice now and don't attempt it. It's dangerous, and of no use at all."

The method of hunting called "running" consists in attacking the buffalo on horseback and shooting him with bullets or arrows when at full-speed. In "approaching," the hunter conceals himself and crawls on the ground toward the game, or lies in wait to kill them.

"Then why did you come out with us? What do you mean to do?"

"I shall 'approach,'" replied the captain.

"You don't mean to 'approach' with your pistols, do you? We have all of us left our rifles in the wagons."

The captain seemed staggered at the suggestion. In his characteristic indecision, at setting out, pistols, rifles, "running" and "approaching" were mingled in an inextricable medley in his brain. He trotted on in silence between us for a while; but at length he dropped behind and slowly walked his horse back to rejoin the party. Shaw and I kept on; when lo! as we advanced, the band of buffalo were transformed into certain clumps of tall bushes, dotting the prairie for a considerable distance. At this ludicrous termination of our chase, we followed the example of our late ally, and turned back toward the party. We were skirting the brink of a deep ravine, when we saw Henry and the broad-chested pony coming toward us at a gallop.

"Here's old Papin and Frederic, down from Fort Laramie!" shouted Henry, long before he came up. We had for some days expected this encounter. Papin was the bourgeois of Fort Laramie. He had come down the river with the buffalo robes and the beaver, the produce of the last winter's trading. I had among our baggage a letter which I wished to commit to their hands; so requesting Henry to detain the boats if he could until my return, I set out after the wagons. They were about four miles in advance. In half an hour I overtook them, got the letter, trotted back upon the trail, and looking carefully, as I rode, saw a patch of broken, storm-blasted trees, and moving near them some little black specks like men and horses. Arriving at the place, I found a strange assembly. The boats, eleven in number, deep-laden with the skins, hugged close to the shore, to escape being borne down by the swift current. The rowers, swarthy ignoble Mexicans, turned their brutish faces upward to look, as I reached the bank. Papin sat in the middle of one of the boats upon the canvas covering that protected the robes. He was a stout, robust fellow, with a little gray eye, that had a peculiarly sly twinkle. "Frederic" also stretched

A herd of buffalo
at water circa 1905.

his tall rawboned proportions close by the bourgeois, and "mountain-men" completed the group; some lounging in the boats, some strolling on shore; some attired in gayly painted buffalo robes, like Indian dandies; some with hair saturated with red paint, and be-plastered with glue to their temples; and one bedaubed with vermilion upon his forehead and each cheek. They were a mongrel race; yet the French blood seemed to predominate; in a few, indeed, might be seen the black snaky eye of the Indian half-breed, and one and all, they seemed to aim at assimilating themselves to their savage associates.

I shook hands with the bourgeois, and delivered the letter; then the boats swung round into the stream and floated away. They had reason for haste, for already the voyage from Fort Laramie had occupied a full month, and the river was growing daily more shallow. Fifty times a day the boats had been aground, indeed; those who navigate the Platte invariably spend half their time upon sand-bars. Two of these boats, the property of private traders, got hopelessly involved in the shallows, not very far from the Pawnee villages, and were soon surrounded by a swarm of the inhabitants. They carried off everything that they considered valuable, including most of the robes; and amused themselves by tying up the men left on guard and soundly whipping them with sticks.

We encamped that night upon the bank of the river. Among the emigrants there was an overgrown boy, some eighteen years old, with a head as round and about as large as a pumpkin, and fever-and-ague fits had dyed his face of a corresponding color. He wore an old white hat, tied under his chin with a handkerchief; his body was short and stout, but his legs of disproportioned and appalling length. I observed him at sunset, breasting the hill with gigantic strides, and standing against the sky on the summit, like a colossal pair of tongs. In a moment after we heard him screaming frantically behind the ridge, and nothing doubting that he was in the clutches of Indians or grizzly bears, some of the party caught up their rifles and ran to the rescue. His outcries, however, proved but an ebullition of joyous excitement; he had chased two little wolf pups to their burrow, and he was on his knees, grubbing away like a dog at the mouth of the hole, to get at them.

Before morning he caused more serious disquiet in the camp. It was his turn to hold the middle guard; but no sooner was he called up, than he coolly arranged a pair of saddle-bags under a wagon, laid his head upon them, closed his eyes, opened his mouth and fell asleep. The guard on our side of the camp, thinking it no part of his duty to look after the cattle of the emigrants, contented himself with watching our own horses and mules; the wolves, he said, were unusually noisy; but still no mischief was anticipated until the sun rose, and not a hoof or horn was in sight! The cattle were gone! While Tom was quietly slumbering, the wolves had driven them away.

Then we reaped the fruits of R.'s precious plan of traveling in company with emigrants. To leave them in their distress was not to be thought of, and we felt bound to wait

They had reason for haste, for already the voyage from Fort Laramie had occupied a full month, and the river was growing daily more shallow. Fifty times a day the boats had been aground, indeed; those who navigate the Platte invariably spend half their time upon sand-bars.

until the cattle could be searched for, and, if possible, recovered. But the reader may be curious to know what punishment awaited the faithless Tom. By the wholesome law of the prairie, he who falls asleep on guard is condemned to walk all day leading his horse by the bridle, and we found much fault with our companions for not enforcing such a sentence on the offender. Nevertheless had he been of our party, I have no doubt he would in like manner have escaped scot-free. But the emigrants went farther than mere forebearance; they decreed that since Tom couldn't stand guard without falling asleep, he shouldn't stand guard at all, and henceforward his slumbers were unbroken. Establishing such a premium on drowsiness could have no very beneficial effect upon the vigilance of our sentinels; for it is far from agreeable, after riding from sunrise to sunset, to feel your slumbers interrupted by the butt of a rifle nudging your side, and a sleepy voice growling in your ear that you must get up, to shiver and freeze for three weary hours at midnight.

"Buffalo! buffalo!" It was but a grim old bull, roaming the prairie by himself in misanthropic seclusion; but there might be more behind the hills. Dreading the monotony and languor of the camp, Shaw and I saddled our horses, buckled our holsters in their places, and set out with Henry Chatillon in search of the game. Henry, not intending to take part in the chase, but merely conducting us, carried his rifle with him, while we left ours behind as incumbrances. We rode for some five or six miles, and saw no living thing but wolves, snakes, and prairie dogs.

"This won't do at all," said Shaw.

"What won't do?"

"A Wagon Train Heading West in the 1860s," engraved by Stephane Pannemaker.

"There's no wood about here to make a litter for the wounded man; I have an idea that one of us will need something of the sort before the day is over."

There was some foundation for such an apprehension, for the ground was none of the best for a race, and grew worse continually as we proceeded; indeed it soon became desperately bad, consisting of abrupt hills and deep hollows, cut by frequent ravines not easy to pass. At length, a mile in advance, we saw a band of bulls. Some were scattered grazing over a green declivity, while the rest were crowded more densely together in the wide hollow below. Making a circuit to keep out of sight, we rode toward them until we ascended a hill within a furlong of them, beyond which nothing intervened that could possibly screen us from their view. We dismounted behind the ridge just out of sight, drew our saddle-girths, examined our pistols, and mounting again rode over the hill, and descended at a canter toward them, bending close to our horses' necks. Instantly they took the alarm; those on the hill descended; those below gathered into a mass, and the whole got in motion, shouldering each other along at a clumsy gallop. We followed, spurring our horses to full speed; and as the herd rushed, crowding and trampling in terror through an opening in the hills, we were close at their heels, half suffocated by the clouds of dust. But as we drew near, their alarm and speed increased; our horses showed signs of the utmost fear, bounding violently aside as we approached, and refusing to enter among the herd.

The buffalo now broke into several small bodies, scampering over the hills in different directions, and I lost sight of Shaw; neither of us knew where the other had gone. Old Pontiac ran like a frantic elephant up hill and down hill, his ponderous hoofs striking the prairie like sledge-hammers. He showed a curious mixture of eagerness and terror, straining to overtake the panic-stricken herd, but constantly recoiling in dismay as we drew near. The fugitives, indeed, offered no very attractive spectacle, with their enormous size and weight, their shaggy manes and the tattered remnants of their last winter's hair covering their backs in irregular shreds and patches, and flying off in the wind as they ran. At length I urged my horse close behind a bull, and after trying in vain, by blows and spurring, to bring him alongside, I shot a bullet into the buffalo from this disadvantageous position. At the report, Pontiac swerved so much that I was again thrown a little behind the game. The bullet, entering too much in the rear, failed to disable the bull, for a buffalo requires to be shot at particular points, or he will certainly escape. The herd ran up a hill, and I followed in pursuit. As Pontiac rushed headlong down on the other side, I saw Shaw and Henry descending the hollow on the right, at a leisurely gallop; and in front, the buffalo were just disappearing behind the crest of the next hill, their short tails erect, and their hoofs twinkling through a cloud of dust.

At that moment, I heard Shaw and Henry shouting to me; but the muscles of a stronger arm than mine could not have checked at once the furious course of Pontiac, whose mouth was as insensible as leather. Added to this, I rode him that morning with a common snaffle, having the day before, for the benefit of my other horse, unbuckled from

OPPOSITE:

"An American Bison, or Buffalo, Grazing with its Herd," a 1916 color lithograph by Louis Agassiz Fuertes.

Purple coneflowers were used for medicinal purposes by Native Americans, and were also eaten by buffalo.

my bridle the curb which I ordinarily used. A stronger and hardier brute never trod the prairie; but the novel sight of the buffalo filled him with terror, and when at full speed he was almost incontrollable. Gaining the top of the ridge, I saw nothing of the buffalo; they had all vanished amid the intricacies of the hills and hollows. Reloading my pistols, in the best way I could, I galloped on until I saw them again scuttling along at the base of the hill, their panic somewhat abated. Down went old Pontiac among them, scattering them to the right and left, and then we had another long chase. About a dozen bulls were before us, scouring over the hills, rushing down the declivities with tremendous weight and impetuosity, and then laboring with a weary gallop upward. Still Pontiac, in spite of spurring and beating, would not close with them. One bull at length fell a little behind the rest, and by dint of much effort I urged my horse within six or eight yards of his side. His back was darkened with sweat; he was panting heavily, while his tongue lolled out a foot from his jaws. Gradually I came up abreast of him, urging Pontiac with leg and rein nearer to his side, then suddenly he did what buffalo in such circumstances will always do; he slackened his gallop, and turning toward us, with an aspect of mingled rage and distress, lowered his huge shaggy head for a charge. Pontiac with a snort, leaped aside in terror, nearly throwing me to the ground, as I was wholly unprepared for such an evolution. I raised my pistol in a passion to strike him on the head, but thinking better of it fired the bullet after the bull, who had resumed his flight, then drew rein and determined to rejoin my companions. It was high time. The breath blew hard from Pontiac's nostrils, and the sweat rolled in big drops down his sides; I myself felt as if drenched in warm water. Pledging myself (and I redeemed the pledge) to take my revenge at a future opportunity, I looked round for some indications to show me where I was, and what course I ought to pursue; I might as well have looked for landmarks in the midst of the ocean. How many miles I had run or in what direction, I had no idea; and around me the prairie was rolling in steep swells and pitches, without a single distinctive feature to guide me. I had a little compass hung at my neck; and ignorant that the Platte at this point diverged considerably from its easterly course, I thought that by keeping to the northward I should certainly reach it. So I turned and rode about two hours in that direction. The prairie changed as I advanced, softening away into easier undulations, but nothing like the Platte appeared, nor any sign of a human being; the same wild endless expanse lay around me still; and to all appearance I was as far from my object as ever. I began now to consider myself in danger of being lost; and therefore, reining in my horse, summoned the scanty share of woodcraft that I possessed (if that term be applicable upon the prairie) to extricate me. Looking round, it occurred to me that the buffalo might prove my best guides. I soon found one of the paths made by them in their passage to the river; it ran nearly at right angles to my course; but turning my horse's head in the direction it indicated, his freer gait and erected ears assured me that I was right.

At that moment, I heard Shaw and Henry shouting to me; but the muscles of a stronger arm than mine could not have checked at once the furious course of Pontiac, whose mouth was as insensible as leather.

But in the meantime my ride had been by no means a solitary one. The whole face of the country was dotted far and wide with countless hundreds of buffalo. They trooped along in files and columns, bulls, cows, and calves, on the green faces of the declivities in front. They scrambled away over the hills to the right and left; and far off, the pale blue swells in the extreme distance were dotted with innumerable specks. Sometimes I surprised shaggy old bulls grazing alone, or sleeping behind the ridges I ascended. They would leap up at my approach, stare stupidly at me through their tangled manes, and then gallop heavily away. The antelope were very numerous; and as they are always bold when in the neighborhood of buffalo, they would approach quite near to look at me, gazing intently with their great round eyes, then suddenly leap aside, and stretch lightly away over the prairie, as swiftly as a racehorse. Squalid, ruffianlike wolves sneaked through the hollows and sandy ravines. Several times I passed through villages of prairie dogs, who sat, each at the mouth of his burrow, holding his paws before him in a supplicating attitude, and yelping away most vehemently, energetically whisking his little tail with every squeaking cry he uttered. Prairie dogs are not fastidious in their choice of companions; various long, checkered snakes were sunning themselves in the midst of the village, and demure little gray owls, with a large white ring around each eye, were perched side by side with the rightful inhabitants. The prairie teemed with life. Again and again I looked toward the crowded hillsides, and was sure I saw horsemen; and riding near, with a mixture of hope and dread, for Indians were abroad, I found them transformed into a group of buffalo. There was nothing in human shape amid all this vast congregation of brute forms.

When I turned down the buffalo path, the prairie seemed changed; only a wolf or two glided past at intervals, like conscious felons, never looking to the right or left. Being now free from anxiety, I was at leisure to observe minutely the objects around me; and

Buffalo hunters typically hunted on horseback for reasons of expediency and safety.

here, for the first time, I noticed insects wholly different from any of the varieties found farther to the eastward. Gaudy butterflies fluttered about my horse's head; strangely formed beetles, glittering with metallic luster, were crawling upon plants that I had never seen before; multitudes of lizards, too, were darting like lightning over the sand.

I had run to a great distance from the river. It cost me a long ride on the buffalo path before I saw from the ridge of a sand-hill the pale surface of the Platte glistening in the midst of its desert valleys, and the faint outline of the hills beyond waving along the sky. From where I stood, not a tree nor a bush nor a living thing was visible throughout the whole extent of the sun-scorched landscape. In half an hour I came upon the trail, not far from the river; and seeing that the party had not yet passed, I turned eastward to meet them, old Pontiac's long swinging trot again assuring me that I was right in doing so. Having been slightly ill on leaving camp in the morning six or seven hours of rough riding had fatigued me extremely. I soon stopped, therefore; flung my saddle on the ground, and with my head resting on it, and my horse's trail-rope tied loosely to my arm, lay waiting the arrival of the party, speculating meanwhile on the extent of the injuries Pontiac had received. At length the white wagon coverings rose from the verge of the plain. By a singular coincidence, almost at the same moment two horsemen appeared coming down from the hills. They were Shaw and Henry, who had searched for me a while in the morning, but well knowing the futility of the attempt in such a broken country, had placed themselves on the top of the highest hill they could find, and picketing their horses near them, as a signal to me, had laid down and fallen asleep. The stray cattle had been recovered, as the emigrants told us, about noon. Before sunset, we pushed forward eight miles farther.

> JUNE 7, 1846.—Four men are missing; R., Sorel and two emigrants. They set out this morning after buffalo, and have not yet made their appearance; whether killed or lost, we cannot tell.

I find the above in my notebook, and well remember the council held on the occasion. Our fire was the scene of it; or the palpable superiority of Henry Chatillon's experience and skill made him the resort of the whole camp upon every question of difficulty. He was molding bullets at the fire, when the captain drew near, with a perturbed and care-worn expression of countenance, faithfully reflected on the heavy features of Jack, who followed close behind. Then emigrants came straggling from their wagons toward the common center; various suggestions were made to account for the absence of the four men, and one or two of the emigrants declared that when out after the cattle they had seen Indians dogging them, and crawling like wolves along the ridges of the hills. At this time the captain slowly shook his head with double gravity, and solemnly remarked:

"It's a serious thing to be traveling through this cursed wilderness"; an opinion in which Jack immediately expressed a thorough coincidence. Henry would not commit himself by declaring any positive opinion.

"Maybe he only follow the buffalo too far; maybe Indian kill him; maybe he got lost; I cannot tell!"

With this the auditors were obliged to rest content; the emigrants, not in the least alarmed, walked back to their wagons and the captain betook himself pensively to his tent. Shaw and I followed his example.

"It will be a bad thing for our plans," said he as we entered, "if these fellows don't get back safe. The captain is as helpless on the prairie as a child. We shall have to take him and his brother in tow; they will hang on us like lead."

"The prairie is a strange place," said I. "A month ago I should have thought it rather a startling affair to have an acquaintance ride out in the morning and lose his scalp before night, but here it seems the most natural thing in the world; not that R. has lost his yet."

If a man is constitutionally liable to nervous apprehensions, a tour on the distant prairies would prove the best prescription; for though when in the neighborhood of the Rocky Mountains he may at times find himself placed in circumstances of some danger, I believe that few ever breathe that reckless atmosphere without becoming almost indifferent to any evil chance that may befall themselves or their friends.

Shaw had a propensity for luxurious indulgence. He spread his blanket with the utmost accuracy on the ground, picked up the sticks and stones that he thought might interfere with his comfort, adjusted his saddle to serve as a pillow, and composed himself for his night's rest. I had the first guard that evening; so, taking my rifle, I went out of the tent. It was perfectly dark. One of the emigrants, named Morton, was my companion; and laying our rifles on the grass, we sat down together by the fire. Morton was a Kentuckian, an athletic fellow, with a fine intelligent face, and in his manners and conversation he showed the essential characteristics of a gentleman. Our conversation turned on the pioneers of his gallant native State. The three hours of our watch dragged away at last, and we went to call up the relief.

R.'s guard succeeded mine. He was absent; but the captain, anxious lest the camp should be left defenseless, had volunteered to stand in his place; so I went to wake him up. The captain had been awake since nightfall. A fire was blazing outside of the tent, and by the light through the canvas, I saw him and Jack lying on their backs, with their eyes wide open. The captain responded instantly to my call; he jumped up, seized the double-barreled rifle, and came out of the tent with an air of solemn determination, as if about to devote himself to the safety of the party. I went and lay down, not doubting that for the next three hours our slumbers would be guarded with sufficient vigilance.

TAKING
FRENCH LEAVE

O n the 8th of June, at eleven o'clock, we reached the South Fork of the Platte, at the usual fording place. For league upon league the desert uniformity of the prospect was almost unbroken; the hills were dotted with little tufts of shriveled grass, but betwixt these the white sand was glaring in the sun; and the channel of the river, almost on a level with the plain, was but one great sand-bed, about half a mile wide. It was covered with water, but so scantily that the bottom was scarcely hidden; for, wide as it is, the average depth of the Platte does not at this point exceed a foot and a half. Stopping near its bank, we gathered bois de vache, and made a meal of buffalo meat. Far off, on the other side, was a green meadow, where we could see the white tents and wagons of an emigrant camp; and just opposite to us we could discern a group of men and animals at the water's edge. Four or five horsemen soon entered the river, and in ten minutes had waded across and clambered up the loose sand-bank. They were ill-looking fellows, thin and swarthy, with care-worn, anxious faces and lips rigidly compressed. They had good cause for anxiety; it was three days since they first encamped here, and on the night of their arrival they had lost 123 of their best cattle, driven off by

"Covered Wagons Heading West,"
oil on canvas, by N. C. Wyeth.

95

the wolves, through the neglect of the man on guard. This discouraging and alarming calamity was not the first that had overtaken them. Since leaving the settlements, they had met with nothing but misfortune. Some of their party had died; one man had been killed by the Pawnees; and about a week before, they had been plundered by the Dakotas of all their best horses, the wretched animals on which our visitors were mounted being the only ones that were left. They had encamped, they told us, near sunset, by the side of the Platte, and their oxen were scattered over the meadow, while the band of horses were feeding a little farther off. Suddenly the ridges of the hills were alive with a swarm of mounted Indians, at least six hundred in number, who, with a tremendous yell, came pouring down toward the camp, rushing up within a few rods, to the great terror of the emigrants; but suddenly wheeling, they swept around the band of horses, and in five minutes had disappeared with their prey through the openings of the hills.

As these emigrants were telling their story, we saw four other men approaching. They proved to be R. and his companions, who had encountered no mischance of any kind, but had only wandered too far in pursuit of the game. They said they had seen no Indians, but only "millions of buffalo"; and both R. and Sorel had meat dangling behind their saddles.

The emigrants re-crossed the river, and we prepared to follow. First the heavy ox-wagons plunged down the bank, and dragged slowly over the sand-beds; sometimes the hoofs of the oxen were scarcely wetted by the thin sheet of water; and the next moment the river would be boiling against their sides, and eddying fiercely around the wheels. Inch by inch they receded from the shore, dwindling every moment, until at length they seemed to be floating far in the very middle of the river. A more critical experiment awaited us; for our little mule-cart was but ill-fitted for the passage of so swift a stream. We watched it with anxiety till it seemed to be a little motionless white speck in the midst of the waters; and it *was* motionless, for it had stuck fast in a quicksand. The little mules were losing their footing, the wheels were sinking deeper and deeper, and the water began to rise through the bottom and drench the goods within. All of us who had remained on the hither bank galloped to the rescue; the men jumped into the water, adding their strength to that of the mules, until by much effort the cart was extricated, and conveyed in safety across.

As we gained the other bank, a rough group of men surrounded us. They were not robust, nor large of frame, yet they had an aspect of hardy endurance. Finding at home no scope for their fiery energies, they had betaken themselves to the prairie; and in them seemed to be revived, with redoubled force, that fierce spirit which impelled their ancestors, scarce more lawless than themselves, from the German forests, to inundate Europe and break to pieces the Roman empire. A fortnight afterward this unfortunate party passed Fort Laramie, while we were there. Not one of their missing oxen had been recovered, though they had remained encamped a week in search of them; and they had been compelled to abandon a great part of their baggage and provisions, and yoke cows

Lightening the Load

By Ezra Meeker

Soon we began to see abandoned property. First it might be a table or a cupboard, or perhaps a bedstead or a cast-iron cookstove. Then feather beds, blankets… Very soon, here and there would be an abandoned wagon; then provision.

… Long after the end of the mania for getting rid of goods, the abandonment of wagons continued, as the teams became weaker and the ravages of cholera among the emigrants began to tell. It was then that many lost their heads and ruined their teams by furious driving … There came a veritable stampede—a strive for possession of the road, to see who should get ahead. It was against the rule to attempt to pass a team ahead; a wagon that had withdrawn from the line and stopped beside the trail could get into the line again, but on the march it could not cut ahead of the wagon in front of it. Yet now whole trains would strive, often with bad blood, for the mastery of the trail, one attempting to pass the other.

and heifers to their wagons to carry them forward upon their journey, the most toilsome and hazardous part of which lay still before them.

It is worth noticing that on the Platte one may sometimes see the shattered wrecks of ancient claw-footed tables, well waxed and rubbed, or massive bureaus of carved oak. These, many of them no doubt the relics of ancestral prosperity in the colonial time, must have encountered strange vicissitudes. Imported, perhaps, originally from England; then, with the declining fortunes of their owners, borne across the Alleghenies to the remote wilderness of Ohio or Kentucky; then to Illinois or Missouri; and now at last fondly stowed away in the family wagon for the interminable journey to Oregon. But the stern privations of the way are little anticipated. The cherished relic is soon flung out to scorch and crack upon the hot prairie.

We resumed our journey; but we had gone scarcely a mile, when R. called out from the rear:

"We'll camp here."

"Why do you want to camp? Look at the sun. It is not three o'clock yet."

"We'll camp here!"

This was the only reply vouchsafed. Delorier was in advance with his cart. Seeing the mule-wagon wheeling from the track, he began to turn his own team in the same direction.

"Go on, Delorier," and the little cart advanced again. As we rode on, we soon heard the wagon of our confederates creaking and jolting on behind us, and the driver, Wright,

Pioneers in Kansas, circling their wagons, in preparation to make camp on the plains in the late 1800s.

Covered wagons proceeding on a trail through the forks of the Platte River in 1849, by J. Goldsborough Bruff.

discharging a furious volley of oaths against his mules; no doubt venting upon them the wrath which he dared not direct against a more appropriate object.

Something of this sort had frequently occurred. Our English friend was by no means partial to us, and we thought we discovered in his conduct a deliberate intention to thwart and annoy us, especially by retarding the movements of the party, which he knew that we, being Yankees, were anxious to quicken. Therefore, he would insist on encamping at all unseasonable hours, saying that fifteen miles was a sufficient day's journey. Finding our wishes systematically disregarded, we took the direction of affairs into our own hands. Keeping always in advance, to the inexpressible indignation of R., we encamped at what time and place we thought proper, not much caring whether the rest chose to follow or not. They always did so, however, pitching their tents near ours, with sullen and wrathful countenances.

Traveling together on these agreeable terms did not suit our tastes; for some time we had meditated a separation. The connection with this party had cost us various

"There are good things," thought I, "in the savage life, but what can it offer to replace those powerful and ennobling influences that can reach unimpaired over more than three thousand miles of mountains, forests and deserts?"

delays and inconveniences; and the glaring want of courtesy and good sense displayed by their virtual leader did not dispose us to bear these annoyances with much patience. We resolved to leave camp early in the morning, and push forward as rapidly as possible for Fort Laramie, which we hoped to reach, by hard traveling, in four or five days. The captain soon trotted up between us, and we explained our intentions.

"A very extraordinary proceeding, upon my word!" he remarked. Then he began to enlarge upon the enormity of the design. The most prominent impression in his mind evidently was that we were acting a base and treacherous part in deserting his party, in what he considered a very dangerous stage of the journey. To palliate the atrocity of our conduct, we ventured to suggest that we were only four in number while his party still included sixteen men; and as, moreover, we were to go forward and they were to follow, at least a full proportion of the perils he apprehended would fall upon us. But the austerity of the captain's features would not relax. "A very extraordinary proceeding, gentlemen!" and repeating this, he rode off to confer with his principal.

By good luck, we found a meadow of fresh grass, and a large pool of rain-water in the midst of it. We encamped here at sunset. Plenty of buffalo skulls were lying around, bleaching in the sun; and sprinkled thickly among the grass was a great variety of strange flowers. I had nothing else to do, and so gathering a handful, I sat down on a buffalo skull to study them. Although the offspring of a wilderness, their texture was frail and delicate, and their colors extremely rich; pure white, dark blue, and a transparent crimson. One traveling in this country seldom has leisure to think of anything but the stern features of the scenery and its accompaniments, or the practical details of each day's journey. Like them, he and his thoughts grow hard and rough. But now these flowers suddenly awakened a train of associations as alien to the rude scene around me as they were themselves; and for the moment my thoughts went back to New England. A throng of fair and well-remembered faces rose, vividly as life, before me. "There are good things," thought I, "in the savage life, but what can it offer to replace those powerful and ennobling influences that can reach unimpaired over more than three thousand miles of mountains, forests and deserts?"

Before sunrise on the next morning our tent was down; we harnessed our best horses to the cart and left the camp. But first we shook hands with our friends the emigrants, who sincerely wished us a safe journey, though some others of the party might easily have been consoled had we encountered an Indian war party on the way. The captain and his brother were standing on the top of a hill, wrapped in their plaids, like spirits of the mist, keeping an anxious eye on the band of horses below. We waved adieu to them as we rode off the ground. The captain replied with a salutation of the utmost dignity, which Jack tried to imitate; but being little practiced in the gestures of polite society, his effort was not a very successful one.

In five minutes we had gained the foot of the hills, but here we came to a stop. Old Hendrick was in the shafts, and being the very incarnation of perverse and brutish obstinacy, he utterly refused to move. Delorier lashed and swore till he was tired, but Hendrick stood like a rock, grumbling to himself and looking askance at his enemy, until he saw a favorable opportunity to take his revenge, when he struck out under the shaft with such cool malignity of intention that Delorier only escaped the blow by a sudden skip into the air, such as no one but a Frenchman could achieve. Shaw and he then joined forces, and lashed on both sides at once. The brute stood still for a while till he could bear it no longer, when all at once he began to kick and plunge till he threatened the utter demolition of the cart and harness. We glanced back at the camp, which was in full sight. Our companions, inspired by emulation, were leveling their tents and driving in their cattle and horses.

"Take the horse out," said I.

I took the saddle from Pontiac and put it upon Hendrick; the former was harnessed to the cart in an instant. "Avance donc!" cried Delorier. Pontiac strode up the hill, twitching the little cart after him as if it were a feather's weight; and though, as we gained the top, we saw the wagons of our deserted comrades just getting into motion, we had little fear that they could overtake us. Leaving the trail, we struck directly across the country, and took the shortest cut to reach the main stream of the Platte. A deep ravine suddenly intercepted us. We skirted its sides until we found them less abrupt, and then plunged through the best way we could. Passing behind the sandy ravines called "Ash Hollow," we stopped for a short nooning at the side of a pool of rain-water; but soon resumed our journey, and some hours before sunset were descending the ravines and gorges opening downward upon the Platte to the west of Ash Hollow. Our horses waded to the fetlock in sand; the sun scorched like fire, and the air swarmed with sand-flies and mosquitoes.

At last we gained the Platte. Following it for about five miles, we saw, just as the sun was sinking, a great meadow, dotted with hundreds of cattle, and beyond them an emigrant encampment. A party of about a dozen came out to meet us, looking upon us at first with cold and suspicious faces. Seeing four men, different in appearance and equipment from themselves, emerging from the hills, they had taken us for the van of the much-dreaded Mormons, whom they were very apprehensive of encountering. We made known our true character, and then they greeted us cordially. They expressed much surprise that so small a party should venture to traverse that region, though in fact such attempts are not unfrequently made by trappers and Indian traders. We rode with them to their camp. The wagons, some fifty in number, were arranged as usual in a circle; in the area within the best horses were picketed, and the whole circumference was glowing with the dusky light of the fires, displaying the forms of the women and children who were crowded

"Bull Boating," by Alfred Jacob Miller. Conestoga wagons, stripped and with buffalo hides wrapped around them, cross a deep river.

around them. This patriarchal scene was curious and striking enough; but we made our escape from the place with all possible dispatch, being tormented by the intrusive curiosity of the men who crowded around us. Yankee curiosity was nothing to theirs. They demanded our names, where we came from, where we were going, and what was our business. The last query was particularly embarrassing; since traveling in that country, or indeed anywhere, from any other motive than gain, was an idea of which they took no cognizance. Yet they were fine-looking fellows, with an air of frankness, generosity, and even courtesy, having come from one of the least barbarous of the frontier counties.

We passed about a mile beyond them, and encamped. Being too few in number to stand guard without excessive fatigue, we extinguished our fire, lest it should attract

Three Sioux chiefs photographed by Edward S. Curtis circa 1905.

the notice of wandering Indians; and picketing our horses close around us, slept undisturbed till morning. For three days we traveled without interruption, and on the evening of the third encamped by the well-known spring on Scott's Bluff.

Henry Chatillon and I rode out in the morning, and descending the western side of the Bluff, were crossing the plain beyond. Something that seemed to me a file of buffalo came into view, descending the hills several miles before us. But Henry reined in his horse, and keenly peering across the prairie with a better and more practiced eye, soon discovered its real nature. "Indians!" he said. "Old Smoke's lodges, I b'lieve. Come! let us go! Wah! get up, now, Five Hundred Dollar!" And laying on the lash with good will, he galloped forward, and I rode by his side. Not long after, a black speck became visible on the prairie, full two miles off. It grew larger and larger; it assumed the form of a man and horse; and soon we could discern a naked Indian, careering at full gallop toward us. When within a furlong he wheeled his horse in a wide circle, and made him describe various mystic figures upon the prairie; and Henry immediately compelled Five Hundred Dollar to execute similar evolutions. "It *is* Old Smoke's village," said he, interpreting these signals; "didn't I say so?"

As the Indian approached we stopped to wait for him, when suddenly he vanished, sinking, as it were, into the earth. He had come upon one of the deep ravines that everywhere intersect these prairies. In an instant the rough head of his horse stretched upward from the edge and the rider and steed came scrambling out, and hounded up to us; a sudden jerk of the rein brought the wild panting horse to a full stop. Then followed the needful formality of shaking hands. I forget our visitor's name. He was a young fellow, of no note in his nation; yet in his person and equipments he was a good specimen of a Dakota warrior in his ordinary traveling dress. Like most of his people, he was nearly six feet high; lithely and gracefully, yet strongly proportioned; and with a skin singularly clear and delicate. He wore no paint; his head was bare; and his long hair was gathered in a clump behind, to the top of which was attached transversely, both by way of ornament and of talisman, the mystic whistle, made of the wingbone of the war eagle, and endowed with various magic virtues. From the back of his head descended a line of glittering brass plates, tapering from the size of a doubloon to that of a half-dime, a cumbrous ornament, in high vogue among the Dakotas, and for which they pay the traders a most extravagant price; his chest and arms were naked, the buffalo robe, worn over them when at rest, had fallen about his waist, and was confined there by a belt. This, with the gay moccasins on his feet, completed his attire. For arms he carried a quiver of dogskin at his back, and a rude but powerful bow in his hand. His horse had no bridle; a cord of hair, lashed around his jaw, served in place of one. The saddle was of most singular construction; it was made of wood covered with raw hide, and both pommel and cantle rose perpendicularly full eighteen inches, so that the warrior was wedged firmly in his seat, whence nothing could dislodge him but the bursting of the girths.

Ezra Meeker with ox-drawn wagon at Chimney Rock, a major landmark in western Nebraska.

Advancing with our new companion, we found more of his people seated in a circle on the top of a hill; while a rude procession came straggling down the neighboring hollow, men, women, and children, with horses dragging the lodge-poles behind them. All that morning, as we moved forward, tall savages were stalking silently about us. At noon we reached Horse Creek; and as we waded through the shallow water, we saw a wild and striking scene. The main body of the Indians had arrived before us. On the farther bank stood a large and strong man, nearly naked, holding a white horse by a long cord, and eyeing us as we approached. This was the chief, whom Henry called "Old Smoke." Just behind him his youngest and favorite squaw sat astride of a fine mule; it was covered with caparisons of whitened skins, garnished with blue and white beads, and fringed with little ornaments of metal that tinkled with every movement of the animal. The girl had a light clear complexion, enlivened by a spot of vermilion on each cheek; she smiled, not to say grinned, upon us, showing two gleaming rows of white teeth. In her hand, she carried the tall lance of her unchivalrous lord, fluttering with feathers; his round white shield hung at the side of her mule; and his pipe was slung at her back. Her dress was a tunic of deerskin, made beautifully white by means of a species of clay found on the prairie, and ornamented with beads, arrayed in figures more gay than tasteful, and with long fringes at all the seams. Not far from the chief stood a group of stately figures, their white buffalo robes thrown over their shoulders, gazing coldly upon us; and in the rear, for several acres, the ground was covered with a temporary encampment; men, women, and children swarmed like bees; hundreds of dogs, of all sizes and colors, ran restlessly about; and, close at hand, the wide shallow stream was alive with boys, girls, and young squaws, splashing, screaming, and laughing in the water. At the same time a long train of emigrant wagons were crossing the creek, and dragging on in their slow, heavy procession, passed the encampment of the people whom they and their descendants, in the space of a century, are to sweep from the face of the earth.

The encampment itself was merely a temporary one during the heat of the day. None of the lodges were erected; but their heavy leather coverings, and the long poles used to support them, were scattered everywhere around, among weapons, domestic utensils, and the rude harness of mules and horses. The squaws of each lazy warrior had made him a shelter from the sun, by stretching a few buffalo robes, or the corner of a lodge-covering upon poles; and here he sat in the shade, with a favorite young squaw, perhaps, at his side, glittering with all imaginable trinkets. Before him stood the insignia of his rank as a warrior, his white shield of bull-hide, his medicine bag, his bow and quiver, his lance and his pipe, raised aloft on a tripod of three poles. Except the dogs, the most active and noisy tenants of the camp were the old women, ugly as Macbeth's witches, with their hair streaming loose in the wind, and nothing but the tattered fragment of an old buffalo robe to hide their shriveled wiry limbs. The day of their favoritism passed two generations ago; now the heaviest labors of the camp devolved upon them; they were to harness the horses, pitch the lodges, dress the buffalo robes, and bring in meat for the hunters. With the cracked voices of these hags, the clamor of dogs, the shouting and laughing of children and girls, and the listless tranquillity of the warriors, the whole scene had an effect too lively and picturesque ever to be forgotten.

We stopped not far from the Indian camp, and having invited some of the chiefs and warriors to dinner, placed before them a sumptuous repast of biscuit and coffee. Squatted in a half circle on the ground, they soon disposed of it. As we rode forward on the afternoon journey, several of our late guests accompanied us. Among the rest was a huge bloated savage of more than three hundred pounds' weight, christened La Cochon, in consideration of his preposterous dimensions and certain corresponding traits of his character. "The Hog" bestrode a little white pony, scarce able to bear up under the enormous burden,

> . . . A long train of emigrant wagons were crossing the creek, and dragging on in their slow, heavy procession, passed the encampment of the people whom they and their descendants, in the space of a century, are to sweep from the face of the earth.

though, by way of keeping up the necessary stimulus, the rider kept both feet in constant motion, playing alternately against his ribs. The old man was not a chief; he never had ambition enough to become one; he was not a warrior nor a hunter, for he was too fat and lazy: but he was the richest man in the whole village. Riches among the Dakotas consist in horses, and of these The Hog had accumulated more than thirty. He had already ten times as many as he wanted, yet still his appetite for horses was insatiable. Trotting up to me he shook me by the hand, and gave me to understand that he was a very devoted friend; and then he began a series of most earnest signs and gesticulations, his oily countenance radiant with smiles, and his little eyes peeping out with a cunning twinkle from between the masses of flesh that almost obscured them. Knowing nothing at that time of the sign language of the Indians, I could only guess at his meaning. So I called on Henry to explain it.

The Hog, it seems, was anxious to conclude a matrimonial bargain. He said he had a very pretty daughter in his lodge, whom he would give me, if I would give him my horse. These flattering overtures I chose to reject; at which The Hog, still laughing with undiminished good humor, gathered his robe about his shoulders, and rode away.

Where we encamped that night, an arm of the Platte ran between high bluffs; it was turbid and swift as heretofore, but trees were growing on its crumbling banks, and there was a nook of grass between the water and the hill. Just before entering this place, we saw the emigrants encamping at two or three miles' distance on the right; while the whole Indian rabble were pouring down the neighboring hill in hope of the same sort of entertainment which they had experienced from us. In the savage landscape before our camp, nothing but the rushing of the Platte broke the silence. Through the ragged boughs of the trees, dilapidated and half dead, we saw the sun setting in crimson behind the peaks of the Black Hills; the restless bosom of the river was suffused with red; our white tent was tinged with it, and the sterile bluffs, up to the rocks that crowned them, partook of the same fiery hue. It soon passed away; no light remained, but that from our fire, blazing high among the dusky trees and bushes. We lay around it wrapped in our blankets, smoking and conversing until a late hour, and then withdrew to our tent.

We crossed a sun-scorched plain on the next morning; the line of old cotton-wood trees that fringed the bank of the Platte forming its extreme verge. Nestled apparently close beneath them, we could discern in the distance something like a building. As we came nearer, it assumed form and dimensions, and proved to be a rough structure of logs. It was a little trading fort, belonging to two private traders; and originally intended, like all the forts of the country, to form a hollow square, with rooms for lodging and storage opening upon the area within. Only two sides of it had been completed; the place was now as ill-fitted for the purposes of defense as any of those little log-houses,

OPPOSITE:
A Sioux maiden wears a beaded headband and buckskin dress, in a photograph by Edward S. Curtis circa 1908.

The white checkermallow, a wildflower commonly found in the Rocky Mountain states.

which upon our constantly shifting frontier have been so often successfully maintained against overwhelming odds of Indians. Two lodges were pitched close to the fort; the sun beat scorching upon the logs; no living thing was stirring except one old squaw, who thrust her round head from the opening of the nearest lodge, and three or four stout young pups, who were peeping with looks of eager inquiry from under the covering. In a moment a door opened, and a little, swarthy black-eyed Frenchman came out. His dress was rather singular; his black curling hair was parted in the middle of his head, and fell below his shoulders; he wore a tight frock of smoked deerskin, very gayly ornamented with figures worked in dyed porcupine quills. His moccasins and leggings were also gaudily adorned in the same manner; and the latter had in addition a line of long fringes, reaching down the seams. The small frame of Richard, for by this name Henry made him known to us, was in the highest degree athletic and vigorous. There was no superfluity, and indeed there seldom is among the active white men of this country, but every limb was compact and hard; every sinew had its full tone and elasticity, and the whole man wore an air of mingled hardihood and buoyancy.

Richard committed our horses to a Navahoe slave, a mean looking fellow taken prisoner on the Mexican frontier; and, relieving us of our rifles with ready politeness, led the way into the principal apartment of his establishment. This was a room ten feet square. The walls and floor were of black mud, and the roof of rough timber; there was a huge fireplace made of four flat rocks, picked up on the prairie. An Indian bow and otter-skin quiver, several gaudy articles of Rocky Mountain finery, an Indian medicine bag, and a pipe and tobacco pouch, garnished the walls, and rifles rested in a corner. There was no furniture except a sort of rough settle covered with buffalo robes, upon which lolled a tall half-breed, with his hair glued in masses upon each temple, and saturated with vermilion. Two or three more "mountain men" sat cross-legged on the floor. Their attire was not unlike that of Richard himself; but the most striking figure of the group was a naked Indian boy of sixteen, with a handsome face, and light, active proportions, who sat in an easy posture in the corner near the door. Not one of his limbs moved the breadth of a hair; his eye was fixed immovably, not on any person present, but, as it appeared, on the projecting corner of the fireplace opposite to him.

On these prairies the custom of smoking with friends is seldom omitted, whether among Indians or whites. The pipe, therefore, was taken from the wall, and its great red bowl crammed with the tobacco and shongsasha, mixed in suitable proportions. Then it passed round the circle, each man inhaling a few whiffs and handing it to his neighbor. Having spent half an hour here, we took our leave; first inviting our new friends to drink a cup of coffee with us at our camp, a mile farther up the river. By this time, as the reader may conceive, we had grown rather shabby; our clothes had burst into rags and tatters; and what was worse, we had very little means of renovation. Fort Laramie was but seven miles before us. Being totally averse to appearing in such plight among any society that

could boast an approximation to the civilized, we soon stopped by the river to make our toilet in the best way we could. We hung up small looking-glasses against the trees and shaved, an operation neglected for six weeks; we performed our ablutions in the Platte, though the utility of such a proceeding was questionable, the water looking exactly like a cup of chocolate, and the banks consisting of the softest and richest yellow mud, so that we were obliged, as a preliminary, to build a cause-way of stout branches and twigs. Having also put on radiant moccasins, procured from a squaw of Richard's establishment, and made what other improvements our narrow circumstances allowed, we took our seats on the grass with a feeling of greatly increased respectability, to wait the arrival of our guests. They came; the banquet was concluded, and the pipe smoked. Bidding them adieu, we turned our horses' heads toward the fort.

An hour elapsed. The barren hills closed across our front, and we could see no farther; until having surmounted them, a rapid stream appeared at the foot of the descent, running into the Platte; beyond was a green meadow, dotted with bushes, and in the midst of these, at the point where the two rivers joined, were the low clay walls of a fort. This was not Fort Laramie, but another post of less recent date, which having sunk before its successful competitor was now deserted and ruinous. A moment after the hills, seeming to draw apart as we advanced, disclosed Fort Laramie itself, its high bastions and perpendicular walls of clay crowning an eminence on the left beyond the stream, while behind stretched a line of arid and desolate ridges, and behind these again, towering aloft seven thousand feet, arose the grim Black Hills.

We tried to ford Laramie Creek at a point nearly opposite the fort, but the stream, swollen with the rains in the mountains, was too rapid. We passed up along its bank to find a better crossing place. Men gathered on the wall to look at us. "There's Bordeaux!" called Henry, his face brightening as he recognized his acquaintance; "him there with the spyglass; and there's old Vaskiss, and Tucker, and May; and, by George! there's Cimoneau!" This Cimoneau was Henry's fast friend, and the only man in the country who could rival him in hunting.

We soon found a ford. Henry led the way, the pony approaching the bank with a countenance of cool indifference, bracing his feet and sliding into the stream with the most unmoved composure.

We followed; the water boiled against our saddles, but our horses bore us easily through. The unfortunate little mules came near going down with the current, cart and all; and we watched them with some solicitude scrambling over the loose round stones at the bottom, and bracing stoutly against the stream. All landed safely at last; we crossed a little plain, descended a hollow, and riding up a steep bank found ourselves before the gateway of Fort Laramie, under the impending blockhouse.

SCENES AT FORT LARAMIE

Looking back, after the expiration of a year, upon Fort Laramie and its inmates, they seem less like a reality than like some fanciful picture of the olden time; so different was the scene from any which this tamer side of the world can present. Tall Indians, enveloped in their white buffalo robes, were striding across the area or reclining at full length on the low roofs of the buildings which inclosed it. Numerous squaws, gayly bedizened, sat grouped in front of the apartments they occupied; their mongrel offspring, restless and vociferous, rambled in every direction through the fort; and the trappers, traders, and *engagés* of the establishment were busy at their labor or their amusements.

We were met at the gate, but by no means cordially welcomed. Indeed, we seemed objects of some distrust and suspicion until Henry Chatillon explained that we were not traders, and we, in confirmation, handed to the bourgeois a letter of introduction from his principals. He took it, turned it upside down, and tried hard to read it; but his literary attainments not being adequate to the task, he applied for relief to the clerk, a sleek, smiling Frenchman, named Montalon. The letter read, Bordeaux (the bourgeois) seemed gradually to awaken to a sense of what was expected of him. Though not deficient in hospitable intentions, he was wholly unaccustomed to act as master of ceremonies. Discarding all formalities of reception, he did not honor us with a single word, but walked swiftly across the area, while we followed in some admiration to a railing

The interior of Fort Laramie, painted by
Alfred Jacob Miller in the late 1850s.

and a flight of steps opposite the entrance. He signed to us that we had better fasten our horses to the railing; then he walked up the steps, tramped along a rude balcony, and kicking open a door displayed a large room, rather more elaborately finished than a barn. For furniture it had a rough bedstead, but no bed; two chairs, a chest of drawers, a tin pail to hold water, and a board to cut tobacco upon. A brass crucifix hung on the wall, and close at hand a recent scalp, with hair full a yard long, was suspended from a nail. I shall again have occasion to mention this dismal trophy, its history being connected with that of our subsequent proceedings.

This apartment, the best in Fort Laramie, was that usually occupied by the legitimate bourgeois, Papin; in whose absence the command devolved upon Bordeaux. The latter, a stout, bluff little fellow, much inflated by a sense of his new authority, began to roar for buffalo robes. These being brought and spread upon the floor formed our beds; much better ones than we had of late been accustomed to. Our arrangements made, we stepped out to the balcony to take a more leisurely survey of the long looked-for haven at which we had arrived at last. Beneath us was the square area surrounded by little rooms, or rather cells, which opened upon it. These were devoted to various purposes, but served chiefly for the accommodation of the men employed at the fort, or of

A wagon train on the Oregon Trail approaches Fort Laramie in Wyoming. Indian teepees appear on both sides of the river, and Laramie Peak is in the distance.

the equally numerous squaws, whom they were allowed to maintain in it. Opposite to us rose the blockhouse above the gateway; it was adorned with a figure which even now haunts my memory; a horse at full speed, daubed upon the boards with red paint, and exhibiting a degree of skill which might rival that displayed by the Indians in executing similar designs upon their robes and lodges. A busy scene was enacting in the area. The wagons of Vaskiss, an old trader, were about to set out for a remote post in the mountains, and the Canadians were going through their preparations with all possible bustle, while here and there an Indian stood looking on with imperturbable gravity.

Fort Laramie is one of the posts established by the American Fur Company, who well-nigh monopolize the Indian trade of this whole region. Here their officials rule with an absolute sway; the arm of the United States has little force; for when we were there, the extreme outposts of her troops were about seven hundred miles to the eastward. The little fort is built of bricks dried in the sun, and externally is of an oblong form, with bastions of clay, in the form of ordinary blockhouses, at two of the corners. The walls are about fifteen feet high, and surmounted by a slender palisade. The roofs of the apartments within, built close against the walls, serve the purpose of a banquette. Within, the fort is divided by a partition; on one side is the square area surrounded by the storerooms, offices, and apartments of the inmates; on the other is the corral, a narrow place, encompassed by the high clay walls, where at night, or in presence of dangerous Indians, the horses and mules of the fort are crowded for safe-keeping. The main entrance has two gates, with an arched passage intervening. A little square window, quite high above the ground, opens laterally from an adjoining chamber into this passage; so that when the inner gate is closed and barred, a person without may still hold communication with those within through this narrow aperture. This obviates the necessity of admitting suspicious Indians, for purposes of trading, into the body of the fort; for when danger is apprehended, the inner gate is shut fast, and all traffic is carried on by means of the little window. This precaution, though highly necessary at some of the company's posts, is now seldom resorted to at Fort Laramie; where, though men are frequently killed in its neighborhood, no apprehensions are now entertained of any general designs of hostility from the Indians.

Fort Laramie is one of the posts established by the American Fur Company, who well-nigh monopolize the Indian trade of this whole region. Here their officials rule with an absolute sway...

We did not long enjoy our new quarters undisturbed. The door was silently pushed open, and two eyeballs and a visage as black as night looked in upon us; then a red arm and shoulder intruded themselves, and a tall Indian, gliding in, shook us by the hand, grunted his salutation, and sat down on the floor. Others followed, with faces of the natural hue; and letting fall their heavy robes from their shoulders, they took their seats, quite at ease, in a semicircle before us. The pipe was now to be lighted and passed round from one to another; and this was the only entertainment that at present they expected from us. These visitors were fathers, brothers, or other relatives of the squaws in the fort, where they were permitted to remain, loitering about in perfect idleness. All those who smoked with us were men of standing and repute. Two or three others dropped in also; young fellows who neither by their years nor their exploits were entitled to rank with the old men and warriors, and who, abashed in the presence of their superiors, stood aloof, never withdrawing their eyes from us. Their cheeks were adorned with vermilion, their ears with pendants of shell, and their necks with beads. Never yet having signalized themselves as hunters, or performed the honorable exploit of killing a man, they were held in slight esteem, and were diffident and bashful in proportion. Certain formidable inconveniences attended this influx of visitors. They were bent on inspecting everything in the room; our equipments and our dress alike underwent their scrutiny; for though the contrary has been carelessly asserted, few beings have more curiosity than Indians in regard to subjects within their ordinary range of thought. As to other matters, indeed, they seemed utterly indifferent. They will not trouble themselves to inquire into what they cannot comprehend, but are quite contented to place their hands over their mouths in token of wonder, and exclaim that it is "great medicine." With this comprehensive solution, an Indian never is at a loss. He never launches forth into speculation and conjecture; his reason moves in its beaten track. His soul is dormant; and no exertions of the missionaries, Jesuit or Puritan, of the Old World or of the New, have as yet availed to rouse it.

As we were looking, at sunset, from the wall, upon the wild and desolate plains that surround the fort, we observed a cluster of strange objects like scaffolds rising in the distance against the red western sky. They bore aloft some singular looking burdens; and at their foot glimmered something white like bones. This was the place of sepulture of some Dakota chiefs, whose remains their people are fond of placing in the vicinity of the fort, in the hope that they may thus be protected from violation at the hands of their enemies. Yet it has happened more than once, and quite recently, that war parties of the Crow Indians, ranging through the country, have thrown the bodies from the scaffolds, and broken them to pieces amid the yells of the Dakotas, who remained pent up in the fort, too few to defend the honored relics from insult. The white objects upon the ground were buffalo skulls, arranged in the mystic circle commonly seen at Indian places of sepulture upon the prairie.

We soon discovered, in the twilight, a band of fifty or sixty horses approaching the fort. These were the animals belonging to the establishment; who having been sent out to feed, under the care of armed guards, in the meadows below, were now being driven into the corral for the night. A little gate opened into this inclosure; by the side of it stood one of the guards, an old Canadian, with gray bushy eyebrows, and a dragoon pistol stuck into his belt; while his comrade, mounted on horseback, his rifle laid across the saddle in front of him, and his long hair blowing before his swarthy face, rode at the rear

OPPOSITE:

Bone Necklace, the Oglala Sioux council chief, photographed circa 1899.

A Hidatsa warrior, in the costume of the Dog dance, in a painting by Karl Bodmer.

"Buffalo Hunt, 1915," an oil painting
by Colin Campbell Cooper.

of the disorderly troop, urging them up the ascent. In a moment the narrow corral was thronged with the half-wild horses, kicking, biting, and crowding restlessly together.

The discordant jingling of a bell, rung by a Canadian in the area, summoned us to supper. This sumptuous repast was served on a rough table in one of the lower apartments of the fort, and consisted of cakes of bread and dried buffalo meat—an excellent thing for strengthening the teeth. At this meal were seated the bourgeois and superior dignitaries of the establishment, among whom Henry Chatillon was worthily included. No sooner was it finished, than the table was spread a second time (the luxury of bread being now, however, omitted), for the benefit of certain hunters and trappers of an inferior standing; while the ordinary Canadian *engagés* were regaled on dried meat in one of their lodging rooms. By way of illustrating the domestic economy of Fort Laramie, it may not be amiss to introduce in this place a story current among the men when we were there.

There was an old man named Pierre, whose duty it was to bring the meat from the storeroom for the men. Old Pierre, in the kindness of his heart, used to select the fattest and the best pieces for his companions. This did not long escape the keen-eyed bourgeois, who was greatly disturbed at such improvidence, and cast about for some means to stop it. At last he hit on a plan that exactly suited him. At the side of the meat-room, and separated from it by a clay partition, was another compartment, used for the storage of furs. It had no other communication with the fort, except through a square hole in the partition; and of course it was perfectly dark. One evening the bourgeois, watching for a moment when no one observed him, dodged into the meat-room, clambered through the hole, and ensconced himself among the furs and buffalo robes. Soon after, old Pierre came in with his lantern; and, muttering to himself, began to pull over the bales of meat, and select the best pieces, as usual. But suddenly a hollow and sepulchral voice proceeded from the inner apartment: "Pierre! Pierre! Let that fat meat alone! Take nothing but lean!" Pierre dropped his lantern, and bolted out into the fort, screaming, in an agony of terror, that the devil was in the storeroom; but tripping on the threshold, he pitched over upon the gravel, and lay senseless, stunned by the fall. The Canadians ran out to the rescue. Some lifted the unlucky Pierre; and others, making an extempore crucifix out of two sticks, were proceeding to attack the devil in his stronghold, when the bourgeois, with a crest-fallen countenance, appeared at the door. To add to the bourgeois' mortification, he was obliged to explain the whole stratagem to Pierre, in order to bring the latter to his senses.

We were sitting, on the following morning, in the passage-way between the gates, conversing with the traders Vaskiss and May. These two men, together with our sleek friend, the clerk Montalon, were, I believe, the only persons then in the fort who could read and write. May was telling a curious story about the traveler Catlin, when an ugly,

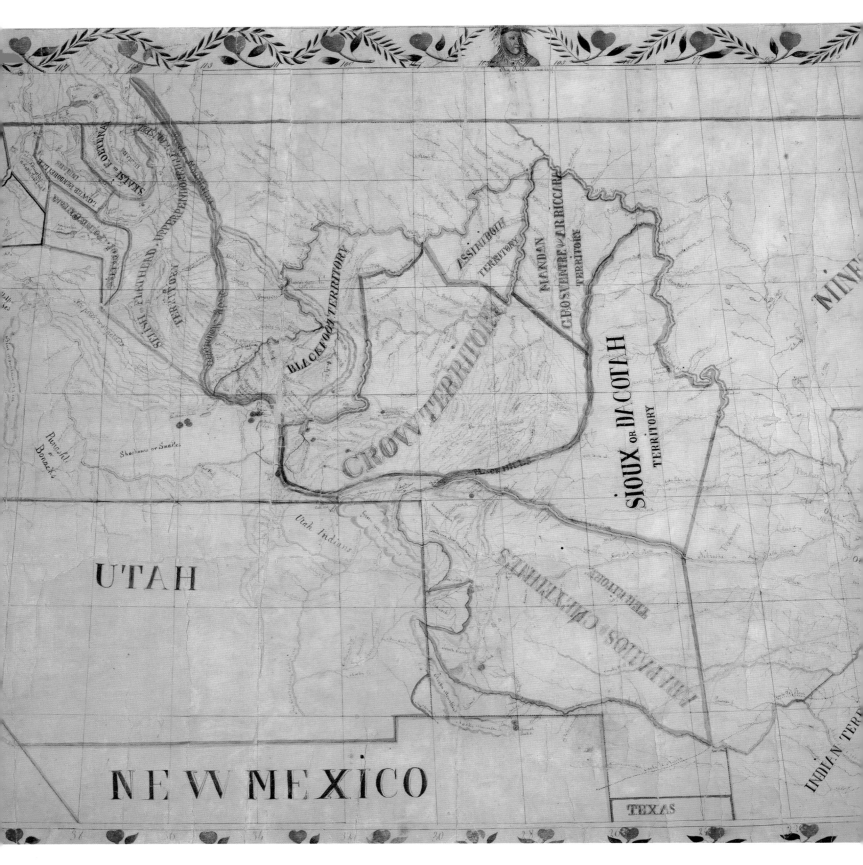

Part of an 1851 map of the upper Great Plains and Rocky Mountain regions, made a few years after Parkman's journey.

diminutive Indian, wretchedly mounted, came up at a gallop, and rode past us into the fort. On being questioned, he said that Smoke's village was close at hand. Accordingly only a few minutes elapsed before the hills beyond the river were covered with a disorderly swarm of savages, on horseback and on foot. May finished his story; and by that time the whole array had descended to Laramie Creek, and commenced crossing it in a mass. I walked down to the bank. The stream is wide, and was then between three and four feet deep, with a very swift current. For several rods the water was alive with dogs, horses, and Indians. The long poles used in erecting the lodges are carried by the horses, being fastened by the heavier end, two or three on each side, to a rude sort of pack saddle, while the other end drags on the ground. About a foot behind the horse, a kind of large basket or pannier is suspended between the poles, and firmly lashed in its place on the back of the horse are piled various articles of luggage; the basket also is well filled with domestic utensils, or, quite as often, with a litter of puppies, a brood of small children, or a superannuated old man. Numbers of these curious vehicles, called, in the bastard language of the country, *travaux* were now splashing together through the stream. Among them swam countless dogs, often burdened with miniature *travaux*; and dashing forward on horseback through the throng came the superbly formed warriors, the slender figure of some lynx-eyed boy, clinging fast behind them. The women sat perched on the pack saddles, adding not a little to the load of the already overburdened horses.

The confusion was prodigious. The dogs yelled and howled in chorus; the puppies in the *travaux* set up a dismal whine as the water invaded their comfortable retreat; the little black-eyed children, from one year of age upward, clung fast with both hands to the edge of their basket, and looked over in alarm at the water rushing so near them, sputtering and making wry mouths as it splashed against their faces. Some of the dogs, encumbered by their loads, were carried down by the current, yelping piteously; and the old squaws would rush into the water, seize their favorites by the neck, and drag them out. As each horse gained the bank, he scrambled up as he could. Stray horses and colts came among the rest, often breaking away at full speed through the crowd, followed by the old hags, screaming after their fashion on all occasions of excitement. Buxom young squaws, blooming in all the charms of vermilion, stood here and there on the bank, holding aloft their master's lance, as a signal to collect the scattered portions of his household. In a few moments the crowd melted away; each family, with its horses and equipage, filing off to the plain at the rear of the fort; and here, in the space of half an hour, arose sixty or seventy of their tapering lodges. Their horses were feeding by hundreds over the surrounding prairie, and their dogs were roaming everywhere. The fort was full of men, and the children were whooping and yelling incessantly under the walls.

These newcomers were scarcely arrived, when Bordeaux was running across the fort, shouting to his squaw to bring him his spyglass. The obedient Marie, the very model of a squaw, produced the instrument, and Bordeaux hurried with it up to the wall.

Pointing it to the eastward, he exclaimed, with an oath, that the families were coming. But a few moments elapsed before the heavy caravan of the emigrant wagons could be seen, steadily advancing from the hills. They gained the river, and without turning or pausing plunged in; they passed through, and slowly ascending the opposing bank, kept directly on their way past the fort and the Indian village, until, gaining a spot a quarter of a mile distant, they wheeled into a circle. For some time our tranquillity was undisturbed. The emigrants were preparing their encampment; but no sooner was this accomplished than Fort Laramie was fairly taken by storm. A crowd of broad-brimmed hats, thin visages, and staring eyes appeared suddenly at the gate. Tall awkward men, in brown homespun; women with cadaverous faces and long lank figures came thronging in together, and, as if inspired by the very demon of curiosity, ransacked every nook and corner of the fort. Dismayed at this invasion, we withdrew in all speed to our chamber, vainly hoping that it might prove an inviolable sanctuary. The emigrants prosecuted their investigations with untiring vigor. They penetrated the rooms or rather dens, inhabited by the astonished squaws. They explored the apartments of the men, and even that of Marie and the bourgeois. At last a numerous deputation appeared at our door, but were immediately expelled. Being totally devoid of any sense of delicacy or propriety, they seemed resolved to search every mystery to the bottom.

Having at length satisfied their curiosity, they next proceeded to business. The men occupied themselves in procuring supplies for their onward journey; either buying them with money or giving in exchange superfluous articles of their own.

The emigrants felt a violent prejudice against the French Indians, as they called the trappers and traders. They thought, and with some justice, that these men bore them no good will. Many of them were firmly persuaded that the French were instigating the Indians to attack and cut them off. On visiting the encampment we were at once struck with the extraordinary perplexity and indecision that prevailed among the emigrants. They seemed like men totally out of their elements; bewildered and amazed, like a troop of school-boys lost in the woods. It was impossible to be long among them without being conscious of the high and bold spirit with which most of them were animated. But the forest is the home of the backwoodsman. On the remote prairie he is totally at a loss. He differs much from the genuine "mountain man," the wild prairie hunter, as a Canadian voyageur, paddling his canoe on the rapids of the Ottawa, differs from an American sailor among the storms of Cape Horn. Still my companion and I were somewhat at a loss to account for this perturbed state of mind. It could not be cowardice; these men were of the same stock with the volunteers of Monterey and Buena Vista. Yet, for the most part, they were the rudest and most ignorant of the frontier population; they knew absolutely nothing of the country and its inhabitants; they had already experienced much misfortune, and apprehended more; they had seen nothing of mankind, and had never put their own resources to the test.

On Missionary Work

From a letter to her friend, Mrs. H.K.W. Perkins

BY NARCISSA WHITMAN

Since I last wrote to you we have enjoyed refreshing seasons from the hand of our Heavenly Father in the conviction and conversion of two or three individuals in our family . . . We have every reason to be assured that were there more faith and prayer and consecration to the work among ourselves, we should witness in the heathen around us many turning to the Lord. If I know my own heart I think I, too, desire to be freed from so many worldly cares and perplexities, and that my time may be spent in seeking the immediate conversion of these dear heathen to God. O, what a thought to think of meeting them among the blood-washed throng around the throne of God! Will not their songs be as sweet as any we can sing? If we were constantly to keep our eyes on the scenes that are before us, we should scarcely grow weary in well doing, or be disheartened by the few trials and privations through which we are called to pass.

Assume, in the presence of Indians a bold bearing, self-confident yet vigilant, and you will find them tolerably safe neighbors. But your safety depends on the respect and fear you are able to inspire.

A full proportion of suspicion fell upon us. Being strangers we were looked upon as enemies. Having occasion for a supply of lead and a few other necessary articles, we used to go over to the emigrant camps to obtain them. After some hesitation, some dubious glances, and fumbling of the hands in the pockets, the terms would be agreed upon, the price tendered, and the emigrant would go off to bring the article in question. After waiting until our patience gave out, we would go in search of him, and find him seated on the tongue of his wagon.

"Well, stranger," he would observe, as he saw us approach, "I reckon I won't trade!"

Some friend of his followed him from the scene of the bargain and suggested in his ear, that clearly we meant to cheat him, and he had better have nothing to do with us.

This timorous mood of the emigrants was doubly unfortunate, as it exposed them to real danger. Assume, in the presence of Indians a bold bearing, self-confident yet vigilant, and you will find them tolerably safe neighbors. But your safety depends on the respect and fear you are able to inspire. If you betray timidity or indecision, you convert them from that moment into insidious and dangerous enemies. The Dakotas saw clearly enough the perturbation of the emigrants and instantly availed themselves of it. They became extremely insolent and exacting in their demands. It has become an established custom with them to go to the camp of every party, as it arrives in succession at the fort, and demand a feast. Smoke's village had come with the express design, having made several days' journey with no other object than that of enjoying a cup of coffee and two or three biscuits. So the "feast" was demanded, and the emigrants dared not refuse it.

One evening, about sunset, the village was deserted. We met old men, warriors, squaws, and children in gay attire, trooping off to the encampment, with faces of anticipation; and, arriving here, they seated themselves in a semicircle. Smoke occupied the center, with his warriors on either hand; the young men and boys next succeeded, and the squaws and children formed the horns of the crescent. The biscuit and coffee were most promptly dispatched, the emigrants staring open-mouthed at their savage guests. With each new emigrant party that arrived at Fort Laramie this scene was renewed; and every day the Indians grew more rapacious and presumptuous. One evening they broke to pieces, out of mere wantonness, the cups from which they had been feasted; and this so exasperated the emigrants that many of them seized their rifles and could scarcely be restrained from firing on the insolent mob of Indians. Before we left the country this dangerous spirit on the part of the Dakota had mounted to a yet higher pitch. They began openly to threaten the emigrants with destruction, and actually fired upon one or two parties of whites. A military force and military law are urgently called for in that perilous region; and unless troops are speedily stationed at Fort Laramie, or elsewhere in the neighborhood, both the emigrants and other travelers will be exposed to most imminent risks.

The Ogallalla, the Brules, and other western bands of the Dakota, are thorough savages, unchanged by any contact with civilization. Not one of them can speak a European tongue, or has ever visited an American settlement. Until within a year or two, when the emigrants began to pass through their country on the way to Oregon, they had seen no whites except the handful employed about the Fur Company's posts. They esteemed them a wise people, inferior only to themselves, living in leather lodges, like their own, and subsisting on buffalo. But when the swarm of *Meneaska*, with their oxen and wagons, began to invade them, their astonishment was unbounded. They could scarcely believe that the earth contained such a multitude of white men. Their wonder is now giving way to indignation; and the result, unless vigilantly guarded against, may be lamentable in the extreme.

Indian hunters on their way to a buffalo hunt in the early 1900s.

But to glance at the interior of a lodge. Shaw and I used often to visit them. Indeed, we spent most of our evenings in the Indian village; Shaw's assumption of the medical character giving us a fair pretext. As a sample of the rest I will describe one of these visits. The sun had just set, and the horses were driven into the corral. The Prairie Cock, a noted beau, came in at the gate with a bevy of young girls, with whom he began to dance in the area, leading them round and round in a circle, while he jerked up from his chest a succession of monotonous sounds, to which they kept time in a rueful chant. Outside the gate boys and young men were idly frolicking; and close by, looking grimly upon them, stood a warrior in his robe, with his face painted jet-black, in token that he had lately taken a Pawnee scalp. Passing these, the tall dark lodges rose between us and the red western sky. We repaired at once to the lodge of Old Smoke himself. It was by no means better than the others; indeed, it was rather shabby; for in this democratic community, the chief never assumes superior state. Smoke sat cross-legged on a buffalo robe, and his grunt of salutation as we entered was unusually cordial, out of respect no doubt to Shaw's medical character. Seated around the lodge were several squaws, and an abundance of children. The complaint of Shaw's patients was, for the most part, a severe inflammation of the eyes, occasioned by exposure to the sun, a species of disorder which he treated with some success. He had brought with him a homeopathic medicine chest, and was, I presume, the first who introduced that harmless system of treatment among the Ogallalla. No sooner had a robe been spread at the head of the lodge for our accommodation, and we had seated ourselves upon it, than a patient made her appearance; the chief's daughter herself, who, to do her justice, was the best-looking girl in the village. Being on excellent terms with the physician, she placed herself readily under his hands, and submitted with a good grace to his applications, laughing in his face during the whole process, for a squaw hardly knows how to smile. This case dispatched, another of a different kind succeeded. A hideous, emaciated old woman sat in the darkest corner of the lodge rocking to and fro with pain and hiding her eyes from

the light by pressing the palms of both hands against her face. At Smoke's command, she came forward, very unwillingly, and exhibited a pair of eyes that had nearly disappeared from excess of inflammation. No sooner had the doctor fastened his grips upon her than she set up a dismal moaning, and writhed so in his grasp that he lost all patience, but being resolved to carry his point, he succeeded at last in applying his favorite remedies.

"It is strange," he said, when the operation was finished, "that I forgot to bring any Spanish flies with me; we must have something here to answer for a counter-irritant!"

So, in the absence of better, he seized upon a red-hot brand from the fire, and clapped it against the temple of the old squaw, who set up an unearthly howl, at which the rest of the family broke out into a laugh.

During these medical operations Smoke's eldest squaw entered the lodge, with a sort of stone mallet in her hand. I had observed some time before a litter of well-grown black puppies, comfortably nestled among some buffalo robes at one side; but this new-comer speedily disturbed their enjoyment; for seizing one of them by the hind paw, she dragged him out, and carrying him to the entrance of the lodge, hammered him on the head till she killed him. Being quite conscious to what this preparation tended, I looked through a hole in the back of the lodge to see the next steps of the process. The squaw, holding the puppy by the legs, was swinging him to and fro through the blaze of a fire, until the hair was singed off. This done, she unsheathed her knife and cut him into small pieces, which she dropped into a kettle to boil. In a few moments a large wooden dish was set before us, filled with this delicate preparation. We felt conscious of the honor. A dog-feast is the greatest compliment a Dakota can offer to his guest; and knowing that to refuse eating would be an affront, we attacked the little dog and devoured him before the eyes of his unconscious parent. Smoke in the meantime was preparing his great pipe. It was lighted when we had finished our repast, and we passed it from one to another till the bowl was empty. This done, we took our leave without further ceremony, knocked at the gate of the fort, and after making ourselves known were admitted.

One morning, about a week after reaching Fort Laramie, we were holding our customary Indian levee, when a bustle in the area below announced a new arrival; and looking down from our balcony, I saw a familiar red beard and mustache in the gateway. They belonged to the captain, who with his party had just crossed the stream. We met him on the stairs as he came up, and congratulated him on the safe arrival of himself and his devoted companions. But he remembered our treachery, and was grave and dignified accordingly; a tendency which increased as he observed on our part a disposition to laugh at him. After remaining an hour or two at the fort he rode away with his friends, and we have heard nothing of him since. As for R., he kept carefully aloof. It was but too evident that we had the unhappiness to have forfeited the kind regards of our London fellow-traveler.

Lakota Sioux encampment with their horses watering in White Clay Creek near Pine Ridge, South Dakota.

A Tourist's Travels

From *Views of Louisiana, Together with a Journal of a Voyage Up the Missouri River*

BY HENRY MARIE BRACKENRIDGE

A writer and lawyer, Brackenridge became the first documented tourist to what is now South Dakota when he visited fur trader Manuel Lisa in 1811. He published his book in 1814.

Some of the ancient cities of the old world were probably like this village, inattentive to that cleanliness so necessary to health, where a great mass of beings are collected in one place; and we need not be surprised at the frequency of desolating plagues and pestilence.

The village is swarming with dogs and children. I rank these together, for they are inseparable companions. Wherever I went, the children ran away, screaming, and frightened at my outre and savage appearance. Let us not flatter ourselves with the belief, that the effect of our civilization and refinement, is to render us agreeable and lovely to the eyes of those whom we exclusively denominate! The dogs, of which every family has thirty or forty, pretended to make a show of fierceness, but on the least threat, ran off. They are of different sizes and colors. A number are fattened on purpose to eat, others are used to draw their baggage. It is nothing more than the domesticated wolf. In wandering through the prairies, I have often mistaken wolves for Indian dogs. The larger kind has long curly hair and resembles the shepherd dog. There is the same diversity among the wolves of this country.

I entered several lodges, the people of which received us with kindness, placed mats and skins for us to sit on, and after smoking the pipe, offered us something to eat; this consisted of fresh buffalo meat served in a wooden dish. They had a variety of earthen vessels, in which they prepared their food, or kept water. After the meat, they offered us hominy made of corn dried in milk, mixed with beans, which was prepared with buffalo marrow, and tasted extremely well . . . The prairie turnip is a root very common in the prairies, with something of the taste of the turnip but more dry.

THE
WAR PARTIES

Indians near Fort Laramie, by Albert Bierstadt from the late 1850s.

The summer of 1846 was a season of much warlike excitement among all the western bands of the Dakota. In 1845 they encountered great reverses. Many war parties had been sent out; some of them had been totally cut off, and others had returned broken and disheartened, so that the whole nation was in mourning. Among the rest, ten warriors had gone to the Snake country, led by the son of a prominent Ogallalla chief, called The Whirlwind. In passing over Laramie Plains they encountered a superior number of their enemies, were surrounded, and killed to a man. Having performed this exploit the Snakes became alarmed, dreading the resentment of the Dakota, and they hastened therefore to signify their wish for peace by sending the scalp of the slain partisan, together with a small parcel of tobacco attached, to his tribesmen and relations. They had employed old Vaskiss, the trader, as their messenger, and the scalp was the same that hung in our room at the fort. But The Whirlwind proved inexorable. Though his character hardly corresponds with his name, he is nevertheless an Indian, and hates the Snakes with his whole soul. Long before the scalp arrived he had made his preparations for revenge. He sent messengers with presents and tobacco to all the Dakota within three hundred miles, proposing a grand combination to

chastise the Snakes, and naming a place and time of rendezvous. The plan was readily adopted and at this moment many villages, probably embracing in the whole five or six thousand souls, were slowly creeping over the prairies and tending towards the common center at La Bonte's Camp, on the Platte. Here their war-like rites were to be celebrated with more than ordinary solemnity, and a thousand warriors, as it was said, were to set out for the enemy country. The characteristic result of this preparation will appear in the sequel.

High Bear, Sioux,
circa 1900.

I was greatly rejoiced to hear of it. I had come into the country almost exclusively with a view of observing the Indian character. Having from childhood felt a curiosity on this subject, and having failed completely to gratify it by reading, I resolved to have recourse to observation. I wished to satisfy myself with regard to the position of the Indians among the races of men; the vices and the virtues that have sprung from their innate character and from their modes of life, their government, their superstitions, and their domestic situation. To accomplish my purpose it was necessary to live in the midst of them, and become, as it were, one of them. I proposed to join a village and make myself an inmate of one of their lodges; and henceforward this narrative, so far as I am concerned, will be chiefly a record of the progress of this design.

We resolved on no account to miss the rendezvous at La Bonte's Camp. Our plan was to leave Delorier at the fort, in charge of our equipage and the better part of our horses, while we took with us nothing but our weapons and the worst animals we had. In all probability jealousies and quarrels would arise among so many hordes of fierce impulsive savages, congregated together under no common head, and many of them strangers, from remote prairies and mountains. We were bound in common prudence to be cautious how we excited any feeling of cupidity. This was our plan, but unhappily we were not destined to visit La Bonte's Camp in this manner; for one morning a young Indian came to the fort and brought us evil tidings. The newcomer was a dandy of the first water. His ugly face was painted with vermilion; on his head fluttered the tail of a prairie cock (a large species of pheasant, not found, as I have heard, eastward of the Rocky Mountains); in his ears were hung pendants of shell, and a flaming red blanket was wrapped around him. He carried a dragoon sword in his hand, solely for display, since the knife, the arrow, and the rifle are the arbiters of every prairie fight; but no one in this country goes abroad unarmed, the dandy carried a bow and arrows in an otter-skin quiver at his back. In this guise, and bestriding his yellow horse with an air of extreme dignity, The Horse, for that was his name, rode in at the gate, turning neither to the right nor the left, but casting glances askance at the groups of squaws who, with their mongrel progeny, were sitting in the sun before their doors. The evil tidings brought by The Horse were of the following import: The squaw of Henry Chatillon, a woman with whom he had been connected for years by the strongest ties which in that country exist between the sexes, was dangerously ill. She and her children were in the village of The Whirlwind, at the distance of a few days' journey. Henry was anxious to see the woman before she died, and provide for the safety and support of his children, of whom he was extremely fond. To have refused him this would have been gross inhumanity. We abandoned our plan of joining Smoke's village, and of proceeding with it to the rendezvous, and determined to meet The Whirlwind, and go in his company.

I wished to satisfy myself with regard to the position of the Indians among the races of men; the vices and the virtues that have sprung from their innate character and from their modes of life . . .

I had been slightly ill for several weeks, but on the third night after reaching Fort Laramie a violent pain awoke me, and I found myself attacked by the same disorder that occasioned such heavy losses to the army on the Rio Grande. In a day and a half I was reduced to extreme weakness, so that I could not walk without pain and effort. Having within that time taken six grains of opium, without the least beneficial effect, and having no medical adviser, nor any choice of diet, I resolved to throw myself upon Providence for recovery, using, without regard to the disorder, any portion of strength that might remain to me. So on the 20th of June we set out from Fort Laramie to meet The Whirl-wind's village. Though aided by the high-bowed "mountain saddle," I could scarcely keep my seat on horseback. Before we left the fort we hired another man, a long-haired Canadian, with a face like an owl's, contrasting oddly enough with Delorier's mercur-ial countenance. This was not the only re-enforcement to our party. A vagrant Indian trader, named Reynal, joined us, together with his squaw Margot, and her two nephews, our dandy friend, The Horse, and his younger brother, The Hail Storm. Thus accompa-nied, we betook ourselves to the prairie, leaving the beaten trail, and passing over the desolate hills that flank the bottoms of Laramie Creek. In all, Indians and whites, we counted eight men and one woman.

Reynal, the trader, the image of sleek and selfish complacency, carried The Horse's dragoon sword in his hand, delighting apparently in this useless parade; for, from spending half his life among Indians, he had caught not only their habits but their ideas. Margot, a female animal of more than two hundred pounds' weight, was couched in the basket of a travail, such as I have before described; besides her ponderous bulk, vari-ous domestic utensils were attached to the vehicle, and she was leading by a trail-rope a packhorse, who carried the covering of Reynal's lodge. Delorier walked briskly by the side of the cart, and Raymond came behind, swearing at the spare horses, which it was his business to drive. The restless young Indians, their quivers at their backs, and their bows in their hand, galloped over the hills, often starting a wolf or an antelope from the thick growth of wild-sage bushes. Shaw and I were in keeping with the rest of the rude cavalcade, having in the absence of other clothing adopted the buckskin attire of the trappers. Henry Chatillon rode in advance of the whole. Thus we passed hill after hill and hollow after hollow, a country arid, broken and so parched by the sun that none of the plants familiar to our more favored soil would flourish upon it, though there were multitudes of strange medicinal herbs, more especially the absanth, which covered ev-ery declivity, and cacti were hanging like reptiles at the edges of every ravine. At length we ascended a high hill, our horses treading upon pebbles of flint, agate, and rough jasper, until, gaining the top, we looked down on the wild bottoms of Laramie Creek, which far below us wound like a writhing snake from side to side of the narrow inter-val, amid a growth of shattered cotton-wood and ash trees. Lines of tall cliffs, white as chalk, shut in this green strip of woods and meadow land, into which we descended

Quicksand

By Ezra Meeker

Fording a river was usually tiresome, and sometimes dangerous. I remember fording the Loup fork of the Platte with a large number of wagons fastened together with ropes or chains, so that if a wagon got into trouble the teams in front would help to pull it out. The quicksand would cease to sustain the wheels so suddenly that the wagon would drop a few inches with a jolt, and up again the wheel would come as new sand was struck; then down again it would go, up and down, precisely as if the wagons were passing over a rough corduroy road that "nearly jolted the life out of us," as the women folks said after it was over, and no wonder, for the river at this point was half a mile wide.

and encamped for the night. In the morning we passed a wide grassy plain by the river; there was a grove in front, and beneath its shadows the ruins of an old trading fort of logs. The grove bloomed with myriads of wild roses, with their sweet perfume fraught with recollections of home. As we emerged from the trees, a rattlesnake, as large as a man's arm, and more than four feet long, lay coiled on a rock, fiercely rattling and hissing at us; a gray hare, double the size of those in New England, leaped up from the tall ferns; curlew were screaming over our heads, and a whole host of little prairie dogs sat yelping at us at the mouths of their burrows on the dry plain beyond. Suddenly an antelope leaped up from the wild-sage bushes, gazed eagerly at us, and then, erecting his white tail, stretched away like a greyhound. The two Indian boys found a white wolf, as large as a calf in a hollow, and giving a sharp yell, they galloped after him; but the wolf leaped into the stream and swam across. Then came the crack of a rifle, the bullet whistling harmlessly over his head, as he scrambled up the steep declivity, rattling down stones and earth into the water below. Advancing a little, we beheld on the farther bank of the stream, a spectacle not common even in that region; for, emerging from among the trees, a herd of some two hundred elk came out upon the meadow, their antlers clattering as they walked forward in dense throng. Seeing us, they broke into a run, rushing across the opening and disappearing among the trees and scattered groves. On our left was a barren prairie, stretching to the horizon; on our right, a deep gulf, with Laramie Creek at the bottom. We found ourselves at length at the edge of a steep descent; a narrow valley, with long rank grass and scattered trees stretching before us for a mile or more along the course of the stream. Reaching the farther end, we stopped and encamped. An old huge cotton-wood tree spread its branches horizontally over our tent. Laramie Creek, circling before our camp, half inclosed us; it swept along the bottom of a line of tall white cliffs that looked down on us from the farther bank. There were dense copses on our right; the cliffs, too, were half hidden by shrubbery, though behind us a few cotton-wood trees, dotting the green prairie, alone impeded the view, and friend or enemy could be discerned in that direction at a mile's distance. Here we resolved to remain and await the arrival of The Whirlwind, who would certainly pass this way in his progress toward La Bonte's Camp. To go in search of him was not expedient, both on account of the broken and impracticable nature of the country and the uncertainty of his position and movements; besides, our horses were almost worn out, and I was in no condition to travel. We had good grass, good water, tolerable fish from the stream, and plenty of smaller game, such as antelope and deer, though no buffalo. There was one little drawback to our satisfaction—a certain extensive tract of bushes and dried grass, just behind us, which it was by no means advisable to enter, since it sheltered a numerous brood of rattlesnakes. Henry Chatillon again dispatched The Horse to the village, with a message to his squaw that she and her relatives should leave the rest and push on as rapidly as possible to our camp.

Rattlesnakes were an ever-present danger on the Oregon Trail.

Our daily routine soon became as regular as that of a well-ordered household. The weather-beaten old tree was in the center; our rifles generally rested against its vast trunk, and our saddles were flung on the ground around it; its distorted roots were so twisted as to form one or two convenient arm-chairs, where we could sit in the shade and read or smoke; but meal-times became, on the whole, the most interesting hours of the day, and a bountiful provision was made for them. An antelope or a deer usually swung from a stout bough, and haunches were suspended against the trunk. That camp is daguerreotyped on my memory; the old tree, the white tent, with Shaw sleeping in the shadow of it, and Reynal's miserable lodge close by the bank of the stream. It was a wretched oven-shaped structure, made of begrimed and tattered buffalo hides stretched

over a frame of poles; one side was open, and at the side of the opening hung the powder horn and bullet pouch of the owner, together with his long red pipe, and a rich quiver of otterskin, with a bow and arrows; for Reynal, an Indian in most things but color, chose to hunt buffalo with these primitive weapons. In the darkness of this cavern-like habitation might be discerned Madame Margot, her overgrown bulk stowed away among her domestic implements, furs, robes, blankets, and painted cases of raw hide, in which dried meat is kept. Here she sat from sunrise to sunset, a bloated impersonation of gluttony and laziness, while her affectionate proprietor was smoking, or begging petty gifts from us, or telling lies concerning his own achievements, or perchance engaged in the more profitable occupation of cooking some preparation of prairie delicacies. Reynal was an adept at this work; he and Delorier have joined forces and are hard at work together over the fire, while Raymond spreads, by way of tablecloth, a buffalo hide, carefully whitened with pipeclay, on the grass before the tent. Here, with ostentatious display, he arranges the teacups and plates; and then, creeping on all fours like a dog, he thrusts his head in at the opening of the tent. For a moment we see his round owlish eyes rolling wildly, as if the idea he came to communicate had suddenly escaped him; then collecting his scattered thoughts, as if by an effort, he informs us that supper is ready, and instantly withdraws.

When sunset came, and at that hour the wild and desolate scene would assume a new aspect, the horses were driven in. They had been grazing all day in the neighboring meadow, but now they were picketed close about the camp. As the prairie darkened we sat and conversed around the fire, until becoming drowsy we spread our saddles on the ground, wrapped our blankets around us and lay down. We never placed a guard, having by this time become too indolent; but Henry Chatillon folded his loaded rifle in the same blanket with himself, observing that he always took it to bed with him when he camped in that place. Henry was too bold a man to use such a precaution without good cause. We had a hint now and then that our situation was none of the safest; several Crow war parties were known to be in the vicinity, and one of them, that passed here some time before, had peeled the bark from a neighboring tree, and engraved upon the white wood certain hieroglyphics, to signify that they had invaded the territories of their enemies, the Dakota, and set them at defiance. One morning a thick mist covered the whole country. Shaw and Henry went out to ride, and soon came back with a startling piece of intelligence; they had found within rifle-shot of our camp the recent trail of about thirty horsemen. They could not be whites, and they could not be Dakota, since we knew no such parties to be in the neighborhood; therefore they must be Crows. Thanks to that friendly mist, we had escaped a hard battle; they would inevitably have attacked us and our Indian companions had they seen our camp. Whatever doubts we might have entertained, were quite removed a day or two after, by two or three Dakota,

Pretty Camp – Rocky Mountains

Artist Daniel A. Jenks sketched this camp near a riverbend in the Rocky Mountains in 1859.

who came to us with an account of having hidden in a ravine on that very morning, from whence they saw and counted the Crows; they said that they followed them, carefully keeping out of sight, as they passed up Chugwater; that here the Crows discovered five dead bodies of Dakota, placed according to the national custom in trees, and flinging them to the ground, they held their guns against them and blew them to atoms.

If our camp were not altogether safe, still it was comfortable enough; at least it was so to Shaw, for I was tormented with illness and vexed by the delay in the accomplishment of my designs. When a respite in my disorder gave me some returning strength, I rode out well-armed upon the prairie, or bathed with Shaw in the stream, or waged a petty warfare with the inhabitants of a neighborhood prairie-dog village. Around our fire at night we employed ourselves in inveighing against the fickleness and inconstancy of Indians, and execrating The Whirlwind and all his village. At last the thing grew insufferable.

"To-morrow morning," said I, "I will start for the fort, and see if I can hear any news there." Late that evening, when the fire had sunk low, and all the camp were asleep, a loud cry sounded from the darkness. Henry started up, recognized the voice, replied to it, and our dandy friend, The Horse, rode in among us, just returned from his mission to the village. He coolly picketed his mare, without saying a word, sat down by the fire and began to eat, but his imperturbable philosophy was too much for our patience. Where was the village? about fifty miles south of us; it was moving slowly and would not arrive in less than a week; and where was Henry's squaw? coming as fast as she could with Mahto-Tatonka, and the rest of her brothers, but she would never reach us, for she was dying, and asking every moment for Henry. Henry's manly face became clouded and downcast; he said that if we were willing he would go in the morning to find her, at which Shaw offered to accompany him.

We saddled our horses at sunrise. Reynal protested vehemently against being left alone, with nobody but the two Canadians and the young Indians, when enemies were in the neighborhood. Disregarding his complaints, we left him, and coming to the mouth of Chugwater, separated, Shaw and Henry turning to the right, up the bank of the stream, while I made for the fort.

Taking leave for a while of my friend and the unfortunate squaw, I will relate by way of episode what I saw and did at Fort Laramie. It was not more than eighteen miles distant, and I reached it in three hours; a shriveled little figure, wrapped from head to foot in a dingy white Canadian capote, stood in the gateway, holding by a cord of bull's hide a shaggy wild horse, which he had lately caught. His sharp prominent features, and his little keen snakelike eyes, looked out from beneath the shadowy hood of the capote, which was drawn over his head exactly like the cowl of a Capuchin friar. His face was extremely thin and like an old piece of leather, and his mouth spread from ear to ear. Extending his long wiry hand, he welcomed me with something more cordial than the ordinary cold salute of an Indian, for we were excellent friends. He had made an exchange of horses to our mutual advantage; and Paul, thinking himself well-treated, had declared everywhere that the white man had a good heart. He was a Dakota from the Missouri, a reputed son of the half-breed interpreter, Pierre Dorion, so often mentioned in Irving's "Astoria." He said that he was going to Richard's trading house to sell his horse to some emigrants who were encamped there, and asked me to go with him. We forded the stream together, Paul dragging his wild charge behind him. As we passed over the sandy plains beyond, he grew quite communicative. Paul was a cosmopolitan in his way; he had been to the settlements of the whites, and visited in peace and war most of the tribes within the range of a thousand miles. He spoke a jargon of French and another of English, yet nevertheless he was a thorough Indian; and as he told of the bloody deeds of his own people against their enemies, his little eye would glitter with a fierce luster. He told how the Dakota exterminated a village of the Hohays on the Upper Missouri, slaughtering men, women, and children; and how an overwhelming force of them cut off sixteen of the brave Delawares, who fought like wolves to the last, amid the throng of their enemies. He told me also another story, which I did not believe until I had it confirmed from so many independent sources that no room was left for doubt. I am tempted to introduce it here.

Crow Hoop on the Forehead, with a Crow tomahawk and rifle circa 1908.

Six years ago a fellow named Jim Beckwith, a mongrel of French, American, and negro blood, was trading for the Fur Company, in a very large village of the Crows. Jim Beckwith was last summer at St. Louis. He is a ruffian of the first stamp; bloody and treacherous, without honor or honesty; such at least is the character he bears upon the prairie. Yet in his case all the standard rules of character fail, for though he will stab a man in his sleep, he will also perform most desperate acts of daring; such, for instance, as the following: While he was in the Crow village, a Blackfoot war party, between thirty and forty in number came stealing through the country, killing stragglers and carrying off horses. The Crow warriors got upon their trail and pressed them so closely that they could not escape, at which the Blackfeet, throwing up a semicircular breastwork of logs at the foot of a precipice, coolly awaited their approach. The logs and sticks, piled four or five high, protected them in front. The Crows might have swept over the breastwork and exterminated their enemies; but though out-numbering them tenfold, they did not dream of storming the little fortification. Such a proceeding would be altogether repugnant to their notions of warfare. Whooping and yelling, and jumping from side to side like devils incarnate, they showered bullets and arrows upon the logs; not a Blackfoot was hurt, but several Crows, in spite of their leaping and dodging, were shot down. In this childish manner the fight went on for an hour or two. Now and then a Crow warrior in an ecstasy of valor and vainglory would scream forth his war song, boasting himself the bravest and greatest of mankind, and grasping his hatchet, would rush up and strike it upon the breastwork, and then as he retreated to his companions, fall dead under a shower of arrows; yet no combined attack seemed to be dreamed of. The Blackfeet remained secure in their intrenchment. At last Jim Beckwith lost patience.

"You are all fools and old women," he said to the Crows; "come with me, if any of you are brave enough, and I will show you how to fight."

He threw off his trapper's frock of buckskin and stripped himself naked like the Indians themselves. He left his rifle on the ground, and taking in his hand a small light hatchet, he ran over the prairie to the right, concealed by a hollow from the eyes of the Blackfeet. Then climbing up the rocks, he gained the top of the precipice behind them. Forty or fifty young Crow warriors followed him. By the cries and whoops that rose from below he knew that the Blackfeet were just beneath him; and running forward, he leaped down the rock into the midst of them. As he fell he caught one by the long loose hair and dragging him down tomahawked him; then grasping another by the belt at his waist, he struck him also a stunning blow, and gaining his feet, shouted the Crow war-cry. He swung his hatchet so fiercely around him that the astonished Blackfeet bore back and gave him room. He might, had he chosen, have leaped over the breastwork and escaped; but this was not necessary, for with devilish yells the Crow warriors came dropping in quick succession over the rock among their enemies. The main body of the Crows, too, answered the cry from the front and rushed up simultaneously. The convulsive struggle within the breastwork was frightful; for an instant the Blackfeet fought and yelled like pent-up tigers; but the butchery was soon complete, and the mangled bodies lay piled up together under the precipice. Not a Blackfoot made his escape.

As Paul finished his story we came in sight of Richard's Fort. It stood in the middle of the plain; a disorderly crowd of men around it, and an emigrant camp a little in front.

"Now, Paul," said I, "where are your Winnicongew lodges?"

"Not come yet," said Paul, "maybe come to-morrow."

A public dance in honor of the Indian warrior He Dog, painted with ink on paper.

Crow woman at camp on the Great Plains with dogs and horses.

**With one hand
he sawed the air,
and with the other
clutched firmly
a brown jug of
whisky, which
he applied every
moment to his lips,
forgetting that he
had drained the
contents long ago.**

Two large villages of a band of Dakota had come three hundred miles from the Missouri, to join in the war, and they were expected to reach Richard's that morning. There was as yet no sign of their approach; so pushing through a noisy, drunken crowd, I entered an apartment of logs and mud, the largest in the fort; it was full of men of various races and complexions, all more or less drunk. A company of California emigrants, it seemed, had made the discovery at this late day that they had encumbered themselves with too many supplies for their journey. A part, therefore, they had thrown away or sold at great loss to the traders, but had determined to get rid of their copious stock of Missouri whisky, by drinking it on the spot. Here were maudlin squaws stretched on piles of buffalo robes; squalid Mexicans, armed with bows and arrows; Indians sedately drunk; long-haired Canadians and trappers, and American backwoodsmen in brown homespun, the well-beloved pistol and bowie knife displayed openly at their sides. In the middle of the room a tall, lank man, with a dingy broadcloth coat, was haranguing the company in the style of the stump orator. With one hand he sawed the air, and with the other clutched firmly a brown jug of whisky, which he applied every moment to his lips, forgetting that he had drained the contents long ago. Richard formally introduced me to this personage, who was no less a man than Colonel R., once the leader of the party. Instantly the colonel seizing me, in the absence of buttons by the leather fringes of my frock, began to define his position. His men, he said, had mutinied and deposed him; but still he exercised over them the influence of a superior mind; in all but the name he was yet their chief. As the colonel spoke, I looked round on the wild assemblage, and could not help thinking that he was but ill qualified to conduct such men across the desert to California. Conspicuous among the rest stood three tall young men, grandsons of Daniel Boone. They had clearly inherited the adventurous character of that prince of pioneers; but I saw no signs of the quiet and tranquil spirit that so remarkably distinguished him.

Fearful was the fate that months after overtook some of the members of that party. General Kearny, on his late return from California, brought in the account how they were interrupted by the deep snows among the mountains, and maddened by cold and hunger fed upon each other's flesh.

I got tired of the confusion. "Come, Paul," said I, "we will be off." Paul sat in the sun, under the wall of the fort. He jumped up, mounted, and we rode toward Fort Laramie. When we reached it, a man came out of the gate with a pack at his back and a rifle on his shoulder; others were gathering about him, shaking him by the hand, as if taking leave. I thought it a strange thing that a man should set out alone and on foot for the prairie. I soon got an explanation. Perrault—this, if I recollect right was the Canadian's name—had quarreled with the bourgeois, and the fort was too hot to hold him. Bordeaux, inflated with his transient authority, had abused him, and received a blow in return. The men then sprang at each other, and grappled in the middle of the fort. Bordeaux was down in an instant, at the mercy of the incensed Canadian; had not an old

Indian, the brother of his squaw, seized hold of his antagonist, he would have fared ill. Perrault broke loose from the old Indian, and both the white men ran to their rooms for their guns; but when Bordeaux, looking from his door, saw the Canadian, gun in hand, standing in the area and calling on him to come out and fight, his heart failed him; he chose to remain where he was. In vain the old Indian, scandalized by his brother-in-law's cowardice, called upon him to go upon the prairie and fight it out in the white man's manner; and Bordeaux's own squaw, equally incensed, screamed to her lord and master that he was a dog and an old woman. It all availed nothing. Bordeaux's prudence got the better of his valor, and he would not stir. Perrault stood showering

Crow family on a travois with shelter in 1874, by Valentine Walter Lewis Bromley.

approbrious epithets at the recent bourgeois. Growing tired of this, he made up a pack of dried meat, and slinging it at his back, set out alone for Fort Pierre on the Missouri, a distance of three hundred miles, over a desert country full of hostile Indians.

I remained in the fort that night. In the morning, as I was coming out from breakfast, conversing with a trader named McCluskey, I saw a strange Indian leaning against the side of the gate. He was a tall, strong man, with heavy features.

"Who is he?" I asked.

"That's The Whirlwind," said McCluskey. "He is the fellow that made all this stir about the war. It's always the way with the Sioux; they never stop cutting each other's throats; it's all they are fit for; instead of sitting in their lodges, and getting robes to trade with us in the winter. If this war goes on, we'll make a poor trade of it next season, I reckon."

And this was the opinion of all the traders, who were vehemently opposed to the war, from the serious injury that it must occasion to their interests. The Whirlwind left his village the day before to make a visit to the fort. His warlike ardor had abated not a little since he first conceived the design of avenging his son's death. The long and complicated preparations for the expedition were too much for his fickle, inconstant disposition. That morning Bordeaux fastened upon him, made him presents and told him that if he went to war he would destroy his horses and kill no buffalo to trade with the white men; in short, that he was a fool to think of such a thing, and had better make up his mind to sit quietly in his lodge and smoke his pipe, like a wise man. The Whirlwind's purpose was evidently shaken; he had become tired, like a child, of his favorite plan. Bordeaux exultingly predicted that he would not go to war. I was vexed at the possibility that I might lose the rare opportunity of seeing the formidable ceremonies of war. The Whirlwind, however, had merely thrown the firebrand; the conflagration was become general. All the western bands of the Dakota were bent on war; and as I heard from McCluskey, six large villages already gathered on a little stream, forty miles distant, were daily calling to the Great Spirit to aid them in their enterprise. There were also the two Minnicongew villages that I mentioned before; but about noon, an Indian came from Richard's Fort with the news that they were quarreling, breaking up, and dispersing. So much for the whisky of the emigrants! Finding themselves unable to drink the whole, they had sold the residue to these Indians. Instantly the old jealousies and rivalries and smothered feuds that exist in an Indian village broke out into furious quarrels. They forgot the warlike enterprise that had already brought them three hundred miles. They seemed like ungoverned children inflamed with the fiercest passions of men. Several of them were stabbed in the drunken tumult; and in the morning they scattered and moved back toward the Missouri in small parties. I feared that, after all, the long-projected meeting and the ceremonies that were to attend it might never take place, and I should lose so admirable an opportunity of seeing the Indian under his most fearful and characteristic aspect; however, in foregoing this, I should avoid a very fair probability of being plundered and stripped, and, it might be, stabbed or shot into the bargain. Consoling myself with this reflection, I prepared to carry the news, such as it was, to the camp.

I caught my horse, and to my vexation found he had lost a shoe and broken his tender white hoof against the rocks. Horses are shod at Fort Laramie at the moderate rate of three dollars a foot; so I tied Hendrick to a beam in the corral, and summoned Roubidou, the blacksmith. Roubidou, with the hoof between his knees, was at work with hammer and file, and I was inspecting the process, when a strange voice addressed me.

"Two more gone under! Well, there is more of us left yet. Here's Jean Gras and me off to the mountains to-morrow. Our turn will come, I suppose. It's a hard life, anyhow!"

I looked up and saw a little man, not much more than five feet high, but of very square and strong proportions. In appearance he was particularly dingy; for his old buckskin frock was black and polished with time and grease, and his belt, knife, pouch, and powder-horn appeared to have seen the roughest service. The first joint of each foot was entirely gone, having been frozen off several winters before. His whole appearance and equipment bespoke the "free trapper." He had a round ruddy face, animated with a spirit of carelessness and gayety not at all in accordance with the words he had just spoken.

"Two more gone," said I; "what do you mean by that?"

"Oh," said he, "the Arapahoes have just killed two of us in the mountains. Old Bull-Tail has come to tell us. They stabbed one behind his back, and shot the other with his own rifle. That's the way we live here! I mean to give up trapping after this year. My squaw says she wants a pacing horse and some red ribbons; I'll make enough beaver to get them for her, and then I'm done! I'll go below and live on a farm."

"Your bones will dry on the prairie, Rouleau!" said another trapper, who was standing by; a strong, brutal-looking fellow, with a face as surly as a bull-dog's.

Rouleau only laughed, and began to hum a tune and shuffle on his stumps of feet.

"You'll see us, before long, passing up our way," said the other man.

"Well," said I, "stop and take a cup of coffee with us"; and as it was quite late in the afternoon, I prepared to leave the fort at once.

As I rode out, a train of emigrant wagons was passing across the stream. "Whar are ye goin' stranger?" Thus I was saluted by two or three voices at once.

"About eighteen miles up the creek."

"It's mighty late to be going that far! Make haste, ye'd better, and keep a bright look-out for Indians!"

I thought the advice too good to be neglected. Fording the stream, I passed at a round trot over the plains beyond. But "the more haste, the worse speed." I proved the truth in the proverb by the time I reached the hills three miles from the fort. The trail was faintly marked, and riding forward with more rapidity than caution, I lost sight of it. I kept on in a direct line, guided by Laramie Creek, which I could see at intervals darkly glistening in the evening sun. Half an hour before sunset I came upon its banks. There was

When I came to the mouth of Chugwater, it was totally dark. Slackening the reins, I let my horse take his own course. He trotted on with unerring instinct, and by nine o'clock was scrambling down the steep ascent into the meadows where we were encamped.

something exciting in the wild solitude of the place. An antelope sprang suddenly from the sagebushes before me. As he leaped gracefully not thirty yards before my horse, I fired, and instantly he spun round and fell. Quite sure of him, I walked my horse toward him, leisurely reloading my rifle, when he sprang up and trotted rapidly away on three legs into the dark recesses of the hills. Ten minutes after, I saw in the dim light that something was following. Supposing it to be wolf, I slid from my seat and sat down behind my horse to shoot it; but as it came up, I saw by its motions that it was another antelope. It approached within a hundred yards, arched its graceful neck, and gazed intently. I leveled at the white spot on its chest, and was about to fire when it started off, ran first to one side and then to the other, like a vessel tacking against a wind. Then it stopped again, looked curiously behind it, and trotted up as before; but not so boldly, for it soon paused and stood gazing at me. I fired; it leaped upward and fell upon its tracks. Measuring the distance, I found it 204 paces. When I stood by his side, the antelope turned his expiring eye upward. It was like a beautiful woman's, dark and rich. "Fortunate that I am in a hurry," thought I; "I might be troubled with remorse, if I had time for it."

Cutting the animal up, I hung the meat at the back of my saddle, and rode on again. The hills (I could not remember one of them) closed around me. "It is too late," thought I, "to go forward. I will stay here to-night, and look for the path in the morning." As a last effort, however, I ascended a high hill, from which, to my great satisfaction, I could see Laramie Creek stretching before me, twisting from side to side amid ragged patches of timber; and far off, close beneath the shadows of the trees, the ruins of the old trading fort were visible. I reached them at twilight. It was far from pleasant, in that uncertain light, to be pushing through the dense trees and shrubbery of the grove beyond. I listened anxiously for the footfall of man or beast. Nothing was stirring but one harmless brown bird, chirping among the branches. I was glad when I gained the open prairie once more, where I could see if anything approached. When I came to the mouth of Chugwater, it was totally dark. Slackening the reins, I let my horse take his own course. He trotted on with unerring instinct, and by nine o'clock was scrambling down the steep ascent into the meadows where we were encamped. While I was looking in vain for the light of the fire, Hendrick, with keener perceptions, gave a loud neigh, which was immediately answered in a shrill note from the distance. In a moment I was hailed from the darkness by the voice of Reynal, who had come out, rifle in hand, to see who was approaching.

He, with his squaw, the two Canadians and the Indian boys, were the sole inmates of the camp, Shaw and Henry Chatillon being still absent. At noon of the following day they came back, their horses looking none the better for the journey. Henry seemed dejected. The woman was dead, and his children must henceforward be exposed to the hardships of Indian life. Even in the midst of his grief he had not forgotten his attachment to his bourgeois, for he had procured two beautifully ornamented buffalo robes, which he spread on the ground as a present to us.

Wapiti, or American elk, is the largest species of the deer family.

A traditional Indian burial on a tree platform or scaffold, color lithograph from 1853.

Shaw lighted his pipe, and told me in a few words the history of his journey. When I went to the fort they left me, as I mentioned, at the mouth of Chugwater. They followed the course of the little stream all day, traversing a desolate and barren country. Several times they came upon the fresh traces of a large war party—the same, no doubt, from whom we had so narrowly escaped an attack. At an hour before sunset, without encountering a human being by the way, they came upon the lodges of the squaw and her brothers, who, in compliance with Henry's message, had left the Indian village in order to join us at our camp. The lodges were already pitched, five in number, by the side of the stream. The woman lay in one of them, reduced to a mere skeleton. For some time she had been unable to move or speak. Indeed, nothing had kept her alive but the hope of seeing Henry, to whom she was strongly and faithfully attached. No sooner did he enter the lodge than she revived, and conversed with him the greater part of the night.

Arrival at Fort Hall

By Narcissa Whitman

We were hospitably entertained by Captain Thing, who keeps the fort. It was built by Captain Wyeth, a gentleman from Boston, whom we saw at Rendezvous on his way east. Our dinner consisted of dry buffalo meat, turnips, and fried bread, which was a luxury. Mountain bread is simply coarse flour and water mixed and roasted or fried in buffalo grease. To one who has had nothing but meat for a long time, this relishes well. For tea we had the same, with the addition of some stewed service berries.

The buildings of the fort are made of hewed logs, with roofs covered with mud brick chimneys and fireplaces also being built of the same; no windows, except a square hole in the roof, and in the bastion a few port holes large enough for guns only. The buildings were all enclosed in a strong log wall. This affords them a place of safety when attacked by hostile Indians, as they frequently are, the fort being in the Blackfeet country.

Early in the morning she was lifted into a travail, and the whole party set out toward our camp. There were but five warriors; the rest were women and children. The whole were in great alarm at the proximity of the Crow war party, who would certainly have destroyed them without mercy had they met. They had advanced only a mile or two, when they discerned a horseman, far off, on the edge of the horizon. They all stopped, gathering together in the greatest anxiety, from which they did not recover until long after the horseman disappeared; then they set out again. Henry was riding with Shaw a few rods in advance of the Indians, when Mahto-Tatonka, a younger brother of the woman, hastily called after them. Turning back, they found all the Indians crowded around the travail in which the woman was lying. They reached her just in time to hear the death-rattle in her throat. In a moment she lay dead in the basket of the vehicle. A complete stillness succeeded; then the Indians raised in concert their cries of lamentation over the corpse, and among them Shaw clearly distinguished those strange sounds resembling the word "Halleluyah," which together with some other accidental coincidences has given rise to the absurd theory that the Indians are descended from the ten lost tribes of Israel.

The Indian usage required that Henry, as well as the other relatives of the woman, should make valuable presents, to be placed by the body at its last resting place. Leaving the Indians, he and Shaw set out for the camp and reached it, at about noon. Having obtained the necessary articles, they immediately returned. It was very late and quite dark when they again reached the lodges, in a deep hollow among the dreary hills. Four of them were just visible through the gloom, but the fifth and largest was illuminated by the ruddy blaze of a fire within, glowing through the half-transparent covering of raw hides. There was a perfect stillness as they approached. The lodges seemed without a tenant. Not a living thing was stirring—there was something awful in the scene. There was no sound but the tramp of their horses. A squaw came out and took charge of the animals, without speaking a word. Entering, they found the lodge crowded with Indians; a fire was burning in the midst, and the mourners encircled it in a triple row. Room was made for the newcomers at the head of the lodge, and a pipe lighted and handed to them in perfect silence. Thus they passed the greater part of the night. At times the fire would subside into a heap of embers, until the dark figures seated around it were scarcely visible; then a squaw would drop upon it a piece of buffalo-fat, and a bright flame would reveal of a sudden the crowd of wild faces, motionless as bronze. The silence continued unbroken. It was a relief to Shaw when daylight returned and he could escape from this house of mourning. He and Henry prepared to return homeward; first, however, they placed the presents they had brought near the body of the squaw, which, most gaudily attired, remained in a sitting posture in one of the lodges. A fine horse was picketed not far off, destined to be killed that morning for the service of her spirit, for the woman was lame, and could not travel on foot over the dismal prairies to the villages of the dead. Food, too, was provided, and household implements, for her use upon this last journey.

Scenes at the Camp

Reynal heard guns fired one day, at the distance of a mile or two from the camp. He grew nervous instantly. Visions of Crow war parties began to haunt his imagination; and when we returned (for we were all absent), he renewed his complaints about being left alone with the Canadians and the squaw. The day after, the cause of the alarm appeared. Four trappers, one called Moran, another Saraphin, and the others nicknamed "Rouleau" and "Jean Gras," came to our camp and joined us. They it was who fired the guns and disturbed the dreams of our confederate Reynal. They soon encamped by our side. Their rifles, dingy and battered with hard service, rested with ours against the old tree; their strong rude saddles, their buffalo robes, their traps, and the few rough and simple articles of their traveling equipment, were piled near our tent. Their mountain horses were turned to graze in the meadow among our own; and the men themselves, no less rough and hardy, used to lie half the day in the shade of our tree lolling on the grass, lazily smoking, and telling stories of their adventures; and I defy the annals of chivalry to furnish the record of a life more wild and perilous than that of a Rocky Mountain trapper.

"A Medicine Man Curing a Patient," from a lithograph.

With this efficient re-enforcement the agitation of Reynal's nerves subsided. He began to conceive a sort of attachment to our old camping ground; yet it was time to change our quarters, since remaining too long on one spot must lead to certain unpleasant results not to be borne with unless in a case of dire necessity. The grass no longer presented a smooth surface of turf; it was trampled into mud and clay. So we removed to another old tree, larger yet, that grew by the river side at a furlong's distance. Its trunk was full six feet in diameter; on one side it was marked by a party of Indians with various inexplicable hieroglyphics, commemorating some warlike enterprise, and aloft among the branches were the remains of a scaffolding, where dead bodies had once been deposited, after the Indian manner.

"There comes Bull-Bear," said Henry Chatillon, as we sat on the grass at dinner. Looking up, we saw several horsemen coming over the neighboring hill, and in a moment four stately young men rode up and dismounted. One of them was Bull-Bear, or Mahto-Tatonka, a compound name which he inherited from his father, the most powerful chief in the Ogallalla band. One of his brothers and two other young men accompanied him. We shook hands with the visitors, and when we had finished our meal—for this is the orthodox manner of entertaining Indians—we handed to each a tin cup of coffee and a biscuit, at which they ejaculated from the bottom of their throats, "How! how!" a monosyllable by which an Indian contrives to express half the emotions that he is susceptible of. Then we lighted the pipe, and passed it to them as they squatted on the ground.

"Where is the village?"

"There," said Mahto-Tatonka, pointing southward; "it will come in two days."

"Will they go to the war?"

"Yes."

No man is a philanthropist on the prairie. We welcomed this news, and congratulated ourselves that Bordeaux's efforts to divert The Whirlwind from his congenial vocation of bloodshed had failed of success, and that no additional obstacles would interpose between us and our plan of repairing to the rendezvous at La Bonte's Camp.

For that and several succeeding days, Mahto-Tatonka and his friends remained our guests. They devoured the relics of our meals; they filled the pipe for us and also helped us to smoke it. Sometimes they stretched themselves side by side in the shade, indulging in raillery and practical jokes ill becoming the dignity of brave and aspiring warriors, such as two of them in reality were.

Two days dragged away, and on the morning of the third we hoped confidently to see the Indian village. It did not come; so we rode out to look for it. In place of the eight hundred Indians we expected, we met one solitary savage riding toward us over the prairie, who told us that the Indians had changed their plans, and would not come within three days; still he persisted that they were going to the war. Taking along with us this messenger of evil tidings, we retraced our footsteps to the camp, amusing ourselves by the

way with execrating Indian inconstancy. When we came in sight of our little white tent under the big tree, we saw that it no longer stood alone. A huge old lodge was erected close by its side, discolored by rain and storms, rotted with age, with the uncouth figures of horses and men, and outstretched hands that were painted upon it, well-nigh obliterated. The long poles which supported this squalid habitation thrust themselves rakishly out from its pointed top, and over its entrance were suspended a "medicine-pipe" and various other implements of the magic art. While we were yet at a distance, we observed a greatly increased population of various colors and dimensions, swarming around our quiet encampment. Moran, the trapper, having been absent for a day or two, had returned, it seemed, bringing all his family with him. He had taken to himself a wife for whom he had paid the established price of one horse. This looks cheap at first sight, but in truth the purchase of a squaw is a transaction which no man should enter into without mature deliberation, since it involves not only the payment of the first price, but the formidable burden of feeding and supporting a rapacious horde of the bride's relatives, who hold themselves entitled to feed upon the indiscreet white man. They gather round like leeches, and drain him of all he has.

Moran, like Reynal, had not allied himself to an aristocratic circle. His relatives occupied but a contemptible position in Ogallalla society; for among those wild democrats of the prairie, as among us, there are virtual distinctions of rank and place; though this great advantage they have over us, that wealth has no part in determining such distinctions. Moran's partner was not the most beautiful of her sex, and he had the exceedingly bad taste to array her in an old calico gown bought from an emigrant woman, instead of the neat and graceful tunic of whitened deerskin worn ordinarily by the squaws. The moving spirit of the establishment, in more senses than one, was a hideous old hag of eighty. Human imagination never conceived hobgoblin or witch more ugly than she. You could count all her ribs through the wrinkles of the leathery skin that covered them. Her withered face more resembled an old skull than the countenance of a living being, even to the hollow, darkened sockets, at the bottom of which glittered her little black eyes. Her arms had dwindled away into nothing but whipcord and wire. Her hair, half black, half gray, hung in total neglect nearly to the ground, and her sole garment consisted of the remnant of a discarded buffalo robe tied round her waist with a string of hide. Yet the old squaw's meager anatomy was wonderfully strong. She pitched the lodge, packed the horses, and did the hardest labor of the camp. From morning till night she bustled about the lodge, screaming like a screech-owl when anything displeased her. Then there was her brother, a "medicine-man," or magician, equally gaunt and sinewy with herself. His mouth spread from ear to ear, and his appetite, as we had full occasion to learn, was ravenous in proportion. The other inmates of the lodge were a young bride and bridegroom; the

latter one of those idle, good-for nothing fellows who infest an Indian village as well as more civilized communities. He was fit neither for hunting nor for war; and one might infer as much from the stolid unmeaning expression of his face. The happy pair had just entered upon the honeymoon. They would stretch a buffalo robe upon poles, so as to protect them from the fierce rays of the sun, and spreading beneath this rough canopy a luxuriant couch of furs, would sit affectionately side by side for half the day, though I could not discover that much conversation passed between them. Probably they had nothing to say; for an Indian's supply of topics for conversation is far from being copious. There were half a dozen children, too, playing and whooping about the camp, shooting birds with little bows and arrows, or making miniature lodges of sticks, as children of a different complexion build houses of blocks.

A day passed, and Indians began rapidly to come in. Parties of two or three or more would ride up and silently seat themselves on the grass. The fourth day came at last, when about noon horsemen suddenly appeared into view on the summit of the neighboring ridge. They descended, and behind them followed a wild procession, hurrying in haste and disorder down the hill and over the plain below; horses, mules, and dogs, heavily burdened travaux, mounted warriors, squaws walking amid the throng, and a host of children. For a full half-hour they continued to pour down; and keeping directly to the bend of the stream, within a furlong of us, they soon assembled there, a dark and confused throng, until, as if by magic, 150 tall lodges sprung up. On a sudden the lonely plain was transformed into the site of a miniature city. Countless horses were soon grazing over the meadows around us, and the whole prairie was animated by restless figures careening on horseback, or sedately stalking in their long white robes. The Whirlwind was come at last! One question yet remained to be answered: "Will he go to the war, in order that we, with so respectable an escort, may pass over to the somewhat perilous rendezvous at La Bonte's Camp?"

Still this remained in doubt. Characteristic indecision perplexed their councils. Indians cannot act in large bodies. Though their object be of the highest importance, they cannot combine to attain it by a series of connected efforts. King Philip, Pontiac, and Tecumseh all felt this to their cost. The Ogallalla once had a war chief who could control them; but he was dead, and now they were left to the sway of their own unsteady impulses.

This Indian village and its inhabitants will hold a prominent place in the rest of the narrative, and perhaps it may not be amiss to glance for an instant at the savage people of which they form a part. The Dakota (I prefer this national designation to the unmeaning French name, Sioux) range over a vast territory, from the river St. Peter's to the Rocky Mountains themselves. They are divided into several independent bands, united under no central government, and acknowledge no common head. The same language, usages, and superstitions form the sole bond between them. They do not unite even in their wars. The bands of the east fight the Ojibwas on the Upper Lakes; those of the west

Sioux women and children at work and play in the village, by George Catlin.

"Buffaloes at Rest,"
a lithograph from 1911.

make incessant war upon the Snake Indians in the Rocky Mountains. As the whole people is divided into bands, so each band is divided into villages. Each village has a chief, who is honored and obeyed only so far as his personal qualities may command respect and fear. Sometimes he is a mere nominal chief; sometimes his authority is little short of absolute, and his fame and influence reach even beyond his own village; so that the whole band to which he belongs is ready to acknowledge him as their head. This was, a few years since, the case with the Ogallalla. Courage, address, and enterprise may raise any warrior to the highest honor, especially if he be the son of a former chief, or a member of a numerous family, to support him and avenge his quarrels; but when he has reached the dignity of chief, and the old men and warriors, by a peculiar ceremony, have formally installed him, let it not be imagined that he assumes any of the outward semblances of rank and honor. He knows too well on how frail a tenure he holds his station.

The buffalo supplies them with almost all the necessaries of life; with habitations, food, clothing, and fuel; with strings for their bows, with thread, cordage, and trail-ropes for their horses, with coverings for their saddles . . . When the buffalo are extinct, they too must dwindle away.

He must conciliate his uncertain subjects. Many a man in the village lives better, owns more squaws and more horses, and goes better clad than he. Like the Teutonic chiefs of old, he ingratiates himself with his young men by making them presents, thereby often impoverishing himself. Does he fail in gaining their favor, they will set his authority at naught, and may desert him at any moment; for the usages of his people have provided no sanctions by which he may enforce his authority. Very seldom does it happen, at least among these western bands, that a chief attains so much power, unless he is the head of a numerous family. Frequently the village is principally made up of his relatives and descendants, and the wandering community assumes much of the patriarchal character. A people so loosely united, torn, too, with ranking feuds and jealousies, can have little power or efficiency.

The western Dakota have no fixed habitations. Hunting and fighting, they wander incessantly through summer and winter. Some are following the herds of buffalo over the waste of prairie; others are traversing the Black Hills, thronging on horseback and on foot through the dark gulfs and somber gorges beneath the vast splintering precipices, and emerging at last upon the "Parks," those beautiful but most perilous hunting grounds. The buffalo supplies them with almost all the necessaries of life; with habitations, food, clothing, and fuel; with strings for their bows, with thread, cordage, and trail-ropes for their horses, with coverings for their saddles, with vessels to hold water, with boats to cross streams, with glue, and with the means of purchasing all that they desire from the traders. When the buffalo are extinct, they too must dwindle away.

War is the breath of their nostrils. Against most of the neighboring tribes they cherish a deadly, rancorous hatred, transmitted from father to son, and inflamed by constant aggression and retaliation. Many times a year, in every village, the Great Spirit is called upon, fasts are made, the war parade is celebrated, and the warriors go out by handfuls at a time against the enemy. This fierce and evil spirit awakens their most eager aspirations, and calls forth their greatest energies. It is chiefly this that saves them from lethargy and utter abasement. Without its powerful stimulus they would be like the unwarlike tribes beyond the mountains, who are scattered among the caves and rocks like beasts, living on roots and reptiles. These latter have little of humanity except the form; but the proud and ambitious Dakota warrior can sometimes boast of heroic virtues. It is very seldom that distinction and influence are attained among them by any other course than that of arms. Their superstition, however, sometimes gives great power, to those among them who pretend to the character of magicians. Their wild hearts, too, can feel the power of oratory, and yield deference to the masters of it.

But to return. Look into our tent, or enter, if you can bear the stifling smoke and the close atmosphere. There, wedged close together, you will see a circle of stout warriors, passing the pipe around, joking, telling stories, and making themselves merry, after their fashion. We were also infested by little copper-colored naked boys and snake-eyed girls.

They would come up to us, muttering certain words, which being interpreted conveyed the concise invitation, "Come and eat." Then we would rise, cursing the pertinacity of Dakota hospitality, which allowed scarcely an hour of rest between sun and sun, and to which we were bound to do honor, unless we would offend our entertainers. This necessity was particularly burdensome to me, as I was scarcely able to walk, from the effects of illness, and was of course poorly qualified to dispose of twenty meals a day. Of these sumptuous banquets I gave a specimen in a former chapter, where the tragical fate of the little dog was chronicled. So bounteous an entertainment looks like an outgushing of good will; but doubtless one-half at least of our kind hosts, had they met us alone and unarmed on the prairie, would have robbed us of our horses, and perchance have bestowed an arrow upon us beside.

One morning we were summoned to the lodge of an old man, in good truth the Nestor of his tribe. We found him half sitting, half reclining on a pile of buffalo robes; his long hair, jet-black even now, though he had seen some eighty winters, hung on either side of his thin features. Those most conversant with Indians in their homes will scarcely believe me when I affirm that there was dignity in his countenance and mien. His gaunt but symmetrical frame, did not more clearly exhibit the wreck of bygone strength, than did his dark, wasted features, still prominent and commanding, bear the stamp of mental energies. I recalled, as I saw him, the eloquent metaphor of the Iroquois sachem: "I am an aged hemlock; the winds of a hundred winters have whistled through my branches, and I am dead at the top!" Opposite the patriarch was his nephew, the young aspirant Mahto-Tatonka; and besides these, there were one or two women in the lodge.

The old man's story is peculiar, and singularly illustrative of a superstitious custom that prevails in full force among many of the Indian tribes. He was one of a powerful family, renowned for their warlike exploits. When a very young man, he submitted to the singular rite to which most of the tribe subject themselves before entering upon life. He painted his face black; then seeking out a cavern in a sequestered part of the Black Hills, he lay for several days, fasting and praying to the Great Spirit. In the dreams and visions produced by his weakened and excited state, he fancied like all Indians that he saw supernatural revelations. Again and again the form of an antelope appeared before him. The antelope is the graceful peace spirit of the Ogallalla; but seldom is it that such a gentle visitor presents itself during the initiatory fasts of their young men. The terrible grizzly bear, the divinity of war, usually appears to fire them with martial ardor and thirst for renown. At length the antelope spoke. He told the young dreamer that he was not to follow the path of war; that a life of peace and tranquillity was marked out for him; that henceforward he was to guide the people by his counsels and protect them from the evils of their own feuds and dissensions. Others were to gain renown by fighting the enemy; but greatness of a different kind was in store for him.

At length the antelope spoke. He told the young dreamer that he was not to follow the path of war; that a life of peace and tranquillity was marked out for him . . .

The visions beheld during the period of this fast usually determine the whole course of the dreamer's life, for an Indian is bound by iron superstitions. From that time, Le Borgne, which was the only name by which we knew him, abandoned all thoughts of war and devoted himself to the labors of peace. He told his vision to the people. They honored his commission and respected him in his novel capacity.

A far different man was his brother, Mahto-Tatonka, who had transmitted his names, his features, and many of his characteristic qualities to his son. He was the father of Henry Chatillon's squaw, a circumstance which proved of some advantage to us, as securing for us the friendship of a family perhaps the most distinguished and powerful in the whole Ogallalla band. Mahto-Tatonka, in his rude way, was a hero. No chief could vie with him in warlike renown, or in power over his people. He had a fearless spirit, and a most impetuous and inflexible resolution. His will was law. He was politic and sagacious, and with true Indian craft he always befriended the whites, well knowing that he might thus reap great advantages for himself and his adherents. When he had resolved on any course of conduct, he would pay to the warriors the empty compliment of calling them together to deliberate upon it, and when their debates were over, he would quietly state his own opinion, which no one ever disputed. The consequences of thwarting his imperious will were too formidable to be encountered. Woe to those who incurred his displeasure! He would strike them or stab them on the spot; and this act, which, if attempted by any other chief, would instantly have cost him his life, the awe inspired by his name enabled him to repeat again and again with impunity. In a community where, from immemorial time, no man has acknowledged any law but his own will, Mahto-Tatonka, by the force of his dauntless resolution, raised himself to power little short of despotic. His haughty career came at last to an end. He had a host of enemies only waiting for their opportunity of revenge, and our old friend Smoke, in particular, together with all his kinsmen, hated him most cordially. Smoke sat one day in his lodge in the midst of his own village, when Mahto-Tatonka entered it alone, and approaching the dwelling of his enemy, called on him in a loud voice to come out, if he were a man, and fight. Smoke would not move. At this, Mahto-Tatonka proclaimed him a coward and an old woman, and striding close to the entrance of the lodge, stabbed the chief's best horse, which was picketed there. Smoke was daunted, and even this insult failed to call him forth. Mahto-Tatonka moved haughtily away; all made way for him, but his hour of reckoning was near.

One hot day, five or six years ago, numerous lodges of Smoke's kinsmen were gathered around some of the Fur Company's men, who were trading in various articles with them, whisky among the rest. Mahto-Tatonka was also there with a few of his people. As he lay in his own lodge, a fray arose between his adherents and the kinsmen of his enemy. The war-whoop was raised, bullets and arrows began to fly, and the camp was in confusion. The chief sprang up, and rushing in a fury from the lodge shouted to the combatants on both sides to cease. Instantly—for the attack was preconcerted—came

Early 1900s drawing of a Plains Indian with a rifle by Frederic Dorr Steele.

the reports of two or three guns, and the twanging of a dozen bows, and the savage hero, mortally wounded, pitched forward headlong to the ground. Rouleau was present, and told me the particulars. The tumult became general, and was not quelled until several had fallen on both sides. When we were in the country the feud between the two families was still rankling, and not likely soon to cease.

Thus died Mahto-Tatonka, but he left behind him a goodly army of descendants, to perpetuate his renown and avenge his fate. Besides daughters he had thirty sons, a number which need not stagger the credulity of those who are best acquainted with Indian usages and practices. We saw many of them, all marked by the same dark complexion and the same peculiar cast of features. Of these our visitor, young Mahto-Tatonka, was the eldest, and some reported him as likely to succeed to his father's honors. Though he appeared not more than twenty-one years old, he had oftener struck the enemy, and stolen more horses and more squaws than any young man in the village. We of the civilized world are not apt to attach much credit to the latter species of exploits; but horse-stealing is well known as an avenue to distinction on the prairies, and the other kind of depredation is esteemed equally meritorious. Not that the act can confer fame from its own intrinsic merits. Any one can steal a squaw, and if he chooses afterward to make an adequate present to her rightful proprietor, the easy husband for the most part rests content, his vengeance falls asleep, and all danger from that quarter is averted. Yet this is esteemed but a pitiful and mean-spirited transaction. The danger is averted, but the glory of the achievement also is lost. Mahto-Tatonka proceeded after a more gallant and dashing fashion. Out of several dozen squaws whom he had stolen, he could boast that he had never paid for one, but snapping his fingers in the face of the injured husband, had defied the extremity of his indignation, and no one yet had dared to lay the finger of violence upon him. He was following close in the footsteps of his father. The young men and the young squaws, each in their way, admired him. The one would always follow him to war, and he was esteemed to have unrivaled charm in the eyes of the other. Perhaps his impunity may excite some wonder. An arrow shot from a ravine, a stab given in the dark, require no great valor, and are especially suited to the Indian genius; but Mahto-Tatonka had a strong protection. It was not alone his courage and audacious will that enabled him to career so dashingly among his compeers. His enemies did not forget that he was one of thirty warlike brethren, all growing up to manhood. Should they wreak their anger upon him, many keen eyes would be ever upon them, many fierce hearts would thirst for their blood. The avenger would dog their footsteps everywhere. To kill Mahto-Tatonka would be no better than an act of suicide.

Though he found such favor in the eyes of the fair, he was no dandy. As among us those of highest worth and breeding are most simple in manner and attire, so our aspiring young friend was indifferent to the gaudy trappings and ornaments of his companions. He was content to rest his chances of success upon his own warlike merits. He never arrayed himself in gaudy blanket and glittering necklaces, but left his statue-like form, limbed like an Apollo of bronze, to win its way to favor. His voice was singularly deep and strong. It sounded from his chest like the deep notes of an organ. Yet after all, he was but an Indian. See him as he lies there in the sun before our tent, kicking his heels in the air and cracking jokes with his brother. Does he look like a hero? See him now in the hour of his glory, when at sunset the whole village empties itself to behold him, for to-morrow their favorite young partisan goes out against the enemy. His superb head-dress is adorned with a crest of the war eagle's feathers, rising in a waving ridge above his brow, and sweeping far behind him. His round white shield hangs at his breast, with feathers radiating from the center like a star. His quiver is at his back; his tall lance in his

A Sioux warrior armed with a saber in the foreground is attacking a Crow Indian.

hand, the iron point flashing against the declining sun, while the long scalp-locks of his enemies flutter from the shaft. Thus, gorgeous as a champion in his panoply, he rides round and round within the great circle of lodges, balancing with a graceful buoyancy to the free movements of his war horse, while with a sedate brow he sings his song to the Great Spirit. Young rival warriors look askance at him; vermilion-cheeked girls gaze in admiration, boys whoop and scream in a thrill of delight, and old women yell forth his name and proclaim his praises from lodge to lodge.

Mahto-Tatonka, to come back to him, was the best of all our Indian friends. Hour after hour and day after day, when swarms of savages of every age, sex, and degree beset our camp, he would lie in our tent, his lynx eye ever open to guard our property from pillage.

The Whirlwind invited us one day to his lodge. The feast was finished, and the pipe began to circulate. It was a remarkably large and fine one, and I expressed my admiration of its form and dimensions.

"If the Meneaska likes the pipe," asked The Whirlwind, "why does he not keep it?"

Such a pipe among the Ogallalla is valued at the price of a horse. A princely gift, thinks the reader, and worthy of a chieftain and a warrior. The Whirlwind's generosity rose to no such pitch. He gave me the pipe, confidently expecting that I in return should make him a present of equal or superior value. This is the implied condition of every gift among the Indians as among the Orientals, and should it not be complied with, the present is usually reclaimed by the giver. So I arranged upon a gaudy calico handkerchief, an assortment of vermilion, tobacco, knives, and gunpowder, and summoning the chief to camp, assured him of my friendship and begged his acceptance of a slight token of it. Ejaculating HOW! HOW! he folded up the offerings and withdrew to his lodge.

Several days passed and we and the Indians remained encamped side by side. They could not decide whether or not to go to war. Toward evening, scores of them would surround our tent, a picturesque group. Late one afternoon a party of them mounted on horseback came suddenly in sight from behind some clumps of bushes that lined the bank of the stream, leading with them a mule, on whose back was a wretched negro, only sustained in his seat by the high pommel and cantle of the Indian saddle. His cheeks were withered and shrunken in the hollow of his jaws; his eyes were unnaturally dilated, and his lips seemed shriveled and drawn back from his teeth like those of a corpse. When they brought him up before our tent, and lifted him from the saddle, he could not walk or stand, but he crawled a short distance, and with a look of utter misery sat down on the grass. All the children and women came pouring out of the lodges round us, and with screams and cries made a close circle about him, while he sat supporting himself with his hands, and looking from side to side with a vacant stare. The wretch was starving to death! For thirty-three days he had wandered alone on the prairie, without weapon of any kind; without shoes,

For thirty-three days he had wandered alone on the prairie, without weapon of any kind; without shoes, moccasins, or any other clothing than an old jacket and pantaloons . . .

moccasins, or any other clothing than an old jacket and pantaloons; without intelligence and skill to guide his course, or any knowledge of the productions of the prairie. All this time he had subsisted on crickets and lizards, wild onions, and three eggs which he found in the nest of a prairie dove. He had not seen a human being. Utterly bewildered in the boundless, hopeless desert that stretched around him, offering to his inexperienced eye no mark by which to direct his course, he had walked on in despair till he could walk no longer, and then crawled on his knees until the bone was laid bare. He chose the night for his traveling, lying down by day to sleep in the glaring sun, always dreaming, as he said, of the broth and corn cake he used to eat under his old master's shed in Missouri. Every man in the camp, both white and red, was astonished at his escape not only from starvation but from the grizzly bears which abound in that neighborhood, and the wolves which howled around him every night.

Reynal recognized him the moment the Indians brought him in. He had run away from his master about a year before and joined the party of M. Richard, who was then leaving the frontier for the mountains. He had lived with Richard ever since, until in the end of May he with Reynal and several other men went out in search of some stray horses, when he got separated from the rest in a storm, and had never been heard of up to this time. Knowing his inexperience and helplessness, no one dreamed that he could still be living. The Indians had found him lying exhausted on the ground.

As he sat there with the Indians gazing silently on him, his haggard face and glazed eye were disgusting to look upon. Delorier made him a bowl of gruel, but he suffered it to remain untasted before him. At length he languidly raised the spoon to his lips; again

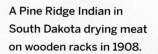

A Pine Ridge Indian in South Dakota drying meat on wooden racks in 1908.

he did so, and again; and then his appetite seemed suddenly inflamed into madness, for he seized the bowl, swallowed all its contents in a few seconds, and eagerly demanded meat. This we refused, telling him to wait until morning, but he begged so eagerly that we gave him a small piece, which he devoured, tearing it like a dog. He said he must have more. We told him that his life was in danger if he ate so immoderately at first. He assented, and said he knew he was a fool to do so, but he must have meat. This we absolutely refused, to the great indignation of the senseless squaws, who, when we were not watching him, would slyly bring dried meat and *pommes blanche*, and place them on the ground by his side. Still this was not enough for him. When it grew dark he contrived to creep away between the legs of the horses and crawl over to the Indian village, about a furlong down the stream. Here he fed to his heart's content, and was brought back again in the morning, when Jean Gras, the trapper, put him on horseback and carried him to the fort. He managed to survive the effects of his insane greediness, and though slightly deranged when we left this part of the country, he was otherwise in tolerable health, and expressed his firm conviction that nothing could ever kill him.

"Sioux Camp Scene, 1841," watercolor, by George Catlin. Women in the right foreground stretch and prepare buffalo hides.

When the sun was yet an hour high, it was a gay scene in the village. The warriors stalked sedately among the lodges, or along the margin of the streams, or walked out to visit the bands of horses that were feeding over the prairie. Half the village population deserted the close and heated lodges and betook themselves to the water; and here you might see boys and girls and young squaws splashing, swimming, and diving beneath the afternoon sun, with merry laughter and screaming. But when the sun was just resting above the broken peaks, and the purple mountains threw their prolonged shadows for miles over the prairie; when our grim old tree, lighted by the horizontal rays, assumed an aspect of peaceful repose, such as one loves after scenes of tumult and excitement; and when the whole landscape of swelling plains and scattered groves was softened into a tranquil beauty, then our encampment presented a striking spectacle. Could Salvator Rosa have transferred it to his canvas, it would have added new renown to his pencil. Savage figures surrounded our tent, with quivers at their backs, and guns, lances, or tomahawks in their hands. Some sat on horseback, motionless as equestrian statues, their arms crossed on their breasts, their eyes fixed in a steady unwavering gaze upon us. Some stood erect, wrapped from head to foot in their long white robes of buffalo hide. Some sat together on the grass, holding their shaggy horses by a rope, with their broad dark busts exposed to view as they suffered their robes to fall from their shoulders. Others again stood carelessly among the throng, with nothing to conceal the matchless symmetry of their forms; and I do not exaggerate when I say that only on the prairie and in the Vatican have I seen such faultless models of the human figure. See that warrior standing by the tree, towering six feet and a half in stature. Your eyes may trace the whole of his graceful and

majestic height, and discover no defect or blemish. With his free and noble attitude, with the bow in his hand, and the quiver at his back, he might seem, but for his face, the Pythian Apollo himself. Such a figure rose before the imagination of West, when on first seeing the Belvidere in the Vatican, he exclaimed, "By God, a Mohawk!"

When the sky darkened and the stars began to appear; when the prairie was involved in gloom and the horses were driven in and secured around the camp, the crowd began to melt away. Fires gleamed around, duskily revealing the rough trappers and the graceful Indians. One of the families near us would always be gathered about a bright blaze, that displayed the shadowy dimensions of their lodge, and sent its lights far up among the masses of foliage above, gilding the dead and ragged branches. Withered, witchlike hags flitted around the blaze, and here for hour after hour sat a circle of children and young girls, laughing and talking, their round merry faces glowing in the ruddy light. We could hear the monotonous notes of the drum from the Indian village, with the chant of the war song, deadened in the distance, and the long chorus of quavering yells, where the war dance was going on in the largest lodge. For several nights, too, we could hear wild and mournful cries, rising and dying away like the melancholy voice of a wolf. They came from the sisters and female relatives of Mahto-Tatonka, who were gashing their limbs with knives, and bewailing the death of Henry Chatillon's squaw. The hour would grow late before all retired to rest in the camp. Then the embers of the fires would be glowing dimly, the men would be stretched in their blankets on the ground, and nothing could be heard but the restless motions of the crowded horses.

I recall these scenes with a mixed feeling of pleasure and pain. At this time I was so reduced by illness that I could seldom walk without reeling like a drunken man, and when I rose from my seat upon the ground the landscape suddenly grew dim before my eyes. In a country where a man's life may at any moment depend on the strength of his arm, or it may be on the activity of his legs, it is more particularly inconvenient. Medical assistance of course there was none; neither had I the means of pursuing a system of diet; and sleeping on a damp ground, with an occasional drenching from a shower, would hardly be recommended as beneficial. I sometimes suffered the extremity of languor and exhaustion, and though at the time I felt no apprehensions of the final result, I have since learned that my situation was a critical one.

I have learned very effectually that a violent attack of dysentery on the prairie is a thing too serious for a joke. I tried repose and a very sparing diet. For a long time, with exemplary patience, I lounged about the camp, or at the utmost staggered over to the Indian village, and walked faint and dizzy among the lodges. It would not do, and I bethought me of starvation. During five days I sustained life on one small biscuit a day. At the end of that time I was weaker than before, but the disorder seemed shaken in its stronghold and very gradually I began to resume a less rigid diet. No sooner had I done so than the same detested symptoms revisited me; my old enemy resumed his pertinacious assaults, yet not with his former violence or constancy, and though before I regained any fair portion of my ordinary strength weeks had elapsed, and months passed before the disorder left me.

I used to lie languid and dreamy before our tent and muse on the past and the future, and when most overcome with lassitude, my eyes turned always toward the distant Black Hills. There is a spirit of energy and vigor in mountains, and they impart it to all who approach their presence. At that time I did not know how many dark superstitions and gloomy legends are associated with those mountains in the minds of the Indians, but I felt an eager desire to penetrate their hidden recesses, to explore the awful chasms and precipices, the black torrents, the silent forests, that I fancied were concealed there.

I did not know how many dark superstitions and gloomy legends are associated with those mountains in the minds of the Indians, but I felt an eager desire to penetrate their hidden recesses, to explore the awful chasms and precipices . . . that I fancied were concealed there.

Left to Die in the Snow

From *Narratives of a Journey Across the Rocky Mountains to the Columbia*

BY JOHN KIRK TOWNSEND

A trapper named Richardson explains to John Kirk Townsend —who was traveling with Nathaniel Wyeth—why he had been rude to an Otto Indian chief they encountered in camp.

"I was once going down alone from the rendezvous with the letter for St. Louis, and when I arrived on the lower part of the Platte River, I fell in with about a dozen Ottos. They were known to be a friendly tribe, and I therefore felt no fear of them. I dismounted from my horse and sat with them upon the ground. It was in the depth of winter; the ground was covered with snow, and the river was frozen solid. While I was thinking of nothing but my dinner, which I was then about preparing, four or five of the cowards jumped on me, mastered my rifle, and held my arms fast, while they took from me my knife and tomahawk, my flint and steel, and all my ammunition. They then loosed me, and told me to be off. I begged them, for the love of God, to give me my rifle and a few loads of ammunition, or I should starve before I could reach the settlements. No—I should have nothing, and if I did not start off immediately, they would throw me under the ice of the river. And that man that sat opposite to you was the chief of them. He recognized me and knew very well the reason why I would not smoke with him. I tell you, sir, if I ever meet that man in any other situation than that in which I saw him this morning, I'll shoot him with as little hesitation as I would shoot a deer. Several years have passed since the penetration of this outrage, but it is still as fresh in my memory as ever, and I again declare, that if ever an opportunity offers, I will kill that man."

"But, Richardson, did they take your horse, also?"

"To be sure they did, and my blankets, and every thing I had, except my clothes."

"But how did you subsist until you reached the settlements? You had a long journey before you."

"Why, set to trappin' prairie squirrels with little nooses made out of the hairs of my head."

I should remark that his hair was so long that it fell in heavy masses on his shoulders. "But squirrels in winter, Richardson, I never heard of squirrels in winter."

"Well but there was plenty of them, though; little white ones."

ILL LUCK

Canadian came from Fort Laramie, and brought a curious piece of intelligence. A trapper, fresh from the mountains, had become enamored of a Missouri damsel belonging to a family who with other emigrants had been for some days encamped in the neighborhood of the fort. If bravery be the most potent charm to win the favor of the fair, then no wooer could be more irresistible than a Rocky Mountain trapper. In the present instance, the suit was not urged in vain. The lovers concerted a scheme, which they proceeded to carry into effect with all possible dispatch. The emigrant party left the fort, and on the next succeeding night but one encamped as usual, and placed a guard. A little after midnight the enamored trapper drew near, mounted on a strong horse and leading another by the bridle. Fastening both animals to a tree, he stealthily moved toward the wagons, as if he were approaching a band of buffalo. Eluding the vigilance of the guard, who was probably half asleep, he met his mistress by appointment at the outskirts of the camp, mounted her on his spare horse, and made off with her through the darkness. The sequel of the adventure did not reach our ears, and we never learned how the imprudent fair one liked an Indian lodge for a dwelling, and a reckless trapper for a bridegroom.

"Indian War Party, 1902,"
by Charles Marion Russell.

At length The Whirlwind and his warriors determined to move. They had resolved after all their preparations not to go to the rendezvous at La Bonte's Camp, but to pass through the Black Hills and spend a few weeks in hunting the buffalo on the other side, until they had killed enough to furnish them with a stock of provisions and with hides to make their lodges for the next season. This done, they were to send out a small independent war party against the enemy. Their final determination left us in some embarrassment. Should we go to La Bonte's Camp, it was not impossible that the other villages would prove as vacillating and indecisive as The Whirlwinds, and that no assembly whatever would take place. Our old companion Reynal had conceived a liking for us, or rather for our biscuit and coffee, and for the occasional small presents which we made him. He was very anxious that we should go with the village which he himself intended to accompany. He declared he was certain that no Indians would meet at the rendezvous, and said moreover that it would be easy to convey our cart and baggage through the Black Hills. In saying this, he told as usual an egregious falsehood. Neither he nor any white man with

A wood engraving of a Sioux Indian village on the move, 1870.

us had ever seen the difficult and obscure defiles through which the Indians intended to make their way. I passed them afterward, and had much ado to force my distressed horse along the narrow ravines, and through chasms where daylight could scarcely penetrate. Our cart might as easily have been conveyed over the summit of Pike's Peak. Anticipating the difficulties and uncertainties of an attempt to visit the rendezvous, we recalled the old proverb about "A bird in the hand," and decided to follow the village.

I was so weak that the aid of a potent auxiliary, a spoonful of whisky swallowed at short intervals, alone enabled me to sit on my hardy little mare Pauline through the short journey.

Both camps, the Indians' and our own, broke up on the morning of the 1st of July. I was so weak that the aid of a potent auxiliary, a spoonful of whisky swallowed at short intervals, alone enabled me to sit on my hardy little mare Pauline through the short journey. For half a mile before us and half a mile behind, the prairie was covered far and wide with the moving throng of savages. The barren, broken plain stretched away to the right and left, and far in front rose the gloomy precipitous ridge of the Black Hills. We pushed forward to the head of the scattered column, passing the burdened travaux, the heavily laden pack horses, the gaunt old women on foot, the gay young squaws on horseback, the restless children running among the crowd, old men striding along in their white buffalo robes, and groups of young warriors mounted on their best horses. Henry Chatillon, looking backward over the distant prairie, exclaimed suddenly that a horseman was approaching, and in truth we could just discern a small black speck slowly moving over the face of a distant swell, like a fly creeping on a wall. It rapidly grew larger as it approached.

"White man, I b'lieve," said Henry; "look how he ride! Indian never ride that way. Yes; he got rifle on the saddle before him."

The horseman disappeared in a hollow of the prairie, but we soon saw him again, and as he came riding at a gallop toward us through the crowd of Indians, his long hair streaming in the wind behind him, we recognized the ruddy face and old buckskin frock of Jean Gras the trapper. He was just arrived from Fort Laramie, where he had been on a visit, and said he had a message for us. A trader named Bisonette, one of Henry's friends, was lately come from the settlements, and intended to go with a party of men to La Bonte's Camp, where, as Jean Gras assured us, ten or twelve villages of Indians would certainly assemble. Bisonette desired that we would cross over and meet him there, and promised that his men should protect our horses and baggage while we went among the Indians. Shaw and I stopped our horses and held a council, and in an evil hour resolved to go.

For the rest of that day's journey our course and that of the Indians was the same. In less than an hour we came to where the high barren prairie terminated, sinking down abruptly in steep descent; and standing on these heights, we saw below us a great level meadow. Laramie Creek bounded it on the left, sweeping along in the shadow of the declivities, and passing with its shallow and rapid current just below us. We sat on horseback, waiting and looking on, while the whole savage array went pouring past us, hurrying down the descent and spreading themselves over the meadow below. In a few moments the plain was swarming with the moving multitude, some just visible, like specks in the distance, others still passing on, pressing down, and fording the stream with bustle and confusion. On the edge of the heights sat half a dozen of the elder warriors, gravely smoking and looking down with unmoved faces on the wild and striking spectacle.

Up went the lodges in a circle on the margin of the stream. For the sake of quiet we pitched our tent among some trees at half a mile's distance. In the afternoon we were in the village. The day was a glorious one, and the whole camp seemed lively and animated in sympathy. Groups of children and young girls were laughing gayly on the outside of the lodges. The shields, the lances, and the bows were removed from the tall tripods on which they usually hung before the dwellings of their owners. The warriors were mounting their horses, and one by one riding away over the prairie toward the neighboring hills.

Shaw and I sat on the grass near the lodge of Reynal. An old woman, with true Indian hospitality, brought a bowl of boiled venison and placed it before us. We amused ourselves with watching half a dozen young squaws who were playing together and chasing each other in and out of one of the lodges. Suddenly the wild yell of the war-whoop came pealing from the hills. A crowd of horsemen appeared, rushing down their sides and riding at full speed toward the village, each warrior's long hair flying behind him in the wind like a ship's streamer. As they approached, the confused throng assumed a regular order, and entering two by two, they circled round the area at full gallop, each warrior singing his war song as he rode. Some of their dresses were splendid. They wore superb crests of feathers and close tunics of antelope skins, fringed with the scalp-locks of their enemies; their shields too were often fluttering with the war eagle's feathers. All had bows and arrows at their back; some carried long lances, and a few were armed with guns. The White Shield, their partisan, rode in gorgeous attire at their head, mounted on a black-and-white horse. Mahto-Tatonka and his brothers took no part in this parade, for they were in mourning for their sister, and were all sitting in their lodges, their bodies bedaubed from head to foot with white clay, and a lock of hair cut from each of their foreheads.

The warriors circled three times round the village; and as each distinguished champion passed, the old women would scream out his name in honor of his bravery, and to incite the emulation of the younger warriors. Little urchins, not two years old, followed the warlike pageant with glittering eyes, and looked with eager wonder and admiration at those whose honors were proclaimed by the public voice of the village. Thus early is the lesson of war instilled into the mind of an Indian, and such are the stimulants which incite his thirst for martial renown.

The procession rode out of the village as it had entered it, and in half an hour all the warriors had returned again, dropping quietly in, singly or in parties of two or three.

A Brulé Indian war party, many wearing war bonnets, circa 1907.

As the sun rose next morning we looked across the meadow, and could see the lodges leveled and the Indians gathering together in preparation to leave the camp. Their course lay to the westward. We turned toward the north with our men, the four trappers following us, with the Indian family of Moran. We traveled until night. I suffered not a little from pain and weakness. We encamped among some trees by the side of a little brook, and here during the whole of the next day we lay waiting for Bisonette, but no Bisonette appeared. Here also two of our trapper friends left us, and set out for the Rocky Mountains. On the second morning, despairing of Bisonette's arrival we resumed our journey, traversing a forlorn and dreary monotony of sun-scorched plains, where no living thing appeared save here and there an antelope flying before us like the wind. When noon came we saw an unwonted and most welcome sight; a rich and luxuriant growth of trees, marking the course of a little stream called Horseshoe Creek. We turned gladly toward it. There were lofty and spreading trees, standing widely asunder, and supporting a thick canopy of leaves, above a surface of rich, tall grass. The stream ran swiftly, as clear as crystal, through the bosom of the wood, sparkling over its bed of white sand and darkening again as it entered a deep cavern of leaves and boughs. I was thoroughly exhausted, and flung myself on the ground,

Chimney Rock, Nebraska, 1837, an important landmark for wagon trains.

scarcely able to move. All that afternoon I lay in the shade by the side of the stream, and those bright woods and sparkling waters are associated in my mind with recollections of lassitude and utter prostration. When night came I sat down by the fire, longing, with an intensity of which at this moment I can hardly conceive, for some powerful stimulant.

In the morning as glorious a sun rose upon us as ever animated that desolate wilderness. We advanced and soon were surrounded by tall bare hills, overspread from top to bottom with prickly-pears and other cacti, that seemed like clinging reptiles. A plain, flat and hard, and with scarcely the vestige of grass, lay before us, and a line of tall misshapen trees bounded the onward view. There was no sight or sound of man or beast, or any living thing, although behind those trees was the long-looked-for place of rendezvous, where we fondly hoped to have found the Indians congregated by thousands. We looked and listened anxiously. We pushed forward with our best speed, and forced our horses through the trees. There were copses of some extent beyond, with a scanty stream creeping through their midst; and as we pressed through the yielding branches, deer sprang up to the right and left. At length we caught a glimpse of the prairie beyond. Soon we emerged, and saw, not a plain covered with encampments and swarming with life, but a vast unbroken desert stretching away before us league upon league, without a bush or a tree or anything that had life. We drew rein and gave to the winds our sentiments concerning the whole aboriginal race of America. Our journey was in vain and much worse than in vain. For myself, I was vexed and disappointed beyond measure; as I well knew that a slight aggravation of my disorder would render this false step irrevocable, and make it quite impossible to accomplish effectively the design which had led me on an arduous journey of between three and four thousand miles. To fortify myself as well as I could against such a contingency, I resolved that I would not under any circumstances attempt to leave the country until my object was completely gained.

And where were the Indians? They were assembled in great numbers at a spot about twenty miles distant, and there at that very moment they were engaged in their warlike ceremonies. The scarcity of buffalo in the vicinity of La Bonte's Camp, which would render their supply of provisions scanty and precarious, had probably prevented them from assembling there; but of all this we knew nothing until some weeks after.

Shaw lashed his horse and galloped forward, I, though much more vexed than he, was not strong enough to adopt this convenient vent to my feelings; so I followed at a quiet pace, but in no quiet mood. We rode up to a solitary old tree, which seemed the only place fit for encampment. Half its branches were dead, and the rest were so scantily furnished with leaves that they cast but a meager and wretched shade, and the old twisted trunk alone furnished sufficient protection from the sun. We threw down our saddles in the strip of shadow that it cast, and sat down upon them. In silent indignation we remained smoking for an hour or more, shifting our saddles with the shifting shadow, for the sun was intolerably hot.

The Ogallalla Village

OPPOSITE:

Chief Red Cloud of the Oglala Sioux Indian tribe in an 1899 painting by Elbridge Ayer Burbank.

S uch a narrative as this is hardly the place for portraying the mental features of the Indians. The same picture, slightly changed in shade and coloring, would serve with very few exceptions for all the tribes that lie north of the Mexican territories. But with this striking similarity in their modes of thought, the tribes of the lake and ocean shores, of the forests and of the plains, differ greatly in their manner of life. Having been domesticated for several weeks among one of the wildest of the wild hordes that roam over the remote prairies, I had extraordinary opportunities of observing them, and I flatter myself that a faithful picture of the scenes that passed daily before my eyes may not be devoid of interest and value. These men were thorough savages. Neither their manners nor their ideas were in the slightest degree modified by contact with civilization. They knew nothing of the power and real character of the white men, and their children would scream in terror at the sight of me. Their religion, their superstitions, and their prejudices were the same that had been handed down to them from immemorial time. They fought with the same weapons that their fathers fought with and wore the same rude garments of skins.

A type of tobacco plant, used by Native Americans.

172

Great changes are at hand in that region. With the stream of emigration to Oregon and California, the buffalo will dwindle away, and the large wandering communities who depend on them for support must be broken and scattered. The Indians will soon be corrupted by the example of the whites, abased by whisky, and overawed by military posts; so that within a few years the traveler may pass in tolerable security through their country. Its danger and its charm will have disappeared together.

As soon as Raymond and I discovered the village from the gap in the hills, we were seen in our turn; keen eyes were constantly on the watch. As we rode down upon the plain the side of the village nearest us was darkened with a crowd of naked figures gathering around the lodges. Several men came forward to meet us. I could distinguish among them the green blanket of the Frenchman Reynal. When we came up the ceremony of shaking hands had to be gone through with in due form, and then all were eager to know what had become of the rest of my party. I satisfied them on this point, and we all moved forward together toward the village.

"You've missed it," said Reynal; "if you'd been here day before yesterday, you'd have found the whole prairie over yonder black with buffalo as far as you could see. There were no cows, though; nothing but bulls. We made a 'surround' every day till yesterday. See the village there; don't that look like good living?"

In fact I could see, even at that distance, that long cords were stretched from lodge to lodge, over which the meat, cut by the squaws into thin sheets, was hanging to dry in the sun. I noticed too that the village was somewhat smaller than when I had last seen it, and I asked Reynal the cause. He said that the old Le Borgne had felt too weak to pass over the mountains, and so had remained behind with all his relations, including Mahto-Tatonka and his brothers. The Whirlwind too had been unwilling to come so far, because, as Reynal said, he was afraid. Only half a dozen lodges had adhered to him, the main body of the village setting their chief's authority at naught, and taking the course most agreeable to their inclinations.

"What chiefs are there in the village now?" said I.

"Well," said Reynal, "there's old Red-Water, and the Eagle-Feather, and the Big Crow, and the Mad Wolf and the Panther, and the White Shield, and—what's his name?—the half-breed Cheyenne."

By this time we were close to the village, and I observed that while the greater part of the lodges were very large and neat in their appearance, there was at one side a cluster of squalid, miserable huts. I looked toward them, and made some remark about their wretched appearance. But I was touching upon delicate ground.

"My squaw's relations live in those lodges," said Reynal very warmly, "and there isn't a better set in the whole village."

> With the stream of emigration to Oregon and California, the buffalo will dwindle away, and the large wandering communities who depend on them for support must be broken and scattered. The Indians will soon be corrupted by the example of the whites . . .

An 1860s engraving by Henry Byron Hall shows emigrants crossing the plains.

"Are there any chiefs among them?" asked I.

"Chiefs?" said Reynal; "yes, plenty!"

"What are their names?" I inquired.

"Their names? Why, there's the Arrow-Head. If he isn't a chief he ought to be one. And there's the Hail-Storm. He's nothing but a boy, to be sure; but he's bound to be a chief one of these days!"

Just then we passed between two of the lodges, and entered the great area of the village. Superb naked figures stood silently gazing on us.

"Where's the Bad Wound's lodge?" said I to Reynal.

"There, you've missed it again! The Bad Wound is away with The Whirlwind. If you could have found him here, and gone to live in his lodge, he would have treated you better than any man in the village. But there's the Big Crow's lodge yonder, next to old Red-Water's. He's a good Indian for the whites, and I advise you to go and live with him."

"Are there many squaws and children in his lodge?" said I.

"No; only one squaw and two or three children. He keeps the rest in a separate lodge by themselves."

So, still followed by a crowd of Indians, Raymond and I rode up to the entrance of the Big Crow's lodge. A squaw came out immediately and took our horses. I put aside the leather nap that covered the low opening, and stooping, entered the Big Crow's dwelling. There I could see the chief in the dim light, seated at one side, on a pile of buffalo robes. He greeted me with a guttural "How, cola!" I requested Reynal to tell him that Raymond and I were come to live with him. The Big Crow gave another low exclamation. If the reader thinks that we were intruding somewhat cavalierly, I beg him to observe that every Indian in the village would have deemed himself honored that white men should give such preference to his hospitality.

The squaw spread a buffalo robe for us in the guest's place at the head of the lodge. Our saddles were brought in, and scarcely were we seated upon them before the place was thronged with Indians, who came crowding in to see us. The Big Crow produced his pipe and filled it with the mixture of tobacco and shongsasha, or red willow bark. Round and round it passed, and a lively conversation went forward. Meanwhile a squaw placed before the two guests a wooden bowl of boiled buffalo meat, but unhappily this was not the only banquet destined to be inflicted on us. Rapidly, one after another, boys and young squaws thrust their heads in at the opening, to invite us to various feasts in different parts of the village. For half an hour or more we were actively engaged in passing from lodge to lodge, tasting in each of the bowl of meat set before us, and inhaling a whiff or two from our entertainer's pipe. A thunderstorm that had been threatening for some time now began in good earnest. We crossed over to Reynal's lodge, though it hardly deserved this name, for it consisted only of a few old buffalo robes, supported on poles, and was quite open on one side. Here we sat down, and the Indians gathered round us.

"What is it," said I, "that makes the thunder?"

"It's my belief," said Reynal, "that it is a big stone rolling over the sky."

"Very likely," I replied; "but I want to know what the Indians think about it."

So he interpreted my question, which seemed to produce some doubt and debate. There was evidently a difference of opinion. At last old Mene-Seela, or Red-Water, who sat by himself at one side, looked up with his withered face, and said he had always known what the thunder was. It was a great black bird; and once he had seen it, in a dream, swooping down from the Black Hills, with its loud roaring wings; and when it flapped them over a lake, they struck lightning from the water.

"The thunder is bad," said another old man, who sat muffled in his buffalo robe; "he killed my brother last summer."

Reynal, at my request, asked for an explanation; but the old man remained doggedly silent, and would not look up. Some time after I learned that the man who was killed belonged to an association which, among other mystic functions, claimed the exclusive power and privilege of fighting the thunder. Whenever a storm which they wished to avert was threatening, the thunder-fighters would take their bows and arrows, their guns, their magic drum, and a sort of whistle, made out of the wingbone of the war eagle. Thus equipped, they would run out and fire at the rising cloud, whooping, yelling, whistling, and beating their drum, to frighten it down again. One afternoon a heavy black cloud was coming up, and they repaired to the top of a hill, where they brought all their magic artillery into play against it. But the undaunted thunder, refusing to be terrified, kept moving straight onward, and darted out a bright flash which struck one of the party dead, as he was in the very act of shaking his long iron-pointed lance against it. The rest scattered and ran yelling in an ecstasy of superstitious terror back to their lodges.

The lodge of my host Kongra-Tonga, or the Big Crow, presented a picturesque spectacle that evening. A score or more of Indians were seated around in a circle, their dark naked forms just visible by the dull light of the smoldering fire in the center, the pipe glowing brightly in the gloom as it passed from hand to hand round the lodge. Then a squaw would drop a piece of buffalo-fat on the dull embers. Instantly a bright glancing flame would leap up, darting its clear light to the very apex of the tall conical structure. It gilded the features of the Indians, as with animated gestures they sat around it, telling their endless stories of war and hunting. It displayed rude garments of skins that hung around the lodge; the bow, quiver, and lance suspended over the resting-place of the chief, and the rifles and powder-horns of the two white guests. For a moment all would be bright as day; then the flames would die away, and fitful flashes from the embers would illumine the lodge, and then leave it in darkness. Then all the light would wholly fade, and the lodge and all within it be involved again in obscurity.

As I left the lodge next morning, I was saluted by howling and yelling from all around the village, and half its canine population rushed forth to the attack. Being as cowardly as they were clamorous, they kept jumping around me at the distance of a few yards, only one little cur, about ten inches long, having spirit enough to make a direct assault. He dashed valiantly at the leather tassel which in the Dakota fashion was trailing behind the heel of my moccasin, and kept his hold, growling and snarling all the while. As I knew that the eyes of the whole village were on the watch, I walked forward without looking to the right or left, surrounded by this magic circle of dogs. When I came to Reynal's lodge I sat down by it, on which the dogs dispersed growling. Only one large white one remained, who kept running about before me and showing his teeth. I looked at him well. He was fat and sleek; just such a dog as I wanted. "My friend," thought I, "you shall pay for this! I will have you eaten this very morning!"

I intended that day to give the Indians a feast and a white dog is the dish which the customs of the Dakota prescribe for all occasions of formality and importance. Reynal soon discovered that an old woman in the next lodge was owner of the white dog. I took a gaudy cotton handkerchief, and laying it on the ground, arranged some vermilion, beads, and other trinkets upon it. Then the old squaw was summoned. I pointed to the dog and to the handkerchief. She gave a scream of delight, snatched up the prize, and vanished with it into her lodge. I engaged the services of two other squaws, each of whom took the white dog by one of his paws, and led him away behind the lodges. Having killed him they threw him into a fire to singe; then chopped him up and put him into two large kettles to boil. I told Raymond to fry in buffalo-fat what little flour we had left, and to make a kettle of tea.

Big Crow's squaw set briskly at work sweeping out the lodge for the approaching festivity. I confided to my host the task of inviting the guests, thinking that I might thereby shift from my own shoulders the odium of fancied neglect and oversight.

When feasting is in question, one hour of the day serves an Indian as well as another. My entertainment came off about eleven o'clock. At that hour, Reynal and Raymond walked across the area of the village, to the admiration of the inhabitants, carrying the two kettles of dog-meat. These they placed in the center of the lodge, and then went back for the bread and the tea. Meanwhile I had put on a pair of brilliant moccasins, and a coat which I had brought with me in view of such public occasions. I also made careful use of the razor, an operation which no man will neglect who desires to gain the good opinion of Indians. Thus attired, I seated myself between Reynal and Raymond at the head of the lodge. Only a few minutes elapsed before all the guests had come in and were seated on the ground, wedged together in a close circle around the lodge. Each brought with him a wooden bowl to hold his share of the repast. When all were assembled, two of the officials called "soldiers" by the white men, came forward with ladles made of the horn of the Rocky Mountain sheep, and began to distribute the feast, always assigning a double share to the old men and chiefs. The dog vanished with astonishing celerity, and each guest turned his dish bottom upward to show that all was gone. Then the bread was distributed in its turn, and finally the tea. As the soldiers poured it out into the same wooden bowls that had served for the substantial part of the meal, I thought it had a particularly curious and uninviting color.

"Oh!" said Reynal, "there was not tea enough, so I stirred some soot in the kettle, to make it look strong."

Fortunately an Indian's palate is not very discriminating. The tea was well sweetened, and that was all they cared for.

Now the former part of the entertainment being concluded, the time for speech-making was come. The Big Crow produced a flat piece of wood on which he cut up tobacco and shongsasha, and mixed them in due proportions. The pipes were filled and passed from hand to hand around the company. Then I began my speech, each sentence being interpreted by Reynal as I went on, and echoed by the whole audience with the usual exclamations of assent and approval. As nearly as I can recollect, it was as follows:

I had come, I told them, from a country so far distant, that at the rate they travel, they could not reach it in a year.

"Howo how!"

"There the Meneaska were more numerous than blades of grass. The squaws were more beautiful than any they had ever seen, and all the men were brave warriors."

"How! how! how!"

"While I was living in the Meneaska lodges, I had heard of the Ogallalla, how great and brave a nation they were, how they loved the whites, and how well they could hunt the buffalo and strike their enemies. I resolved to come and see if all that I heard was true."

"How! how! how! how!"

"As I had come on horseback through the mountains, I had been able to bring them only a very few presents."

"How!"

"But I had enough tobacco to give them all a small piece. They might smoke it, and see how much better it was than the tobacco which they got from the traders."

"How! how! how!"

"I had plenty of powder, lead, knives, and tobacco at Fort Laramie. These I was anxious to give them, and if any of them should come to the fort before I went away, I would make them handsome presents."

"How! how! how! how!"

Raymond cut up and distributed among them two or three pounds of tobacco, and old Mene-Seela began to make a reply. It was quite long, but the following was the pith of it:

"He had always loved the whites. They were the wisest people on earth. He believed they could do everything, and he was always glad when any came to live in the Ogallalla

Woman of Many Deeds, the granddaughter of Sioux Chief Red Cloud.

OPPOSITE:
Plains Indian bow case and quiver, early Sioux woman's dress, moccasins.

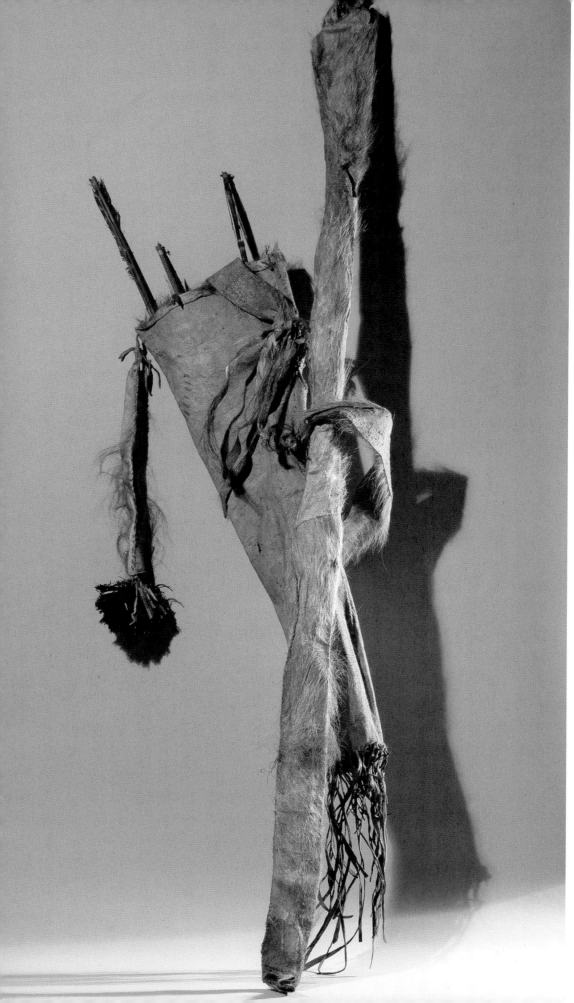

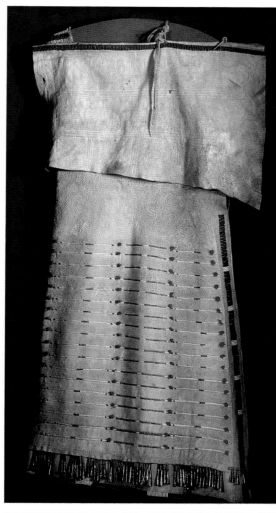

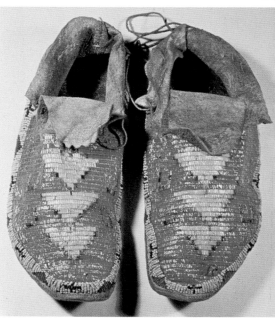

Photograph of bluffs along the banks of the Green River in Wyoming circa 1900.

lodges. It was true I had not made them many presents, but the reason was plain. It was clear that I liked them, or I never should have come so far to find their village."

Several other speeches of similar import followed, and then this more serious matter being disposed of, there was an interval of smoking, laughing, and conversation; but old Mene-Seela suddenly interrupted it with a loud voice:

"Now is a good time," he said, "when all the old men and chiefs are here together, to decide what the people shall do. We came over the mountain to make our lodges for next year. Our old ones are good for nothing; they are rotten and worn out. But we have been disappointed. We have killed buffalo bulls enough, but we have found no herds of cows, and the skins of bulls are too thick and heavy for our squaws to make lodges of. There must be plenty of cows about the Medicine-Bow Mountain. We ought to go there. To be sure it is farther westward than we have ever been before, and perhaps the Snakes will attack us, for those hunting-grounds belong to them. But we must have new lodges at any rate; our old ones will not serve for another year. We ought not to be afraid of the Snakes. Our warriors are brave, and they are all ready for war. Besides, we have three white men with their rifles to help us."

I could not help thinking that the old man relied a little too much on the aid of allies, one of whom was a coward, another a blockhead, and the third an invalid. This speech produced a good deal of debate. As Reynal did not interpret what was said, I could only judge of the meaning by the features and gestures of the speakers. At the end of it, however, the greater number seemed to have fallen in with Mene-Seela's opinion. A short silence followed, and then the old man struck up a discordant chant, which I was told was a song of thanks for the entertainment I had given them.

"Now," said he, "let us go and give the white men a chance to breathe."

So the company all dispersed, and for some time the old chief was walking round the village, singing his song in praise of the feast, after the usual custom of the nation.

At last the day drew to a close, and as the sun went down the horses came trooping from the surrounding plains to be picketed before the dwellings of their respective masters. Soon within the great circle of lodges appeared another concentric circle of restless horses; and here and there fires were glowing and flickering amid the gloom of the dusky figures around them. I went over and sat by the lodge of Reynal. The Eagle-Feather, who was a son of Mene-Seela, and brother of my host the Big Crow, was seated there already, and I asked him if the village would move in the morning. He shook his head, and said that nobody could tell, for since old Mahto-Tatonka had died, the people had been like children that did not know their own minds. They were no better than a body without a head. So I, as well as the Indians themselves, fell asleep that night without knowing whether we should set out in the morning toward the country of the Snakes.

At daybreak, however, as I was coming up from the river after my morning's ablutions, I saw that a movement was contemplated. Some of the lodges were reduced to

I could not help thinking that the old man relied a little too much on the aid of allies, one of whom was a coward, another a blockhead, and the third an invalid.

Portrait of "Little," an Oglala leader and instigator of the Pine Ridge revolt in 1890.

nothing but bare skeletons of poles; the leather covering of others was flapping in the wind as the squaws were pulling it off. One or two chiefs of note had resolved, it seemed, on moving; and so having set their squaws at work, the example was tacitly followed by the rest of the village. One by one the lodges were sinking down in rapid succession, and where the great circle of the village had been only a moment before, nothing now remained but a ring of horses and Indians, crowded in confusion together. The ruins of the lodges were spread over the ground, together with kettles, stone mallets, great ladles of horn, buffalo robes, and cases of painted hide, filled with dried meat. Squaws bustled about in their busy preparations, the old hags screaming to one another at the stretch of their leathern lungs. The shaggy horses were patiently standing while the lodge-poles were lashed to their sides, and the baggage piled upon their backs. The dogs, with their tongues lolling out, lay lazily panting, and waiting for the time of departure. Each warrior sat on the ground by the decaying embers of his fire, unmoved amid all the confusion, while he held in his hand the long trail-rope of his horse.

As their preparations were completed, each family moved off the ground. The crowd was rapidly melting away. I could see them crossing the river, and passing in quick succession along the profile of the hill on the farther bank. When all were gone, I mounted and set out after them, followed by Raymond, and as we gained the summit, the whole village came in view at once, straggling away for a mile or more over the barren plains before us. Everywhere the iron points of lances were glittering. The sun never shone upon a more strange array. Here were the heavy-laden pack horses, some wretched old women leading them, and two or three children clinging to their backs. Here were mules or ponies covered from head to tail with gaudy trappings, and mounted by some gay young squaw, grinning bashfulness and pleasure as the Meneaska looked at her. Boys with miniature bows and arrows were wandering over the plains, little naked children were running along on foot, and numberless dogs were scampering among the feet of the horses. The young braves, gaudy with paint and feathers, were riding in groups among the crowd, and often galloping, two or three at once along the line, to try the speed of their horses. Here and there you might see a rank of sturdy pedestrians stalking along in their white buffalo robes. These were the dignitaries of the village, the old men and warriors, to whose age and experience that wandering democracy yielded a silent deference. With the rough prairie and the broken hills for its background, the restless scene was striking and picturesque beyond description. Days and weeks made me familiar with it, but never impaired its effect upon my fancy.

As we moved on, the broken column grew yet more scattered and disorderly, until, as we approached the foot of a hill, I saw the old men before mentioned seating themselves in a line upon the ground, in advance of the whole. They lighted a pipe and sat smoking, laughing, and telling stories, while the people, stopping as they successively came up, were soon gathered in a crowd behind them. Then the old men rose, drew their buffalo

robes over their shoulders, and strode on as before. Gaining the top of the hill, we found a very steep declivity before us. There was not a minute's pause. The whole descended in a mass, amid dust and confusion. The horses braced their feet as they slid down, women and children were screaming, dogs yelping as they were trodden upon, while stones and earth went rolling to the bottom. In a few moments I could see the village from the summit, spreading again far and wide over the plain below.

At our encampment that afternoon I was attacked anew by my old disorder. In half an hour the strength that I had been gaining for a week past had vanished again, and I became like a man in a dream. But at sunset I lay down in the Big Crow's lodge and slept, totally unconscious till the morning. The first thing that awakened me was a hoarse flapping over my head, and a sudden light that poured in upon me. The camp was breaking up, and the squaws were moving the covering from the lodge. I arose and shook off my blanket with the feeling of perfect health; but scarcely had I gained my feet when a sense of my helpless condition was once more forced upon me, and I found myself scarcely able to stand. Raymond had brought up Pauline and the mule, and I stooped to raise my saddle from the ground. My strength was quite inadequate to the task. "You must saddle her," said I to Raymond, as I sat down again on a pile of buffalo robes:

"*Et hoc etiam fortasse meminisse juvabit,*" I thought, while with a painful effort I raised myself into the saddle. Half an hour after, even the expectation that Virgil's line expressed seemed destined to disappointment. As we were passing over a great plain, surrounded by long broken ridges, I rode slowly in advance of the Indians, with thoughts that wandered far from the time and from the place. Suddenly the sky darkened, and thunder began to mutter. Clouds were rising over the hills, as dreary and dull as the first forebodings of an approaching calamity; and in a moment all around was wrapped in shadow. I looked behind. The Indians had stopped to prepare for the approaching storm, and the dark, dense mass of savages stretched far to the right and left. Since the first attack of my disorder the effects of rain upon me had usually been injurious in the extreme. I had no strength to spare, having at that moment scarcely enough to keep my seat on horseback. Then, for the first time, it pressed upon me as a strong probability that I might never leave those deserts. "Well," thought I to myself, "a prairie makes quick and sharp work. Better to die here, in the saddle to the last, than to stifle in the hot air of a sick chamber, and a thousand times better than to drag out life, as many have done, in the helpless inaction of lingering disease." So, drawing the buffalo robe on which I sat over my head, I waited till the storm should come. It broke at last with a sudden burst of fury, and passing away as rapidly as it came, left the sky clear again. My reflections served me no other purpose than to look back upon as a piece of curious experience; for the rain did not produce the ill effects that I had expected. We encamped within an hour. Having no change of clothes, I contrived to

borrow a curious kind of substitute from Reynal: and this done, I went home, that is, to the Big Crow's lodge to make the entire transfer that was necessary. Half a dozen squaws were in the lodge, and one of them taking my arm held it against her own, while a general laugh and scream of admiration were raised at the contrast in the color of the skin.

Our encampment that afternoon was not far distant from a spur of the Black Hills, whose ridges, bristling with fir trees, rose from the plains a mile or two on our right. That they might move more rapidly toward their proposed hunting-grounds, the Indians determined to leave at this place their stock of dried meat and other superfluous articles. Some left even their lodges, and contented themselves with carrying a few hides to make a shelter from the sun and rain. Half the inhabitants set out in the afternoon, with loaded pack horses, toward the mountains. Here they suspended the dried meat

"Supplying Camp with Buffalo Meat," a watercolor painting by Alfred Jacob Miller circa 1858–1860.

186

upon trees, where the wolves and grizzly bears could not get at it. All returned at evening. Some of the young men declared that they had heard the reports of guns among the mountains to the eastward, and many surmises were thrown out as to the origin of these sounds. For my part, I was in hopes that Shaw and Henry Chatillon were coming to join us. I would have welcomed them cordially, for I had no other companions than two brutish white men and five hundred savages. I little suspected that at that very moment my unlucky comrade was lying on a buffalo robe at Fort Laramie, fevered with ivy poison, and solacing his woes with tobacco and Shakespeare.

As we moved over the plains on the next morning, several young men were riding about the country as scouts; and at length we began to see them occasionally on the tops of the hills, shaking their robes as a signal that they saw buffalo. Soon after, some bulls came in sight. Horsemen darted away in pursuit, and we could see from the distance that one or two of the buffalo were killed. Raymond suddenly became inspired. I looked at him as he rode by my side; his face had actually grown intelligent!

"This is the country for me!" he said; "if I could only carry the buffalo that are killed here every month down to St. Louis I'd make my fortune in one winter. I'd grow as rich as old Papin, or Mackenzie either. I call this the poor man's market. When I'm hungry I have only got to take my rifle and go out and get better meat than the rich folks down below can get with all their money. You won't catch me living in St. Louis another winter."

"No," said Reynal, "you had better say that after you and your Spanish woman almost starved to death there. What a fool you were ever to take her to the settlements."

"Your Spanish woman?" said I; "I never heard of her before. Are you married to her?"

"No," answered Raymond, again looking intelligent; "the priests don't marry their women, and why should I marry mine?"

This honorable mention of the Mexican clergy introduced the subject of religion, and I found that my two associates, in common with other white men in the country, were as indifferent to their future welfare as men whose lives are in constant peril are apt to be. Raymond had never heard of the Pope. A certain bishop, who lived at Taos or at Santa Fe, embodied his loftiest idea of an ecclesiastical dignitary. Reynal observed that a priest had been at Fort Laramie two years ago, on his way to the Nez Perce mission, and that he had confessed all the men there and given them absolution. "I got a good clearing out myself that time," said Reynal, "and I reckon that will do for me till I go down to the settlements again."

Here he interrupted himself with an oath and exclaimed: "Look! look! The Panther is running an antelope!"

The Panther, on his black-and-white horse, one of the best in the village, came at full speed over the hill in hot pursuit of an antelope that darted away like lightning before him. The attempt was made in mere sport and bravado, for very few are the horses that can for a moment compete in swiftness with this little animal. The antelope ran down the hill toward the main body of the Indians who were moving over the plain below. Sharp yells were given and horsemen galloped out to intercept his flight. At this he turned sharply to the left and scoured away with such incredible speed that he distanced all his pursuers and even the vaunted horse of the Panther himself. A few moments after, we witnessed a more serious sport. A shaggy buffalo bull bounded out from a neighboring hollow, and close behind him came a slender Indian boy, riding without stirrups or saddle and lashing his eager little horse to full speed. Yard after yard he drew closer to his gigantic victim, though the bull, with his short tail erect and his tongue lolling out a foot from his foaming jaws, was straining his unwieldy strength to the utmost. A moment more and the boy was close alongside of him. It was our friend the Hail-Storm. He dropped the rein on his horse's neck and jerked an arrow like lightning from the quiver at his shoulder.

"I tell you," said Reynal, "that in a year's time that boy will match the best hunter in the village. There he has given it to him! and there goes another! You feel well, now, old bull, don't you, with two arrows stuck in your lights? There, he has given him another! Hear how the Hail-Storm yells when he shoots! Yes, jump at him; try it again, old fellow! You may jump all day before you get your horns into that pony!"

The bull sprang again and again at his assailant, but the horse kept dodging with wonderful celerity. The bull followed up his attack with a furious rush, and the Hail-Storm was put to flight, the shaggy monster close behind. The boy clung in his seat like a leech, and secure in the speed of his little pony, looked round toward us and laughed. In a moment he was again alongside of the bull, who was now driven to complete desperation. His eyeballs glared through his tangled mane, and the blood flew from his mouth and nostrils. Thus, still battling with each other, the two enemies disappeared over the hill.

Many of the Indians rode at full gallop toward the spot. We followed at a more moderate pace, and soon saw the bull lying dead on the side of the hill. The Indians were gathered around him, and several knives were already at work. These little instruments were plied with such wonderful address that the twisted sinews were cut apart, the ponderous bones fell asunder as if by magic, and in a moment the vast carcass was reduced to a heap of bloody ruins. The surrounding group of savages offered no very attractive spectacle to a civilized eye. Some were cracking the huge thigh-bones and devouring the marrow within; others were cutting away pieces of the liver and other approved morsels, and swallowing them on the spot with the appetite of wolves. The faces of most of them, besmeared with blood from ear to ear, looked grim and horrible enough. My friend the White Shield proffered me a marrowbone, so skillfully laid open that all the rich substance within was exposed to view at once. Another Indian held out a large piece of the delicate lining of the paunch; but these courteous offerings I begged leave to decline. I noticed one boy who was very busy with his knife about the jaws and throat of the buffalo, from which he extracted some morsel of peculiar delicacy. It is but fair to say that only certain parts of the animal are considered eligible in these extempore

Antelope on the plains near the Rocky Mountains, detail from an Albert Bierstadt painting.

banquets. The Indians would look with abhorrence on anyone who should partake indiscriminately of the newly killed carcass.

We encamped that night, and marched westward through the greater part of the following day. On the next morning we again resumed our journey. It was the 17th of July, unless my notebook misleads me. At noon we stopped by some pools of rain-water, and in the afternoon again set forward. This double movement was contrary to the usual practice of the Indians, but all were very anxious to reach the hunting ground, kill the necessary number of buffalo, and retreat as soon as possible from the dangerous neighborhood. I pass by for the present some curious incidents that occurred during these marches and encampments. Late in the afternoon of the last-mentioned day we came upon the banks of a little sandy stream, of which the Indians could not tell the name; for they were very ill acquainted with that part of the country. So parched and arid were the prairies around that they could not supply grass enough for the horses to feed upon, and we were compelled to move farther and farther up the stream in search of ground for encampment. The country was much wilder than before. The plains were gashed with ravines and broken into hollows and steep declivities, which flanked our course, as, in long-scattered array, the Indians advanced up the side of the stream. Mene-Seela consulted an extraordinary oracle to instruct him where the buffalo were to be found. When he with the other chiefs sat down on the grass to smoke and converse, as they often did during the march, the old man picked up one of those enormous black-and-green crickets, which the Dakota call by a name that signifies "They who point out the buffalo." The Root-Diggers, a wretched tribe beyond the mountains, turn them to good account by making them into a sort of soup, pronounced by certain unscrupulous trappers to be extremely rich. Holding the bloated insect respectfully between his fingers and thumb, the old Indian looked attentively at him and inquired, "Tell me, my father, where must we go to-morrow to find the buffalo?" The cricket twisted about his long horns in evident embarrassment. At last he pointed, or seemed to point, them westward. Mene-Seela, dropping him gently on the grass, laughed with great glee, and said that if we went that way in the morning we should be sure to kill plenty of game.

Toward evening we came upon a fresh green meadow, traversed by the stream, and deep-set among tall sterile bluffs. The Indians descended its steep bank; and as I was at the rear, I was one of the last to reach this point. Lances were glittering, feathers fluttering, and the water below me was crowded with men and horses passing through, while the meadow beyond was swarming with the restless crowd of Indians. The sun was just setting, and poured its softened light upon them through an opening in the hills.

I remarked to Reynal that at last we had found a good camping-ground.

"Oh, it is very good," replied he ironically; "especially if there is a Snake war party about, and they take it into their heads to shoot down at us from the top of these hills. It is no plan of mine, camping in such a hole as this!"

The Indians also seemed apprehensive. High up on the top of the tallest bluff, conspicuous in the bright evening sunlight, sat a naked warrior on horseback, looking around, as it seemed, over the neighboring country; and Raymond told me that many of the young men had gone out in different directions as scouts.

The shadows had reached the summit of the bluffs before the lodges were erected and the village reduced again to quiet and order. A cry was suddenly raised, and men, women, and children came running out with animated faces, and looked eagerly through the opening on the hills by which the stream entered from the westward. I could discern afar off some dark, heavy masses, passing over the sides of a low hill. They disappeared, and then others followed. These were bands of buffalo cows. The hunting-ground was reached at last, and everything promised well for the morrow's sport. Being fatigued and exhausted, I went and lay down in Kongra-Tonga's lodge, when Raymond thrust in his head, and called upon me to come and see some sport. A number of Indians were gathered, laughing, along the line of lodges on the western side of the village, and at some distance, I could plainly see in the twilight two huge black monsters stalking, heavily and solemnly, directly toward us. They were buffalo bulls. The wind blew from them to the village, and such was their blindness and stupidity that they were advancing upon the enemy without the least consciousness of his presence. Raymond told me that two men had hidden themselves with guns in a ravine about twenty yards in front of us. The two bulls walked slowly on, heavily swinging from side to side in their peculiar gait of stupid dignity. They approached within four or five rods of the ravine where the Indians lay in ambush. Here at last they seemed conscious that something was wrong, for they both stopped and stood perfectly still, without looking either to the right or to the left. Nothing of them was to be seen but two huge black masses of shaggy mane, with horns, eyes, and nose in the center, and a pair of hoofs visible at the bottom. At last the more intelligent of them seemed to have concluded that it was time to retire. Very slowly, and with an air of the gravest and most majestic deliberation, he began to turn round, as if he were revolving on a pivot. Little by little his ugly brown side was exposed to view. A white smoke sprang out; a sharp report came with it. The old bull gave a very undignified jump and galloped off. At this his comrade wheeled about with considerable expedition. The other Indian shot at him from the ravine, and then both the bulls were running away at full speed, while half the juvenile population of the village raised a yell and ran after them. The first bull was soon stopped, and while the crowd stood looking at him at a respectable distance, he reeled and rolled over on his side. The other, wounded in a less vital part, galloped away to the hills and escaped.

In half an hour it was totally dark. I lay down to sleep, and ill as I was, there was something very animating in the prospect of the general hunt on the morrow.

An emigrant family in the Rocky Mountains on the way to California.

A Common Western Scene

From a memoir, *Life in the Rocky Mountains*

By Warren Angus Ferris

Ferris was a trapper and fur trader who traveled west in 1833.

We departed southeastward for the Jefferson River on the morning of the fifteenth, accompanied by all the Indians; and picturesque enough was the order and appearance of our March. Fancy to yourself, reader, three thousand horses of every variety of size and color, with trappings almost as varied as their appearance, either packed or ridden by a thousand souls from squalling infancy to decrepit age, their persons fantastically ornamented with scarlet coats, blankets of all colors, buffalo robes painted with hideous little figures, resembling grasshoppers quite as much as men for which they were intended, and sheep-skin dresses garnished with porcupine quills, beads, hawk bells, and human hair. Imagine this motley collection of human figures, crowned with long black locks waving in the wind, their faces painted with vermillion and yellow ochre. Listen to the rattle of numberless lodge poles [carried] by packhorses, to the various noises of children screaming, women scolding, and dogs howling. Observe occasional frightened horses running away and scattering their lading over the prairie. See here and there groups of Indian boys dashing about at full speed, sporting across the plain, or quietly listening to traditional tales of battles and surprises, recounted by their elder companions. Yonder see a hundred horsemen pursuing a herd of antelopes, which sprint and wind before them, conscious of superior fleetness—there as many others racing towards a distant mound, wild with emulation and excitement, and in every direction crowds of hungry dogs chasing and worrying timid rabbits, and other small animals. Imagine these scenes, with all their bustle, vociferation and confusion, lighted by the flashes of hundreds of gleaming gun barrels, upon which the rays of a fervent sun are playing, a beautiful level prairie, with dark blue snow-capped mountains in the distance, and you will have a faint idea of the character of our March, as we followed Old Guignon the Flathead slowly over the plains, on the sources of Clark's River.

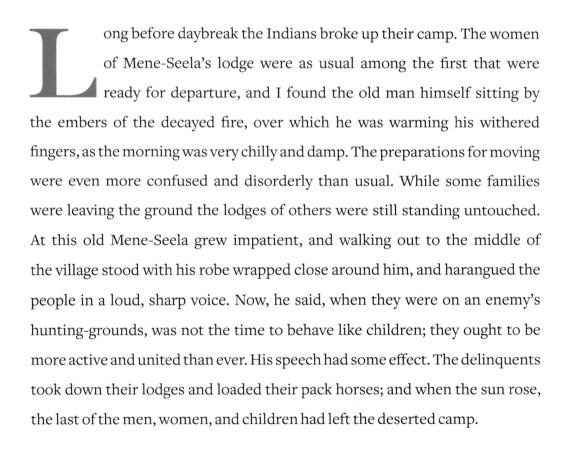

THE HUNTING CAMP

Long before daybreak the Indians broke up their camp. The women of Mene-Seela's lodge were as usual among the first that were ready for departure, and I found the old man himself sitting by the embers of the decayed fire, over which he was warming his withered fingers, as the morning was very chilly and damp. The preparations for moving were even more confused and disorderly than usual. While some families were leaving the ground the lodges of others were still standing untouched. At this old Mene-Seela grew impatient, and walking out to the middle of the village stood with his robe wrapped close around him, and harangued the people in a loud, sharp voice. Now, he said, when they were on an enemy's hunting-grounds, was not the time to behave like children; they ought to be more active and united than ever. His speech had some effect. The delinquents took down their lodges and loaded their pack horses; and when the sun rose, the last of the men, women, and children had left the deserted camp.

"Buffalo Bull, Grazing,"
by George Catlin, 1844.

This movement was made merely for the purpose of finding a better and safer position. So we advanced only three or four miles up the little stream, before each family assumed its relative place in the great ring of the village, and all around the squaws were actively at work in preparing the camp. But not a single warrior dismounted from his horse. All the men that morning were mounted on inferior animals, leading their best horses by a cord, or confiding them to the care of boys. In small parties they began to leave the ground and ride rapidly away over the plains to the westward. I had taken no food that morning, and not being at all ambitious of further abstinence, I went into my host's lodge, which his squaws had erected with wonderful celerity, and sat down in the center, as a gentle hint that I was hungry. A wooden bowl was soon set before me, filled

A detail of a hide painting by a Shoshone artist circa 1875, showing steps of a buffalo hunt.

At length we could discern several of [the] scouts making their signals to us at once; no longer waving their robes boldly from the top of the hill, but standing lower down, so that they could not be seen from the plains beyond. Game worth pursuing had evidently been discovered.

with the nutritious preparation of dried meat called pemmican by the northern voyageurs and wasna by the Dakota. Taking a handful to break my fast upon, I left the lodge just in time to see the last band of hunters disappear over the ridge of the neighboring hill. I mounted Pauline and galloped in pursuit, riding rather by the balance than by any muscular strength that remained to me. From the top of the hill I could overlook a wide extent of desolate and unbroken prairie, over which, far and near, little parties of naked horsemen were rapidly passing. I soon came up to the nearest, and we had not ridden a mile before all were united into one large and compact body. All was haste and eagerness. Each hunter was whipping on his horse, as if anxious to be the first to reach the game. In such movements among the Indians this is always more or less the case; but it was especially so in the present instance, because the head chief of the village was absent, and there were but few "soldiers," a sort of Indian police, who among their other functions usually assumed the direction of a buffalo hunt. No man turned to the right hand or to the left. We rode at a swift canter straight forward, uphill and downhill, and through the stiff, obstinate growth of the endless wild-sage bushes. For an hour and a half the same red shoulders, the same long black hair rose and fell with the motion of the horses before me. Very little was said, though once I observed an old man severely reproving Raymond for having left his rifle behind him, when there was some probability of encountering an enemy before the day was over. As we galloped across a plain thickly set with sagebushes, the foremost riders vanished suddenly from sight, as if diving into the earth. The arid soil was cracked into a deep ravine. Down we all went in succession and galloped in a line along the bottom, until we found a point where, one by one, the horses could scramble out. Soon after we came upon a wide shallow stream, and as we rode swiftly over the hard sand-beds and through the thin sheets of rippling water, many of the savage horsemen threw themselves to the ground, knelt on the sand, snatched a hasty draught, and leaping back again to their seats, galloped on again as before.

Meanwhile scouts kept in advance of the party; and now we began to see them on the ridge of the hills, waving their robes in token that buffalo were visible. These however proved to be nothing more than old straggling bulls, feeding upon the neighboring plains, who would stare for a moment at the hostile array and then gallop clumsily off. At length we could discern several of these scouts making their signals to us at once; no longer waving their robes boldly from the top of the hill, but standing lower down, so that they could not be seen from the plains beyond. Game worth pursuing had evidently been discovered. The excited Indians now urged forward their tired horses even more rapidly than before. Pauline, who was still sick and jaded, began to groan heavily; and her yellow sides were darkened with sweat. As we were crowding together over a lower intervening hill, I heard Reynal and Raymond shouting to me from the left; and looking in that direction, I

saw them riding away behind a party of about twenty mean-looking Indians. These were the relatives of Reynal's squaw Margot, who, not wishing to take part in the general hunt, were riding toward a distant hollow, where they could discern a small band of buffalo which they meant to appropriate to themselves. I answered to the call by ordering Raymond to turn back and follow me. He reluctantly obeyed, though Reynal, who had relied on his assistance in skinning, cutting up, and carrying to camp the buffalo that he and his party should kill, loudly protested and declared that we should see no sport if we went with the rest of the Indians. Followed by Raymond I pursued the main body of hunters, while Reynal in a great rage whipped his horse over the hill after his ragamuffin relatives. The Indians, still about a hundred in number, rode in a dense body at some distance in advance. They galloped forward, and a cloud of dust was flying in the wind behind them. I could not overtake them until they had stopped on the side of the hill where the scouts were standing. Here, each hunter sprang in haste from the tired animal which he had ridden, and leaped upon the fresh horse that he had brought with him. There was not a saddle or a bridle in the whole party. A piece of buffalo robe girthed over the horse's back served in the place of the one, and a cord of twisted hair lashed firmly round his lower jaw answered for the other. Eagle feathers were dangling from every mane and tail, as insignia of courage and speed. As for the rider, he wore no other clothing than a light cincture at his waist, and a pair of moccasins. He had a heavy whip, with a handle of solid elk-horn, and a lash of knotted bull-hide, fastened to his wrist by an ornamental band. His bow was in his hand, and his quiver of otter or panther skin hung at his shoulder. Thus equipped, some thirty of the hunters galloped away toward the left, in order to make a circuit under cover of the hills, that the buffalo might be assailed on both sides at once. The rest impatiently waited until time enough had elapsed for their companions to reach the required position. Then riding upward in a body, we gained the ridge of the hill, and for the first time came in sight of the buffalo on the plain beyond.

They were a band of cows, four or five hundred in number, who were crowded together near the bank of a wide stream that was soaking across the sand-beds of the valley. This was a large circular basin, sun-scorched and broken, scantily covered with herbage and encompassed with high barren hills, from an opening in which we could see our allies galloping out upon the plain. The wind blew from that direction. The buffalo were aware of their approach, and had begun to move, though very slowly and in a compact mass. I have no further recollection of seeing the game until we were in the midst of them, for as we descended the hill other objects engrossed my attention. Numerous old bulls were scattered over the plain, and ungallantly deserting their charge

George Catlin's 1844 lithograph emphasizes
the speed and skills in the pursuit.

at our approach, began to wade and plunge through the treacherous quick-sands or the stream, and gallop away toward the hills. One old veteran was struggling behind all the rest with one of his forelegs, which had been broken by some accident, dangling about uselessly at his side. His appearance, as he went shambling along on three legs, was so ludicrous that I could not help pausing for a moment to look at him. As I came near, he would try to rush upon me, nearly throwing himself down at every awkward attempt. Looking up, I saw the whole body of Indians full a hundred yards in advance. I lashed Pauline in pursuit and reached them just in time, for as we mingled among them, each hunter, as if by a common impulse, violently struck his horse, each horse sprang forward convulsively, and scattering in the charge in order to assail the entire herd at once, we all rushed headlong upon the buffalo. We were among them in an instant. Amid the trampling and the yells I could see their dark figures running hither and thither through clouds of dust, and the horsemen darting in pursuit. While we were charging on one side, our companions had attacked the bewildered and panic-stricken herd on the other. The uproar and confusion lasted but for a moment. The dust cleared away, and the buffalo could be seen scattering as from a common center, flying over the plain singly, or in long files and small compact bodies, while behind each followed the Indians, lashing their horses to furious speed, forcing them close upon their prey, and yelling as they launched arrow after arrow into their sides. The large black carcasses were strewn thickly over the ground. Here and there wounded buffalo were standing, their bleeding sides feathered with arrows; and as I rode past them their eyes would glare, they would bristle like gigantic cats, and feebly attempt to rush up and gore my horse.

I left camp that morning with a philosophic resolution. Neither I nor my horse were at that time fit for such sport, and I had determined to remain a quiet spectator; but amid the rush of horses and buffalo, the uproar and the dust, I found it impossible to sit still; and as four or five buffalo ran past me in a line, I drove Pauline in pursuit. We went plunging close at their heels through the water and the quick-sands, and clambering the bank, chased them through the wild-sage bushes that covered the rising ground beyond. But neither her native spirit nor the blows of the knotted bull-hide could supply the place of poor Pauline's exhausted strength. We could not gain an inch upon the poor fugitives. At last, however, they came full upon a ravine too wide to leap over; and as this compelled them to turn abruptly to the left, I contrived to get within ten or twelve yards of the hindmost. At this she faced about, bristled angrily, and made a show of charging. I shot at her with a large holster pistol, and hit her somewhere in the neck. Down she tumbled into the ravine, whither her companions had descended before her. I saw their dark backs appearing and disappearing as they galloped along the bottom; then, one by one, they came scrambling out on the other side and ran off as before, the wounded animal following with unabated speed.

Grizzly Bear Grunts

From *Narratives of a Journey Across the Rocky Mountains to the Columbia*

BY JOHN KIRK TOWNSEND

The dreaded grizzly bear is quite common in this neighborhood; two have just been seen in some bushes near, and they visit our camp almost every night, attracted by the piles of meat which are heaped all around us. The first intimation we have of his approach is a great grunt or snort, unlike any sound I ever heard, but much more querulous than fierce; then we hear the scraping and tramping of his huge feet, and the snuffing of his nostrils, as the savory scent of the meat is wafted to them. He approaches nearer and nearer, with a stealthy and fearful pace, but just as he is about to accomplish the object of his visit, he suddenly stops short; the snuffing is repeated at long and trembling intervals, and if the slightest motion is then made by one of the party, away goes "Ephraim" like a cowardly burglar as he is, and we hear no more of him that night.

Turning back, I saw Raymond coming on his black mule to meet me; and as we rode over the field together, we counted dozens of carcasses lying on the plain, in the ravines and on the sandy bed of the stream. Far away in the distance, horses and buffalo were still scouring along, with little clouds of dust rising behind them; and over the sides of the hills we could see long files of the frightened animals rapidly ascending. The hunters began to return. The boys, who had held the horses behind the hill, made their appearance, and the work of flaying and cutting up began in earnest all over the field. I noticed my host Kongra-Tonga beyond the stream, just alighting by the side of a cow which he had killed. Riding up to him I found him in the act of drawing out an arrow, which, with the exception of the notch at the end, had entirely disappeared in the animal. I asked him to give it to me, and I still retain it as a proof, though by no means the most striking one that could be offered, of the force and dexterity with which the Indians discharge their arrows.

The hides and meat were piled upon the horses, and the hunters began to leave the ground. Raymond and I, too, getting tired of the scene, set out for the village, riding straight across the intervening desert. There was no path, and as far as I could see, no landmarks sufficient to guide us; but Raymond seemed to have an instinctive perception

An Apsaroke Indian woman scraping a buffalo hide in 1908.

of the point on the horizon toward which we ought to direct our course. Antelope were bounding on all sides, and as is always the case in the presence of buffalo, they seemed to have lost their natural shyness and timidity. Bands of them would run lightly up the rocky declivities, and stand gazing down upon us from the summit. At length we could distinguish the tall white rocks and the old pine trees that, as we well remembered, were just above the site of the encampment. Still, we could see nothing of the village itself until, ascending a grassy hill, we found the circle of lodges, dingy with storms and smoke, standing on the plain at our very feet.

I entered the lodge of my host. His squaw instantly brought me food and water, and spread a buffalo robe for me to lie upon; and being much fatigued, I lay down and fell asleep. In about an hour the entrance of Kongra-Tonga, with his arms smeared with blood to the elbows, awoke me. He sat down in his usual seat on the left side of the lodge. His squaw gave him a vessel of water for washing, set before him a bowl of boiled meat, and as he was eating pulled off his bloody moccasins and placed fresh ones on his feet; then outstretching his limbs, my host composed himself to sleep.

And now the hunters, two or three at a time, began to come rapidly in, and each, consigning his horses to the squaws, entered his lodge with the air of a man whose day's work was done. The squaws flung down the load from the burdened horses, and vast piles of meat and hides were soon accumulated before every lodge. By this time it was darkening fast, and the whole village was illumined by the glare of fires blazing all around. All the squaws and children were gathered about the piles of meat, exploring them in search of the daintiest portions. Some of these they roasted on sticks before the fires, but often they dispensed with this superfluous operation. Late into the night the fires were still glowing upon the groups of feasters engaged in this savage banquet around them.

Several hunters sat down by the fire in Kongra-Tonga's lodge to talk over the day's exploits. Among the rest, Mene-Seela came in. Though he must have seen full eighty winters, he had taken an active share in the day's sport. He boasted that he had killed two cows that morning, and would have killed a third if the dust had not blinded him so that he had to drop his bow and arrows and press both hands against his eyes to stop the pain. The firelight fell upon his wrinkled face and shriveled figure as he sat telling his story with such inimitable gesticulation that every man in the lodge broke into a laugh.

Old Mene-Seela was one of the few Indians in the village with whom I would have trusted myself alone without suspicion, and the only one from whom I would have received a gift or a service without the certainty that it proceeded from an interested motive. He was a great friend to the whites. He liked to be in their society, and was very vain of the favors he had received from them. He told me one afternoon, as we were sitting together in his son's lodge, that he considered the beaver and the whites the wisest people on earth; indeed, he was convinced they were the same; and an incident which had happened to him long before had assured him of this. So he began the following story,

> He told me one afternoon, as we were sitting together in his son's lodge, that he considered the beaver and the whites the wisest people on earth; indeed, he was convinced they were the same . . .

Charcoal drawing of a beaver with its offspring by Charles Livingston Bull.

and as the pipe passed in turn to him, Reynal availed himself of these interruptions to translate what had preceded. But the old man accompanied his words with such admirable pantomime that translation was hardly necessary.

He said that when he was very young, and had never yet seen a white man, he and three or four of his companions were out on a beaver hunt, and he crawled into a large beaver lodge, to examine what was there. Sometimes he was creeping on his hands and knees, sometimes he was obliged to swim, and sometimes to lie flat on his face and drag himself along. In this way he crawled a great distance underground. It was very dark, cold and close, so that at last he was almost suffocated, and fell into a swoon. When he began to recover, he could just distinguish the voices of his companions outside, who had given him up for lost, and were singing his death song. At first he could see nothing, but soon he discerned something white before him, and at length plainly distinguished three people, entirely white; one man and two women, sitting at the edge of a black pool of water. He became alarmed and thought it high time to retreat. Having succeeded, after great trouble, in reaching daylight again, he went straight to the spot directly above the pool of water where he had seen the three mysterious beings. Here he beat a hole with his war club in the ground, and sat down to watch. In a moment the nose of an old male beaver appeared at the opening. Mene-Seela instantly seized him and dragged him up, when two other beavers, both females, thrust out their heads, and these he served in the same way. "These," continued the old man, "must have been the three white people whom I saw sitting at the edge of the water."

Mene-Seela was the grand depository of the legends and traditions of the village. I succeeded, however, in getting from him only a few fragments. Like all Indians, he was excessively superstitious, and continually saw some reason for withholding his stories. "It is a bad thing," he would say, "to tell the tales in summer. Stay with us till next winter, and I will tell you everything I know; but now our war parties are going out, and our young men will be killed if I sit down to tell stories before the frost begins."

But to leave this digression. We remained encamped on this spot five days, during three of which the hunters were at work incessantly, and immense quantities of meat and hides were brought in. Great alarm, however, prevailed in the village. All were on the alert. The young men were ranging through the country as scouts, and the old men paid careful attention to omens and prodigies, and especially to their dreams. In order to convey to the enemy (who, if they were in the neighborhood, must inevitably have known of our presence) the impression that we were constantly on the watch, piles of sticks and stones were erected on all the surrounding hills, in such a manner as to appear at a distance like sentinels. Often, even to this hour, that scene will rise before my mind like a visible reality: the tall white rocks; the old pine trees on their summits; the sandy stream that ran along their bases and half encircled the village; and the wild-sage bushes, with their dull green hue and their medicinal odor, that covered all the neighboring declivities. Hour after hour the squaws would pass and repass with their vessels of water between the stream and the lodges. For the most part no one was to be seen in the camp but women and children, two or three super-annuated old men, and a few lazy and worthless young ones. These, together with the dogs, now grown fat and good-natured with the abundance in the camp, were its only tenants. Still it presented a busy and bustling scene. In all quarters the meat, hung on cords of hide, was drying in the sun, and around the lodges the squaws, young and old, were laboring on the fresh hides that were stretched upon the ground, scraping the hair from one side and the still adhering flesh from the other, and rubbing into them the brains of the buffalo, in order to render them soft and pliant.

In mercy to myself and my horse, I never went out with the hunters after the first day. Of late, however, I had been gaining strength rapidly, as was always the case upon every respite of my disorder. I was soon able to walk with ease. Raymond and I would go out upon the neighboring prairies to shoot antelope, or sometimes to assail straggling buffalo, on foot, an attempt in which we met with rather indifferent success. To kill a bull with a rifle-ball is a difficult art, in the secret of which I was as yet very imperfectly initiated. As I came out of Kongra-Tonga's lodge one morning, Reynal called to me from the opposite side of the village, and asked me over to breakfast. The breakfast was a substantial one. It consisted of the rich, juicy hump-ribs of a fat cow; a repast absolutely unrivaled. It was roasting before the fire, impaled upon a stout stick, when he, with Raymond and myself, unsheathed our knives and assailed it with good will. It spite of all medical experience, this solid fare, without bread or salt, seemed to agree with me admirably.

"We shall have strangers here before night," said Reynal.

"How do you know that?" I asked.

"I dreamed so. I am as good at dreaming as an Indian. There is the Hail-Storm; he dreamed the same thing, and he and his crony, the Rabbit, have gone out on discovery."

I laughed at Reynal for his credulity, went over to my host's lodge, took down my rifle, walked out a mile or two on the prairie, saw an old bull standing alone, crawled up a ravine, shot him and saw him escape. Then, quite exhausted and rather ill-humored, I walked back to the village. By a strange coincidence, Reynal's prediction had been verified; for the first persons whom I saw were the two trappers, Rouleau and Saraphin, coming to meet me. These men, as the reader may possibly recollect, had left our party about a fortnight before. They had been trapping for a while among the Black Hills, and were now on their way to the Rocky Mountains, intending in a day or two to set out for the neighboring Medicine Bow. They were not the most elegant or refined of companions, yet they made a very welcome addition to the limited society of the village. For the rest of that day we lay smoking and talking in Reynal's lodge. This indeed was no better than a little hut, made of hides stretched on poles, and entirely open in front. It was

"In the Foothills of the Rockies, 1898," by French-born painter and illustrator Henry Francois Farny.

well carpeted with soft buffalo robes, and here we remained, sheltered from the sun, surrounded by various domestic utensils of Madame Margot's household. All was quiet in the village. Though the hunters had not gone out that day, they lay sleeping in their lodges, and most of the women were silently engaged in their heavy tasks. A few young men were playing a lazy game of ball in the center of the village; and when they became tired, some girls supplied their place with a more boisterous sport. At a little distance, among the lodges, some children and half-grown squaws were playfully tossing up one of their number in a buffalo robe, an exact counterpart of the ancient pastime from which Sancho Panza suffered so much. Farther out on the prairie, a host of little naked boys were roaming about, engaged in various rough games, or pursuing birds and ground-squirrels with their bows and arrows; and woe to the unhappy little animals that fell into their merciless, torture-loving hands! A squaw from the next lodge, a notable active housewife named Weah Washtay, or the Good Woman, brought us a large bowl of wasna, and went into an ecstasy of delight when I presented her with a green glass ring, such as I usually wore with a view to similar occasions.

The sun went down and half the sky was growing fiery red, reflected on the little stream as it wound away among the sagebushes. Some young men left the village, and soon returned, driving in before them all the horses, hundreds in number, and of every size, age, and color. The hunters came out, and each securing those that belonged to him, examined their condition, and tied them fast by long cords to stakes driven in front of his lodge. It was half an hour before the bustle subsided and tranquillity was restored again. By this time it was nearly dark. Kettles were hung over the blazing fires, around which the squaws were gathered with their children, laughing and talking merrily. A circle of a different kind was formed in the center of the village. This was composed of the old men and warriors of repute, who with their white buffalo robes drawn close around their shoulders, sat together, and as the pipe passed from hand to hand, their conversation had not a particle of the gravity and reserve usually ascribed to Indians. I sat down with them as usual. I had in my hand half a dozen squibs and serpents, which I had made one day when encamped upon Laramie Creek, out of gunpowder and charcoal, and the leaves of "Fremont's Expedition," rolled round a stout lead pencil. I waited till I contrived to get hold of the large piece of burning *bois de vaches* which the Indians kept by them on the ground for lighting their pipes. With this I lighted all the fireworks at once, and tossed them whizzing and sputtering into the air, over the heads of the company. They all jumped up and ran off with yelps of astonishment and consternation. After a moment or two, they ventured to come back one by one, and some of the boldest, picking up the cases of burnt paper that were scattered about, examined them with eager curiosity to discover their mysterious secret. From that time forward I enjoyed great repute as a "fire-medicine."

The camp was filled with the low hum of cheerful voices. There were other sounds, however, of a very different kind, for from a large lodge, lighted up like a gigantic lantern by the blazing fire within, came a chorus of dismal cries and wailings, long drawn out, like the howling of wolves, and a woman, almost naked, was crouching close outside, crying violently, and gashing her legs with a knife till they were covered with blood. Just a year before, a young man belonging to this family had gone out with a war party and had been slain by the enemy, and his relatives were thus lamenting his loss. Still other sounds might be heard; loud earnest cries often repeated from amid the gloom, at a distance beyond the village. They proceeded from some young men who, being about to set out in a few days on a warlike expedition, were standing at the top of a hill, calling on the Great Spirit to aid them in their enterprise. While I was listening, Rouleau, with a laugh

on his careless face, called to me and directed my attention to another quarter. In front of the lodge where Weah Washtay lived another squaw was standing, angrily scolding an old yellow dog, who lay on the ground with his nose resting between his paws, and his eyes turned sleepily up to her face, as if he were pretending to give respectful attention, but resolved to fall asleep as soon as it was all over.

"You ought to be ashamed of yourself!" said the old woman. "I have fed you well, and taken care of you ever since you were small and blind, and could only crawl about and squeal a little, instead of howling as you do now. When you grew old, I said you were a good dog. You were strong and gentle when the load was put on your back, and you never ran among the feet of the horses when we were all traveling together over the prairie. But you had a bad heart! Whenever a rabbit jumped out of the bushes, you were always the first to run after him and lead away all the other dogs behind you. You ought to have known that it was very dangerous to act so. When you had got far out on the prairie, and no one was near to help you, perhaps a wolf would jump out of the ravine; and then what could you do? You would certainly have been killed, for no dog can fight well with a load on his back. Only three days ago you ran off in that way, and turned over the bag of wooden pins with which I used to fasten up the front of the lodge. Look up there, and you will see that it is all flapping open. And now to-night you have stolen a great piece of fat meat which was roasting before the fire for my children. I tell you, you have a bad heart, and you must die!"

So saying, the squaw went into the lodge, and coming out with a large stone mallet, killed the unfortunate dog at one blow. This speech is worthy of notice as illustrating a curious characteristic of the Indians: the ascribing intelligence and a power of understanding speech to the inferior animals, to whom, indeed, according to many of their traditions, they are linked in close affinity, and they even claim the honor of a lineal descent from bears, wolves, deer, or tortoises.

As it grew late, and the crowded population began to disappear, I too walked across the village to the lodge of my host, Kongra-Tonga. As I entered I saw him, by the flickering blaze of the fire in the center, reclining half asleep in his usual place. His couch was by no means an uncomfortable one. It consisted of soft buffalo robes laid together on the ground, and a pillow made of whitened deerskin stuffed with feathers and ornamented with beads. At his back was a light framework of poles and slender reeds, against which he could lean with ease when in a sitting posture; and at the top of it, just above his head, his bow and quiver were hanging. His squaw, a laughing, broad-faced woman, apparently had not yet completed her domestic arrangements, for she was bustling about the lodge, pulling over the utensils and the bales of dried meats that were ranged carefully round it. Unhappily, she and her partner were not the only tenants of the dwelling, for half a dozen children

Crow Indian men dancing in the firelight, 1907, photographed by Richard Throssel.

were scattered about, sleeping in every imaginable posture. My saddle was in its place at the head of the lodge and a buffalo robe was spread on the ground before it. Wrapping myself in my blanket I lay down, but had I not been extremely fatigued the noise in the next lodge would have prevented my sleeping. There was the monotonous thumping of the Indian drum, mixed with occasional sharp yells, and a chorus chanted by twenty voices. A grand scene of gambling was going forward with all the appropriate formalities. The players were staking on the chance issue of the game their ornaments, their horses, and as the excitement rose, their garments, and even their weapons, for desperate gambling is not confined to the hells of Paris. The men of the plains and the forests no less resort to it as a violent but grateful relief to the tedious monotony of their lives, which alternate between fierce excitement and listless inaction. I fell asleep with the dull notes of the drum still sounding on my ear, but these furious orgies lasted without intermission till daylight. I was soon awakened by one of the children crawling over me, while another larger one was tugging at my blanket and nestling himself in a very disagreeable proximity. I immediately repelled these advances by punching the heads of these miniature savages with a short stick which I always kept by me for the purpose; and as sleeping half the day and eating much more than is good for them makes them extremely restless, this operation usually had to be repeated four or five times in the course of the night. My host himself was the author of another most formidable annoyance. All these Indians, and he among the rest, think themselves bound to the constant performance of certain acts as the condition on which their success in life depends, whether in war, love, hunting, or any other employment. These "medicines," as they are called in that country, which are usually communicated in dreams, are often absurd enough. Some Indians will strike the butt of the pipe against the ground every time they smoke; others will insist that everything they say shall be interpreted by contraries; and Shaw once met an old man who conceived that all would be lost unless he compelled every white man he met to drink a bowl of cold water. My host was particularly unfortunate in his allotment. The Great Spirit had told him in a dream that he must sing a certain song in the middle of every night; and regularly at about twelve o'clock his dismal monotonous chanting would awaken me, and I would see him seated bolt upright on his couch, going through his dolorous performances with a most business-like air. There were other voices of the night still more inharmonious. Twice or thrice, between sunset and dawn, all the dogs in the village, and there were hundreds of them, would bay and yelp in chorus; a most horrible clamor, resembling no sound that I have ever heard, except perhaps the frightful howling of wolves that we used sometimes to hear long afterward when descending the Arkansas on the trail of General Kearny's army. The canine uproar is, if possible, more discordant than that of the wolves. Heard at a distance, slowly rising on the night, it has a strange unearthly effect, and would fearfully haunt the dreams of a nervous man; but when you are sleeping in the midst of it the din is outrageous. One long loud howl from the next lodge perhaps begins it, and voice after voice takes up the sound till it passes around the whole circumference of the village, and the air is filled with confused and discordant cries, at once fierce and mournful. It lasts but for a moment and then dies away into silence.

Morning came, and Kongra-Tonga, mounting his horse, rode out with the hunters. It may not be amiss to glance at him for an instant in his domestic character of husband and father. Both he and his squaw, like most other Indians, were very fond of their children, whom they indulged to excess, and never punished, except in extreme cases when they would throw a bowl of cold water over them. Their offspring became sufficiently undutiful and disobedient under this system of education, which tends not a little to foster that wild idea of liberty and utter intolerance of restraint which lie at the very foundation of the Indian

The men of the plains and the forests no less resort to [gambling] as a violent but grateful relief to the tedious monotony of their lives, which alternate between fierce excitement and listless inaction.

character. It would be hard to find a fonder father than Kongra-Tonga. There was one urchin in particular, rather less than two feet high, to whom he was exceedingly attached; and sometimes spreading a buffalo robe in the lodge, he would seat himself upon it, place his small favorite upright before him, and chant in a low tone some of the words used as an accompaniment to the war dance. The little fellow, who could just manage to balance himself by stretching out both arms, would lift his feet and turn slowly round and round in time to his father's music, while my host would laugh with delight, and look smiling up into my face to see if I were admiring this precocious performance of his offspring. In his capacity of husband he was somewhat less exemplary. The squaw who lived in the lodge with him had been his partner for many years. She took good care of his children and his household concerns. He liked her well enough, and as far as I could see they never quarreled; but all his warmer affections were reserved for younger and more recent favorites. Of these he had at present only one, who lived in a lodge apart from his own. One day while in his camp he became displeased with her, pushed her out, threw after her her ornaments, dresses, and everything she had, and told her to go home to her father. Having consummated this summary divorce, for which he could show good reasons, he came back, seated himself in his usual place, and began to smoke with an air of utmost tranquillity and self-satisfaction.

I was sitting in the lodge with him on that very afternoon, when I felt some curiosity to learn the history of the numerous scars that appeared on his naked body. Of some of them, however, I did not venture to inquire, for I already understood their origin. Each of his arms was marked as if deeply gashed with a knife at regular intervals, and there were other scars also, of a different character, on his back and on either breast. They were the traces of those formidable tortures which these Indians, in common with a few other tribes, inflict upon themselves at certain seasons; in part, it may be, to gain the glory of courage and endurance, but chiefly as an act of self-sacrifice to secure the favor of the Great Spirit. The scars upon the breast and back were produced by running through the flesh strong splints of wood, to which ponderous buffalo-skulls are fastened by cords of hide, and the wretch runs forward with all his strength, assisted by two companions, who take hold of each arm, until the flesh tears apart and the heavy loads are left behind. Others of Kongra-Tonga's scars were the result of accidents; but he had many which he received in war. He was one of the most noted warriors in the village. In the course of his life he had slain as he boasted to me, fourteen men, and though, like other Indians, he was a great braggart and utterly regardless of truth, yet in this

"Snake Indians," a 19th-century oil painting by Alfred Jacob Miller.

statement common report bore him out. Being much flattered by my inquiries he told me tale after tale, true or false, of his warlike exploits; and there was one among the rest illustrating the worst features of the Indian character too well for me to omit. Pointing out of the opening of the lodge toward the Medicine-Bow Mountain, not many miles distant he said that he was there a few summers ago with a war party of his young men. Here they found two Snake Indians, hunting. They shot one of them with arrows and chased the other up the side of the mountain till they surrounded him on a level place, and Kongra-Tonga himself, jumping forward among the trees, seized him by the arm. Two of his young men then ran up and held him fast while he scalped him alive. Then they built a great fire, and cutting the tendons of their captive's wrists and feet, threw him in, and held him down with long poles until he was burnt to death. He garnished his story with a great many descriptive particulars much too revolting to mention. His features were remarkably mild and open, without the fierceness of expression common among these Indians; and as he detailed these devilish cruelties, he looked up into my face with the same air of earnest simplicity which a little child would wear in relating to its mother some anecdote of its youthful experience.

Old Mene-Seela's lodge could offer another illustration of the ferocity of Indian warfare. A bright-eyed, active little boy was living there. He had belonged to a village of the Gros-Ventre Blackfeet, a small but bloody and treacherous band, in close alliance with the Arapahoes. About a year before, Kongra-Tonga and a party of warriors had found about twenty lodges of these Indians upon the plains a little to the eastward of our present camp; and surrounding them in the night, they butchered men, women, and children without mercy, preserving only this little boy alive. He was adopted into the old man's family, and was now fast becoming identified with the Ogallalla children, among whom he mingled on equal terms. There was also a Crow warrior in the village, a man of gigantic stature and most symmetrical proportions. Having been taken prisoner many years before and adopted by a squaw in place of a son whom she had lost, he had forgotten his old national antipathies, and was now both in act and inclination an Ogallalla.

I t will be remembered that the scheme of the grand warlike combination against the Snake and Crow Indians originated in this village; and though this plan had fallen to the ground, the embers of the martial ardor continued to glow brightly. Eleven young men had prepared themselves to go out against the enemy. The fourth day of our stay in this camp was fixed upon for their departure. At the head of this party was a well-built active little Indian, called the White Shield, whom I had always noticed for the great neatness of his dress and appearance. His lodge too, though not a large one, was the best in the village, his squaw was one of the prettiest girls, and altogether his dwelling presented a complete model of an Ogallalla domestic establishment. I was often a visitor there, for the White Shield being rather partial to white men, used

A drawing of a grizzly bear,
the most fierce and powerful
North American bear.

to invite me to continual feasts at all hours of the day. Once when the substantial part of the entertainment was concluded, and he and I were seated cross-legged on a buffalo robe smoking together very amicably, he took down his warlike equipments, which were hanging around the lodge, and displayed them with great pride and self-importance. Among the rest was a most superb headdress of feathers. Taking this from its case, he put it on and stood before me, as if conscious of the gallant air which it gave to his dark face and his vigorous, graceful figure. He told me that upon it were the feathers of three war-eagles, equal in value to the same number of good horses. He took up also a shield gayly painted and hung with feathers. The effect of these barbaric ornaments was admirable, for they were arranged with no little skill and taste. His quiver was made of the spotted skin of a small panther, such as are common among the Black Hills, from which the tail and distended claws were still allowed to hang. The White Shield concluded his entertainment in a manner characteristic of an Indian. He begged of me a little powder and ball, for he had a gun as well as bow and arrows; but this I was obliged to refuse, because I had scarcely enough for my own use. Making him, however, a parting present of a paper of vermilion, I left him apparently quite contented.

Unhappily on the next morning the White Shield took cold and was attacked with a violent inflammation of the throat. Immediately he seemed to lose all spirit, and though before no warrior in the village had borne himself more proudly, he now moped about from lodge to lodge with a forlorn and dejected air. At length he came and sat down, close wrapped in his robe, before the lodge of Reynal, but when he found that neither he nor I knew how to relieve him, he arose and stalked over to one of the medicine-men of the village. This old imposter thumped him for some time with both fists, howled and yelped over him, and beat a drum close to his ear to expel the evil spirit that had taken possession of him. This vigorous treatment failing of the desired effect, the White Shield withdrew to his own lodge, where he lay disconsolate for some hours. Making his appearance once more in the afternoon, he again took his seat on the ground before Reynal's lodge, holding his throat with his hand. For some time he sat perfectly silent with his eyes fixed mournfully on the ground. At last he began to speak in a low tone:

"I am a brave man," he said; "all the young men think me a great warrior, and ten of them are ready to go with me to the war. I will go and show them the enemy. Last summer the Snakes killed my brother. I cannot live unless I revenge his death. To-morrow we will set out and I will take their scalps."

The White Shield, as he expressed this resolution, seemed to have lost all the accustomed fire and spirit of his look, and hung his head as if in a fit of despondency.

As I was sitting that evening at one of the fires, I saw him arrayed in his splendid war dress, his cheeks painted with vermilion, leading his favorite war horse to the front of his

Beadwork on a Sioux jacket shows an Indian fighting a white man.

> ...When he feels himself attacked by a mysterious evil, before whose insidious assaults his manhood is wasted, and his strength drained away, when he can see no enemy to resist and defy, the boldest warrior falls prostrate at once.

lodge. He mounted and rode round the village, singing his war song in a loud hoarse voice amid the shrill acclamations of the women. Then dismounting, he remained for some minutes prostrate upon the ground, as if in an act of supplication. On the following morning I looked in vain for the departure of the warriors. All was quiet in the village until late in the forenoon, when the White Shield, issuing from his lodge, came and seated himself in his old place before us. Reynal asked him why he had not gone out to find the enemy.

"I cannot go," answered the White Shield in a dejected voice. "I have given my war arrows to the Meneaska."

"You have only given him two of your arrows," said Reynal. "If you ask him, he will give them back again."

For some time the White Shield said nothing. At last he spoke in a gloomy tone:

"One of my young men has had bad dreams. The spirits of the dead came and threw stones at him in his sleep."

If such a dream had actually taken place it might have broken up this or any other war party, but both Reynal and I were convinced at the time that it was a mere fabrication to excuse his remaining at home.

The White Shield was a warrior of noted prowess. Very probably, he would have received a mortal wound without a show of pain, and endured without flinching the worst tortures that an enemy could inflict upon him. The whole power of an Indian's nature would be summoned to encounter such a trial; every influence of his education from childhood would have prepared him for it; the cause of his suffering would have been visibly and palpably before him, and his spirit would rise to set his enemy at defiance, and gain the highest glory of a warrior by meeting death with fortitude. But when he feels himself attacked by a mysterious evil, before whose insidious assaults his manhood is wasted, and his strength drained away, when he can see no enemy to resist and defy, the boldest warrior falls prostrate at once. He believes that a bad spirit has taken possession of him, or that he is the victim of some charm. When suffering from a protracted disorder, an Indian will often abandon himself to his supposed destiny, pine away and die, the victim of his own imagination. The same effect will often follow from a series of calamities, or a long run of ill success, and the sufferer has been known to ride into the midst of an enemy's camp, or attack a grizzly bear single-handed, to get rid of a life which he supposed to lie under the doom of misfortune.

Thus after all his fasting, dreaming, and calling upon the Great Spirit, the White Shield's war party was pitifully broken up.

An 1859 Daniel A. Jenks drawing of
Cherokee Pass, 1859, near present-
day Fort Collins, Colorado.

Westward Ho!

*From Travels in the Great Western Prairie,
The Anahuac and Rocky Mountains.*

By Thomas J. Farnham

New Englander Thomas J. Farnham was elected as captain of a group of 19 called The Oregon Dragoons that set out for Oregon in 1839. He later wrote a petition signed by Oregon settlers asking the federal government to make Oregon part of the United States.

On the 21st of May, 1839, the author and sixteen others arrived in the town of Independence, Mo. Our destination was the Oregon Territory. Some of our number sought health in the wilderness —others sought the wilderness for its own sake—and still others sought a residence among the ancient forests and lofty heights of the valley of the Columbia, and each actuated by his own peculiar reasons of interest began preparing for leaving the frontier. Pack mules and horses and pack-saddles were purchased and prepared for service. Bacon and flour, salt and pepper, sufficient for 400 miles, were secured in sacks; our powder cakes were wrapped in painted canvas; and large oil cloths were purchased to protect these and our sacks of clothing from the rains; our arms were thoroughly repaired; bullets were moulded; powder horns and cap boxes filled; and all else done that was deemed needful, before we struck our tent for the Indian Territory.

But before leaving this little woodland town, it will be interesting to remember that it is the usual place of rendezvous and "outfit" for the overland traders to Santa Fe and other Mexican states. In the month of May each year, these traders congregate here, and buy large Pennsylvania wagons, and teams of mules to convey their calicoes, cottons, cloths, boots, shoes, etc., over the plains to that distant and hazardous market. And it is quite amusing to a "greenhorn," as those are called who have never been engaged in the trade, to see the mules make their first attempt at practical pulling…They are harnessed in a team two upon the shaft, and the remainder two abreast in long swinging iron traces. And then by the way of initiary intimation that they have passed from a life of mountainous contemplation, in the seclusion of their nursery pastures, to the bustling duties of the "Santa Fe Trade," a hot iron is applied to the thigh or shoulder of each with an embrace so cordially warm, as to leave there, in blistered perfection, the initials of their last owner's name.

THE TRAPPERS

In speaking of the Indians, I have almost forgotten two bold adventurers of another race, the trappers Rouleau and Saraphin. These men were bent on a most hazardous enterprise. A day's journey to the westward was the country over which the Arapahoes are accustomed to range, and for which the two trappers were on the point of setting out. These Arapahoes, of whom Shaw and I afterward fell in with a large village, are ferocious barbarians, of a most brutal and wolfish aspect, and of late they had declared themselves enemies to the whites, and threatened death to the first who should venture within their territory. The occasion of the declaration was as follows:

In the previous spring, 1845, Colonel Kearny left Fort Leavenworth with several companies of dragoons, and marching with extraordinary celerity reached Fort Laramie, whence he passed along the foot of the mountains to Bent's Fort and then, turning eastward again, returned to the point from whence he set out. While at Fort Laramie, he sent a part of his command as far westward as Sweetwater, while he himself remained at the fort, and dispatched messages to the surrounding Indians to meet him there in council. Then for the first time the tribes of that vicinity saw the white warriors, and, as might have been expected, they were lost in astonishment at their regular order, their gay attire, the completeness of their martial equipment, and the great size and power of their horses. Among the rest, the Arapahoes came in considerable numbers to the fort. They had lately committed numerous acts of outrage, and Colonel Kearny threatened that if they killed any more white men he would turn loose his dragoons upon them, and annihilate their whole nation. In the evening, to add effect to his speech, he ordered a howitzer to be fired and a rocket to be thrown up. Many of the Arapahoes fell prostrate

"Trappers Starting for the Beaver Hunt, 1837," by Alfred Jacob Miller.

Related to and larger than weasels, the American marten has a luxuriant coat.

on the ground, while others ran screaming with amazement and terror. On the following day they withdrew to their mountains, confounded with awe at the appearance of the dragoons, at their big gun which went off twice at one shot, and the fiery messenger which they had sent up to the Great Spirit. For many months they remained quiet, and did no further mischief. At length, just before we came into the country, one of them, by an act of the basest treachery, killed two white men, Boot and May, who were trapping among the mountains. For this act it was impossible to discover a motive. It seemed to spring from one of those inexplicable impulses which often actuate Indians and appear no better than the mere outbreaks of native ferocity. No sooner was the murder committed than the whole tribe were in extreme consternation. They expected every day that the avenging dragoons would arrive, little thinking that a desert of nine hundred miles in extent lay between the latter and their mountain fastnesses. A large deputation of them came to Fort Laramie, bringing a valuable present of horses, in compensation for the lives of the murdered men. These Bordeaux refused to accept. They then asked him if he would be satisfied with their delivering up the murderer himself; but he declined this offer also. The Arapahoes went back more terrified than ever. Weeks passed away, and still no dragoons appeared. A result followed which all those best acquainted with Indians had predicted. They conceived that fear had prevented Bordeaux from accepting their gifts, and that they had nothing to apprehend from the vengeance of the whites. From terror they rose to the height of insolence and presumption. They called the white men cowards and old women; and a friendly Dakota came to Fort Laramie and reported that they were determined to kill the first of the white dogs whom they could lay hands on.

Had a military officer, intrusted with suitable powers, been stationed at Fort Laramie, and having accepted the offer of the Arapahoes to deliver up the murderer, had ordered him to be immediately led out and shot, in presence of his tribe, they would have been awed into tranquillity, and much danger and calamity averted; but now the neighborhood of the Medicine-Bow Mountain and the region beyond it was a scene of extreme peril. Old Mene-Seela, a true friend of the whites, and many other of the Indians gathered about the two trappers, and vainly endeavored to turn them from their purpose; but Rouleau and Saraphin only laughed at the danger. On the morning preceding that on which they were to leave the camp, we could all discern faint white columns of smoke rising against the dark base of the Medicine-Bow. Scouts were out immediately, and reported that these proceeded from an Arapahoe camp, abandoned only a few hours before. Still the two trappers continued their preparations for departure.

Saraphin was a tall, powerful fellow, with a sullen and sinister countenance. His rifle had very probably drawn other blood than that of buffalo or even Indians. Rouleau had a broad ruddy face marked with as few traces of thought or care as a child's. His figure was remarkably square and strong, but the first joints of both his feet were frozen off, and his horse had lately thrown and trampled upon him, by which he had been severely

injured in the chest. But nothing could check his inveterate propensity for laughter and gayety. He went all day rolling about the camp on his stumps of feet, talking and singing and frolicking with the Indian women. In fact Rouleau had an unlucky partiality for squaws. He always had one whom he must needs bedizen with beads, ribbons, and all the finery of an Indian wardrobe; and though he was of course obliged to leave her behind him during his expeditions, yet this hazardous necessity did not at all trouble him, for his disposition was the very reverse of jealous. If at any time he had not lavished the whole of the precarious profits of his vocation upon his dark favorite, he always devoted the rest to feasting his comrades. If liquor was not to be had—and this was usually the case—strong coffee was substituted. As the men of that region are by no means remarkable for providence or self-restraint, whatever was set before them on these occasions was sure to be disposed of at one sitting. Like other trappers, Rouleau's life was one of contrast and variety. It was only at certain seasons, and for a limited time, that he was absent on his expeditions. For the rest of the year he would be lounging about the fort, or encamped with his friends in its vicinity, lazily hunting or enjoying all the luxury of inaction; but when once in pursuit of beaver, he was involved in extreme privations and desperate perils. When in the midst of his game and his enemies, hand and foot, eye and ear, are incessantly active. Frequently he must content himself with devouring his evening meal uncooked, lest the light of his fire should attract the eyes of some wandering Indian; and sometimes having made his rude repast, he must leave his fire still blazing, and withdraw to a distance under cover of the darkness, that his disappointed enemy, drawn thither by the light, may find his victim gone, and be unable to trace his footsteps in the gloom. This is the life led by scores of men in the Rocky Mountains and their vicinity. I once met a trapper whose breast was marked with the scars of six bullets and arrows, one of his arms broken by a shot and one of his knees shattered; yet still, with the undaunted mettle of New England he continued to follow his perilous occupation. To some of the children of cities it may seem strange that men should follow a life of such hardship and desperate adventure; yet there is a mysterious, restless charm in the basilisk eye of danger, and few men perhaps remain long in that wild region without learning to love peril for its own sake, and to laugh carelessly in the face of death.

On the last day of our stay in this camp, the trappers were ready for departure. When in the Black Hills they had caught seven beaver, and they now left their skins in charge of Reynal, to be kept until their return. Their strong, gaunt horses were equipped with rusty Spanish bits and rude Mexican saddles, to which wooden stirrups were attached, while a buffalo robe was rolled up behind them, and a bundle of beaver traps slung at the pommel. These, together with their rifles, their knives, their powder-horns and bullet-pouches, flint and steel and a tincup, composed their whole traveling equipment. They shook hands with

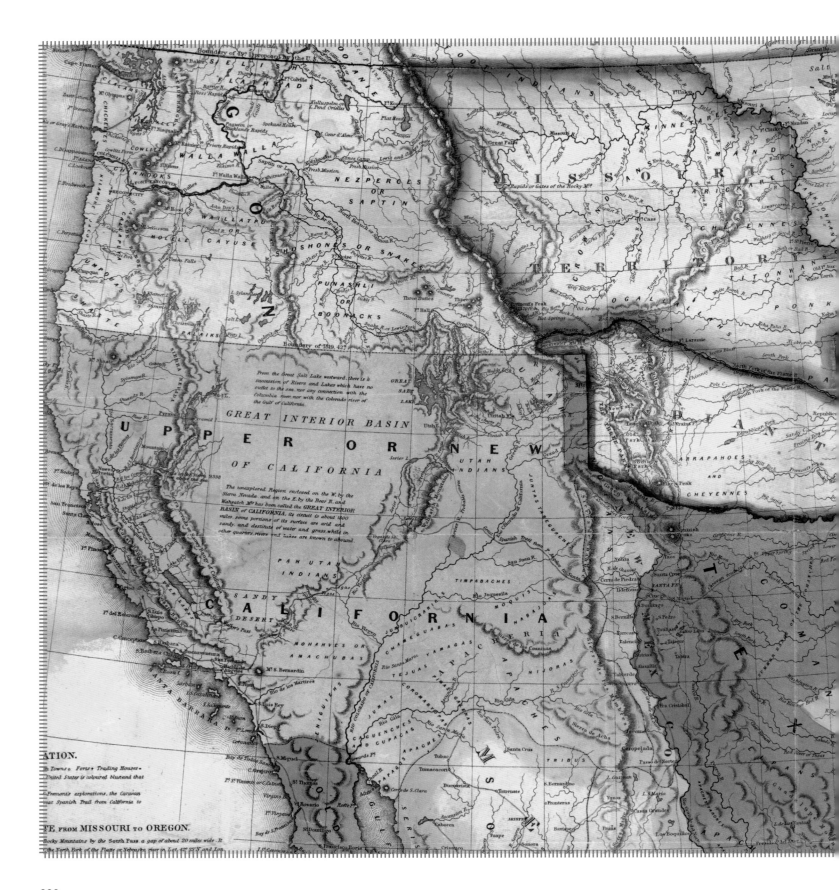

us and rode away; Saraphin with his grim countenance, like a surly bulldog's, was in advance; but Rouleau, clambering gayly into his seat, kicked his horse's sides, flourished his whip in the air, and trotted briskly over the prairie, trolling forth a Canadian song at the top of his lungs. Reynal looked after them with his face of brutal selfishness.

"Well," he said, "if they are killed, I shall have the beaver. They'll fetch me fifty dollars at the fort, anyhow."

This was the last I saw of them.

We had been for five days in the hunting camp, and the meat, which all this time had hung drying in the sun, was now fit for transportation. Buffalo hides also had been procured in sufficient quantities for making the next season's lodges; but it remained to provide the long slender poles on which they were to be supported. These were only to be had among the tall pine woods of the Black Hills, and in that direction therefore our next move was to be made. It is worthy of notice that amid the general abundance which during this time had prevailed in the camp there were no instances of individual privation; for although the hide and the tongue of the buffalo belong by exclusive right to the hunter who has killed it, yet anyone else is equally entitled to help himself from the rest of the carcass. Thus, the weak, the aged, and even the indolent come in for a share of the spoils, and many a helpless old woman, who would otherwise perish from starvation, is sustained in profuse abundance.

On the 25th of July, late in the afternoon, the camp broke up, with the usual tumult and confusion, and we were all moving once more, on horseback and on foot, over the plains. We advanced, however, but a few miles. The old men, who during the whole march had been stoutly striding along on foot in front of the people, now seated themselves in a circle on the ground, while all the families, erecting their lodges in the prescribed order around them, formed the usual great circle of the camp; meanwhile these village patriarchs sat smoking and talking. I threw my bridle to Raymond, and sat down as usual along with them. There was none of that reserve and apparent dignity which an Indian always assumes when in council, or in the presence of white men whom he distrusts. The party, on the contrary, was an extremely merry one; and as in a social circle of a quite different character, "if there was not much wit, there was at least a great deal of laughter."

When the first pipe was smoked out, I rose and withdrew to the lodge of my host. Here I was stooping, in the act of taking off my powder-horn and bullet-pouch, when suddenly, and close at hand, pealing loud and shrill, and in right good earnest, came the terrific yell of the war-whoop. Kongra-Tonga's squaw snatched up her youngest child, and ran out of the lodge. I followed, and found the whole village in confusion, resounding with cries and yells. The circle of old men in the center had vanished. The warriors with glittering eyes

An 1846 map showing
the western territories.

came darting, their weapons in their hands, out of the low opening of the lodges, and running with wild yells toward the farther end of the village. Advancing a few rods in that direction, I saw a crowd in furious agitation, while others ran up on every side to add to the confusion. Just then I distinguished the voices of Raymond and Reynal, shouting to me from a distance, and looking back, I saw the latter with his rifle in his hand, standing on the farther bank of a little stream that ran along the outskirts of the camp. He was calling to Raymond and myself to come over and join him, and Raymond, with his usual deliberate gait and stolid countenance, was already moving in that direction.

This was clearly the wisest course, unless we wished to involve ourselves in the fray; so I turned to go, but just then a pair of eyes, gleaming like a snake's, and an aged familiar countenance was thrust from the opening of a neighboring lodge, and out bolted old Mene-Seela, full of fight, clutching his bow and arrows in one hand and his knife in the other. At that instant he tripped and fell sprawling on his face, while his weapons flew scattering away in every direction. The women with loud screams were hurrying with their children in their arms to place them out of danger, and I observed some hastening to prevent mischief, by carrying away all the weapons they could lay hands on. On a rising ground close to the camp stood a line of old women singing a medicine song to allay the tumult. As I approached the side of the brook I heard gun-shots behind me, and turning back, I saw that the crowd had separated into two lines of naked warriors confronting each other at a respectful distance, and yelling and jumping about to dodge the shot of their adversaries, while they discharged bullets and arrows against each other. At the same time certain sharp, humming sounds in the air over my head, like the flight of beetles on a summer evening, warned me that the danger was not wholly confined to the immediate scene of the fray. So wading through the brook, I joined Reynal and Raymond, and we sat down on the grass, in the posture of an armed neutrality, to watch the result.

Happily it may be for ourselves, though contrary to our expectation, the disturbance was quelled almost as soon as it had commenced. When I looked again, the combatants were once more mingled together in a mass. Though yells sounded, occasionally from the throng, the firing had entirely ceased, and I observed five or six persons moving busily about, as if acting the part of peacemakers. One of the village heralds or criers proclaimed in a loud voice something which my two companions were too much engrossed in their own observations to translate for me. The crowd began to disperse, though many a deep-set black eye still glittered with an unnatural luster, as the warriors slowly withdrew to their lodges. This fortunate suppression of the disturbance was owing to a few of the old men, less pugnacious than Mene-Seela, who boldly ran in between the combatants and aided by some of the "soldiers," or Indian police, succeeded in effecting their object.

Early 1900s drawing of a Plains Indian on a ridge by Frederic Dorr Steele.

It seemed very strange to me that although many arrows and bullets were discharged, no one was mortally hurt, and I could only account for this by the fact that both the marksman and the object of his aim were leaping about incessantly during the whole time. By far the greater part of the villagers had joined in the fray, for although there were not more than a dozen guns in the whole camp, I heard at least eight or ten shots fired.

In a quarter of an hour all was comparatively quiet. A large circle of warriors were again seated in the center of the village, but this time I did not venture to join them, because I could see that the pipe, contrary to the usual order, was passing from the left hand to the right around the circle, a sure sign that a "medicine-smoke" of reconciliation was going forward, and that a white man would be an unwelcome intruder. When I again entered the still agitated camp it was nearly dark, and mournful cries, howls and wailings resounded from many female voices. Whether these had any connection with the late disturbance, or were merely lamentations for relatives slain in some former war expeditions, I could not distinctly ascertain.

To inquire too closely into the cause of the quarrel was by no means prudent, and it was not until some time after that I discovered what had given rise to it. Among the Dakota there are many associations, or fraternities, connected with the purposes of their superstitions, their warfare, or their social life. There was one called "The Arrow-Breakers," now in a great measure disbanded and dispersed. In the village there were, however, four men belonging to it, distinguished by the peculiar arrangement of their hair, which rose in a high bristling mass above their foreheads, adding greatly to their apparent height, and giving them a most ferocious appearance. The principal among them was the Mad Wolf, a warrior of remarkable size and strength, great courage, and the fierceness of a demon. I had always looked upon him as the most dangerous man in the village; and though he often invited me to feasts, I never entered his lodge unarmed. The Mad Wolf had taken a fancy to a fine horse belonging to another Indian, who was called the Tall Bear; and anxious to get the animal into his possession, he made the owner a present of another horse nearly equal in value. According to the customs of the Dakota, the acceptance of this gift involved a sort of obligation to make an equitable return; and the Tall Bear well understood that the other had in view the obtaining of his favorite buffalo horse. He however accepted the present without a word of thanks, and having picketed the horse before his lodge, he suffered day after day to pass without making the expected return. The Mad Wolf grew impatient and angry; and at last, seeing that his bounty was not likely to produce the desired return, he resolved to reclaim it. So this evening, as soon as the village was encamped, he went to the lodge of the Tall Bear, seized upon the horse that he had given him, and led him away. At this the Tall Bear broke into one of those fits of sullen rage not uncommon among the Indians. He ran up to the unfortunate horse, and gave

...I could see that the pipe, contrary to the usual order, was passing from the left hand to the right around the circle, a sure sign that a "medicine-smoke" of reconciliation was going forward, and that a white man would be an unwelcome intruder.

"The Challenge," an 1870 painting by John Mix Stanley.

him three mortal stabs with his knife. Quick as lightning the Mad Wolf drew his bow to its utmost tension, and held the arrow quivering close to the breast of his adversary. The Tall Bear, as the Indians who were near him said, stood with his bloody knife in his hand, facing the assailant with the utmost calmness. Some of his friends and relatives, seeing his danger, ran hastily to his assistance. The remaining three Arrow-Breakers, on the other hand, came to the aid of their associate. Many of their friends joined them, the war-cry was raised on a sudden, and the tumult became general.

The "soldiers," who lent their timely aid in putting it down, are by far the most important executive functionaries in an Indian village. The office is one of considerable honor, being confided only to men of courage and repute. They derive their authority from the old men and chief warriors of the village, who elect them in councils occasionally convened for the purpose, and thus can exercise a degree of authority which no one else in the village would dare to assume. While very few Ogallalla chiefs could venture without instant jeopardy of their lives to strike or lay hands upon the meanest of their people, the "soldiers," in the discharge of their appropriate functions, have full license to make use of these and similar acts of coercion.

Castle Creek • A Temple of The Hills •

The
Black Hills

We traveled eastward for two days, and then the gloomy ridges of the Black Hills rose up before us. The village passed along for some miles beneath their declivities, trailing out to a great length over the arid prairie, or winding at times among small detached hills or distorted shapes. Turning sharply to the left, we entered a wide defile of the mountains, down the bottom of which a brook came winding, lined with tall grass and dense copses, amid which were hidden many beaver dams and lodges. We passed along between two lines of high precipices and rocks, piled in utter disorder one upon another, and with scarcely a tree, a bush, or a clump of grass to veil their nakedness. The restless Indian boys were wandering along their edges and clambering up and down their rugged sides, and sometimes a group of them would stand on the verge of a cliff and look down on the array as it passed in review beneath them. As we advanced, the passage grew more narrow; then it suddenly expanded into a round grassy meadow, completely encompassed by mountains; and here the families stopped as they came up in turn, and the camp rose like magic.

"South Castle Creek, a Temple of
the Hills, Black Hills, South Dakota,"
by Franklin De Haven.

The lodges were hardly erected when, with their usual precipitation, the Indians set about accomplishing the object that had brought them there; that is, the obtaining poles for supporting their new lodges. Half the population, men, women and boys, mounted their horses and set out for the interior of the mountains. As they rode at full gallop over the shingly rocks and into the dark opening of the defile beyond, I thought I had never read or dreamed of a more strange or picturesque cavalcade. We passed between precipices more than a thousand feet high, sharp and splintering at the tops, their sides beetling over the defile or descending in abrupt declivities, bristling with black fir trees. On our left they rose close to us like a wall, but on the right a winding brook with a narrow strip of marshy soil intervened. The stream was clogged with old beaver dams, and spread frequently into wide pools. There were thick bushes and many dead and blasted trees along its course, though frequently nothing remained but stumps cut close to the ground by the beaver, and marked with the sharp chisel-like teeth of those indefatigable laborers. Sometimes we were driving among trees, and then emerging upon open spots, over which, Indian-like, all galloped at full speed. As Pauline bounded over the rocks I felt her saddle-girth slipping, and alighted to draw it tighter; when the whole array swept past me in a moment, the women with their gaudy ornaments tinkling as they rode, the men whooping, and laughing, and lashing forward their horses. Two black-tailed deer bounded away among the rocks; Raymond shot at them from horseback; the sharp report of his rifle was answered by another equally sharp from the opposing cliffs, and then the echoes, leaping in rapid succession from side to side, died away rattling far amid the mountains.

After having ridden in this manner for six or eight miles, the appearance of the scene began to change, and all the declivities around us were covered with forests of tall, slender pine trees. The Indians began to fall off to the right and left, and dispersed with their hatchets and knives among these woods, to cut the poles which they had come to seek. Soon I was left almost alone; but in the deep stillness of those lonely mountains, the stroke of hatchets and the sound of voices might be heard from far and near.

Reynal, who imitated the Indians in their habits as well as the worst features of their character, had killed buffalo enough to make a lodge for himself and his squaw, and now he was eager to get the poles necessary to complete it. He asked me to let Raymond go with him and assist in the work. I assented, and the two men immediately entered the thickest part of the wood. Having left my horse in Raymond's keeping, I began to climb the mountain. I was weak and weary and made slow progress, often pausing to rest, but after an hour had elapsed, I gained a height, whence the little valley out of which I had climbed seemed like a deep, dark gulf, though the inaccessible peak of the mountain was still towering to a much greater distance above. Objects familiar from childhood

Here I made a welcome discovery, no other than a bed of strawberries, with their white flowers and their red fruit, close nestled among the grass by the side of the brook, and I sat down by them, hailing them as old acquaintances . . .

surrounded me; crags and rocks, a black and sullen brook that gurgled with a hollow voice deep among the crevices, a wood of mossy distorted trees and prostrate trunks flung down by age and storms, scattered among the rocks, or damming the foaming waters of the little brook. The objects were the same, yet they were thrown into a wilder and more startling scene, for the black crags and the savage trees assumed a grim and threatening aspect, and close across the valley the opposing mountain confronted me, rising from the gulf for thousands of feet, with its bare pinnacles and its ragged covering of pines. Yet the scene was not without its milder features. As I ascended, I found frequent little grassy terraces, and there was one of these close at hand, across which the brook was stealing, beneath the shade of scattered trees that seemed artificially

A hand-colored lithograph of a male and female Rocky Mountain sheep, originally rendered by John James Audubon.

planted. Here I made a welcome discovery, no other than a bed of strawberries, with their white flowers and their red fruit, close nestled among the grass by the side of the brook, and I sat down by them, hailing them as old acquaintances; for among those lonely and perilous mountains they awakened delicious associations of the gardens and peaceful homes of far-distant New England.

Yet wild as they were, these mountains were thickly peopled. As I climbed farther, I found the broad dusty paths made by the elk, as they filed across the mountainside. The grass on all the terraces was trampled down by deer; there were numerous tracks of wolves, and in some of the rougher and more precipitous parts of the ascent, I found foot-prints different from any that I had ever seen, and which I took to be those of the Rocky Mountain sheep. I sat down upon a rock; there was a perfect stillness. No wind was stirring, and not even an insect could be heard. I recollected the danger of becoming lost in such a place, and therefore I fixed my eye upon one of the tallest pinnacles of the opposite mountain. It rose sheer upright from the woods below, and by an extraordinary freak of nature sustained aloft on its very summit a large loose rock. Such a landmark could never be mistaken, and feeling once more secure, I began again to move forward. A white wolf jumped up from among some bushes, and leaped clumsily away; but he stopped for a moment, and turned back his keen eye and his grim bristling muzzle. I longed to take his scalp and carry it back with me, as an appropriate trophy of the Black Hills, but before I could fire, he was gone among the rocks. Soon I heard a rustling sound, with a cracking of twigs at a little distance, and saw moving above the tall bushes the branching antlers of an elk. I was in the midst of a hunter's paradise.

Such are the Black Hills, as I found them in July; but they wear a different garb when winter sets in, when the broad boughs of the fir tree are bent to the ground by the load of snow, and the dark mountains are whitened with it. At that season the mountain-trappers, returned from their autumn expeditions, often build their rude cabins in the midst of these solitudes, and live in abundance and luxury on the game that harbors there. I have heard them relate, how with their tawny mistresses, and perhaps a few young Indian companions, they have spent months in total seclusion. They would dig pitfalls, and set traps for the white wolves, the sables, and the martens, and though through the whole night the awful chorus of the wolves would resound from the frozen mountains around them, yet within their massive walls of logs they would lie in careless ease and comfort before the blazing fire, and in the morning shoot the elk and the deer from their very door.

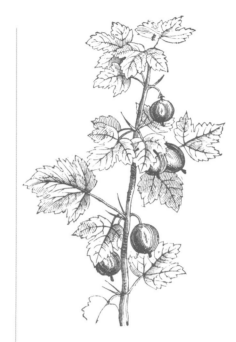

Gooseberrries commonly grow wild on low shrubs. The fruit is a half-inch berry with a unique sweet flavor.

OPPOSITE:
A wagon train raises clouds of dust as it moves through a valley in this 1877 lithograph.

Great Day In the Morning

By Narcissa Whitman

Traveling with Fur Company, nearly 400 animals, mostly mules, and 70 men. Several wagons … I wish I could describe to you how we live so that you can realize it. Our manner of living is far preferable to any in the States. I never was so contented and happy before; neither have I enjoyed such health for years. In the morning as soon as the day breaks the first that we hear is the words, "Arise! Arise!"—then the mules set up such a noise as you never heard, which puts the whole camp in motion. We encamp in a large ring, baggage and men, tents and wagons on the outside, and all the animals except the cows, which are fastened to pickets, within the circle.

This arrangement is to accommodate the guard, who stand regularly every night and day, also when we are in motion, to protect our animals from the approach of Indians, who would steal them. As I said, the mules' noise brings every man on his feet to loose them and turn them out to feed.

Tell mother I am a very good housekeeper on the prairie. I wish she could just take a peep at us while we are sitting at our meals. Our table is the ground, our table-cloth is an India-rubber cloth used when it rains as a cloak; our dishes are made of tin-basins for teacups, iron spoons and plates, each of us, and several pans for milk and to put our meat in when we

wish to set it on the table. Each one carries his own knife in his scabbard, and it is always ready to use … While the Fur Company has felt the want of food, our milk has been of great service to us; but it was considerable work for us to supply ten persons with bread three times a day. We are done using it now. What little flour we have left we shall preserve for thickening our broth, which is excellent. I never saw any thing like buffalo meat to satisfy hunger. We do not want any thing else with it. I have eaten three meals of it and it relishes well. Supper and breakfast we eat in our tent. We do not pitch it at noon. Have worship after supper and breakfast …

Passage
of the
Mountains

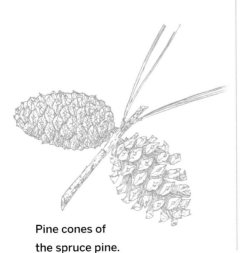

Pine cones of
the spruce pine.

When I took leave of Shaw at La Bonte's Camp, I promised that I would meet him at Fort Laramie on the 1st of August. That day, according to my reckoning, was now close at hand. It was impossible, at best, to fulfill my engagement exactly, and my meeting with him must have been postponed until many days after the appointed time, had not the plans of the Indians very well coincided with my own. They too, intended to pass the mountains and move toward the fort. To do so at this point was impossible, because there was no opening; and in order to find a passage we were obliged to go twelve or fourteen miles southward. Late in the afternoon the camp got in motion, defiling back through the mountains along the same narrow passage by which they had entered. I rode in company with three or four young Indians at the rear, and the moving swarm stretched before me, in the ruddy light of sunset, or in the deep shadow of the mountains far beyond my sight. It was an ill-omened spot they chose to encamp upon. When they were there just a year before, a war party of ten men, led by The Whirlwind's son, had gone out against the enemy, and not one had ever returned. This was the immediate cause of this season's warlike preparations. I was not a little astonished when I came to the camp, at the confusion of horrible sounds with which it was filled; howls, shrieks, and wailings were heard from all the women present, many of whom not content with this exhibition of grief for the loss of their friends and relatives, were gashing their legs deeply with knives. A warrior in the village, who had lost a brother in the expedition; chose another mode of displaying his sorrow. The Indians, who, though often rapacious, are utterly devoid of avarice, are accustomed in times of mourning, or on other solemn occasions, to give away the whole of their possessions, and reduce themselves to nakedness and want. The warrior in question led his two best horses into the center of the village, and gave them away to his friends; upon which songs and acclamations in praise of his generosity mingled with the cries of the women.

"Indian Hunt, 1894," watercolor by Charles M. Russell.

On the next morning we entered once more among the mountains. There was nothing in their appearance either grand or picturesque, though they were desolate to the last degree, being mere piles of black and broken rocks, without trees or vegetation of any kind. As we passed among them along a wide valley, I noticed Raymond riding by the side of a younger squaw, to whom he was addressing various insinuating compliments. All the old squaws in the neighborhood watched his proceedings in great admiration, and the girl herself would turn aside her head and laugh. Just then the old mule thought proper to display her vicious pranks; she began to rear and plunge most furiously. Raymond was an excellent rider, and at first he stuck fast in his seat; but the moment after, I saw the mule's hind-legs flourishing in the air, and my unlucky follower pitching head foremost over her ears. There was a burst of screams and laughter from all the women, in which his mistress herself took part, and Raymond was instantly assailed by such a shower of witticisms, that he was glad to ride forward out of hearing.

Not long after, as I rode near him, I heard him shouting to me. He was pointing toward a detached rocky hill that stood in the middle of the valley before us, and from behind it a long file of elk came out at full speed and entered an opening in the side of the mountain. They had scarcely disappeared when whoops and exclamations came from fifty voices around me. The young men leaped from their horses, flung down their heavy buffalo robes, and ran at full speed toward the foot of the nearest mountain. Reynal also broke away at a gallop in the same direction, "Come on! come on!" he called to us. "Do you see that band of bighorn up yonder? If there's one of them, there's a hundred!"

In fact, near the summit of the mountain, I could see a large number of small white objects, moving rapidly upward among the precipices, while others were filing along its rocky profile. Anxious to see the sport, I galloped forward, and entering a passage in the side of the mountain, ascended the loose rocks as far as my horse could carry me. Here I fastened her to an old pine tree that stood alone, scorching in the sun. At that moment Raymond called to me from the right that another band of sheep was close at hand in that direction. I ran up to the top of the opening, which gave me a full view into the rocky gorge beyond; and here I plainly saw some fifty or sixty sheep, almost within rifle-shot, clattering upward among the rocks, and endeavoring, after their usual custom, to reach the highest point. The naked Indians bounded up lightly in pursuit. In a moment the game and hunters disappeared. Nothing could be seen or heard but the occasional report of a gun, more and more distant, reverberating among the rocks.

I turned to descend, and as I did so I could see the valley below alive with Indians passing rapidly through it, on horseback and on foot. A little farther on, all were stopping as they came up; the camp was preparing, and the lodges rising. I descended to this spot, and soon after Reynal and Raymond returned. They bore between them a sheep which they had pelted to death with stones from the edge of a ravine, along the bottom of which it was attempting to escape. One by one the hunters came dropping in; yet such is the activity of the Rocky Mountain sheep that, although sixty or seventy men were out in pursuit, not more than half a dozen animals were killed. Of these only one was a full-grown male. He had a pair of horns twisted like a ram's, the dimensions of which were almost beyond belief. I have seen among the Indians ladles with long handles, capable of containing more than a quart, cut from such horns.

There is something peculiarly interesting in the character and habits of the mountain sheep, whose chosen retreats are above the region of vegetation and storms, and who leap among the giddy precipices of their aerial home as actively as the antelope skims over the prairies below.

Through the whole of the next morning we were moving forward, among the hills. On the following day the heights gathered around us, and the passage of the mountains began in earnest. Before the village left its camping ground, I set forward in company with the Eagle-Feather, a man of powerful frame, but of bad and sinister face. His son, a light-limbed boy, rode with us, and another Indian, named the Panther, was also of the party. Leaving the village out of sight behind us, we rode together up a rocky defile. After a while, however, the Eagle-Feather discovered in the distance some appearance of game, and set off with his son in pursuit of it, while I went forward with the Panther. This was a mere *nom de guerre*; for, like many Indians, he concealed his real name out of some superstitious notion. He was a very noble looking fellow. As he suffered his ornamented buffalo robe to fall into folds about his loins, his stately and graceful figure was fully displayed; and while he sat his horse in an easy attitude, the long feathers of the prairie cock fluttering from the crown of his head, he seemed the very model of a wild prairie-rider. He had not the same features as those of other Indians. Unless his handsome face greatly belied him, he was free from the jealousy, suspicion, and malignant cunning of his people. For the most part, a civilized white man can discover but very few points of sympathy between his own nature and that of an Indian. With every disposition to do justice to their good qualities, he must be conscious that an impassable gulf lies between him and his red brethren of the prairie. Nay, so alien to himself do they appear that, having breathed for a few months or a few weeks the air of this region, he begins to look upon them as a troublesome and dangerous species of wild beast, and, if expedient, he could shoot them with as little compunction as they themselves would experience after performing the same office upon him. Yet, in the countenance of the Panther, I gladly read that there were at least some points of sympathy between him and me. We were excellent friends, and as we rode forward together through rocky passages, deep dells, and little barren plains, he occupied himself very zealously in teaching me the Dakota language. After a while, we came to a little grassy recess, where some gooseberry bushes were growing at the foot of a rock; and these offered such

temptation to my companion, that he gave over his instruction, and stopped so long to gather the fruit that before we were in motion again the van of the village came in view. An old woman appeared, leading down her pack horse among the rocks above. Savage after savage followed, and the little dell was soon crowded with the throng.

That morning's march was one not easily to be forgotten. It led us through a sublime waste, a wilderness of mountains and pine forests, over which the spirit of loneliness and silence seemed brooding. Above and below little could be seen but the same dark green foliage. It overspread the valleys, and the mountains were clothed with it from the black rocks that crowned their summits to the impetuous streams that circled round their base. Scenery like this, it might seem, could have no very cheering effect on the mind of a sick man (for to-day my disease had again assailed me) in the midst of a horde of savages; but if the reader has ever wandered, with a true hunter's spirit, among the forests of Maine, or the more picturesque solitudes of the Adirondack Mountains, he will understand how the somber woods and mountains around me might have awakened any other feelings than those of gloom. In truth they recalled gladdening recollections of similar scenes in a distant and far different land. After we had been advancing for several hours through passages always narrow, often obstructed and difficult, I saw at a little distance on our right a narrow opening between two high wooded precipices. All within seemed darkness and mystery. In the mood in which I found myself something strongly impelled me to enter. Passing over the intervening space I guided my horse through the rocky portal, and as I did so instinctively drew the covering from my rifle, half expecting that some unknown evil lay in ambush within those dreary recesses. The place was shut in among tall cliffs, and so deeply shadowed by a host of old pine trees that, though the sun shone bright on the side of the mountain, nothing but a dim twilight could penetrate within. As far as I could see it had no tenants except a few hawks and owls, who, dismayed at my intrusion, flapped hoarsely away among the shaggy branches. I moved forward, determined to explore the mystery to the bottom, and soon became involved among the pines. The genius of the place exercised a strange influence upon my mind. Its faculties were stimulated into extraordinary activity, and as I passed along many half-forgotten incidents, and the images of persons and things far distant, rose rapidly before me with surprising distinctness. In that perilous wilderness, eight hundred miles removed beyond the faintest vestige of civilization, the scenes of another hemisphere, the seat of ancient refinement, passed before me more like a succession of vivid paintings than any mere dreams of the fancy. I saw the church of St. Peter's illumined on the evening of Easter Day, the whole majestic pile, from the cross to the foundation stone, penciled in fire and shedding a radiance, like the serene light of the moon, on the sea of upturned faces below. I saw the peak of Mount Etna towering above its inky mantle of clouds and lightly curling its wreaths of milk-white smoke against the soft sky flushed with the Sicilian sunset. I saw also the gloomy vaulted passages and the

"Storm on Laramie Peak," an oil painting by Albert Bierstadt.

narrow cells of the Passionist convent where I once had sojourned for a few days with the fanatical monks, its pale, stern inmates in their robes of black, and the grated window from whence I could look out, a forbidden indulgence, upon the melancholy Coliseum and the crumbling ruins of the Eternal City. The mighty glaciers of the Splugen too rose before me, gleaming in the sun like polished silver, and those terrible solitudes, the birthplace of the Rhine, where bursting from the bowels of its native mountains, it lashes and foams down the rocky abyss into the little valley of Andeer. These recollections, and many more, crowded upon me, until remembering that it was hardly wise to remain long in such a place, I mounted again and retraced my steps. Issuing from between the rocks I saw a few rods before me the men, women, and children, dogs and horses, still filing slowly across the little glen. A bare round hill rose directly above them. I rode to the top, and from this point I could look down on the savage procession as it passed just beneath my feet, and far on the left I could see its thin and broken line, visible only at intervals, stretching away for miles among the mountains. On the farthest ridge horsemen were still descending like mere specks in the distance.

I remained on the hill until all had passed, and then, descending, followed after them. A little farther on I found a very small meadow, set deeply among steep mountains; and here the whole village had encamped. The little spot was crowded with the confused and disorderly host. Some of the lodges were already completely prepared, or the squaws perhaps were busy in drawing the heavy coverings of skin over the bare poles. Others were as yet mere skeletons, while others still—poles, covering, and all— lay scattered in complete disorder on the ground among buffalo robes, bales of meat, domestic utensils, harness, and weapons. Squaws were screaming to one another, horses rearing and plunging, dogs yelping, eager to be disburdened of their loads, while the fluttering of feathers and the gleam of barbaric ornaments added liveliness to the scene. The small children ran about amid the crowd, while many of the boys were scrambling among the overhanging rocks, and standing, with their little bows in their hands, looking down upon a restless throng. In contrast with the general confusion, a circle of old men and warriors sat in the midst, smoking in profound indifference and tranquillity. The disorder at length subsided. The horses were driven away to feed along the adjacent valley, and the camp assumed an air of listless repose. It was scarcely past noon; a vast white canopy of smoke from a burning forest to the eastward overhung the place, and partially obscured the sun; yet the heat was almost insupportable. The lodges stood crowded together without order in the narrow space. Each was a perfect hothouse, within which the lazy proprietor lay sleeping. The camp was silent as death. Nothing stirred except now and then an old woman passing from lodge to lodge. The girls and young men sat together in groups under the pine trees upon the surrounding heights. The dogs lay panting on the ground, too lazy even to growl at the white man. At the entrance of the meadow there was a cold spring among the rocks, completely overshadowed by tall trees and dense undergrowth. In this cold and shady retreat a number of girls were assembled, sitting together on rocks and fallen logs, discussing the latest gossip of the village, or laughing and throwing water with their hands at the intruding Meneaska. The minutes seemed lengthened into hours. I lay for a long time under a tree, studying the Ogallalla tongue, with the zealous instructions of my friend the Panther. When we were both tired of this I went and lay down by the side of a deep, clear pool formed by the water of the spring. A shoal of little fishes of about a pin's length were playing in it, sporting together, as it seemed, very amicably; but on closer observation, I saw that they were engaged in a cannibal warfare among themselves. Now and then a small one would fall a victim, and immediately disappear down the maw of his voracious conqueror. Every moment, however, the tyrant of the pool, a monster about three inches long, with staring goggle eyes, would slowly issue forth with quivering fins and tail from under the shelving bank. The small fry at this would suspend their hostilities, and scatter in a panic at the appearance of overwhelming force.

"Soft-hearted philanthropists," thought I, "may sigh long for their peaceful millennium; for from minnows up to men, life is an incessant battle."

Evening approached at last, the tall mountain-tops around were still gay and bright in sunshine, while our deep glen was completely shadowed. I left the camp and ascended a neighboring hill, whose rocky summit commanded a wide view over the surrounding wilderness. The sun was still glaring through the stiff pines on the ridge of the western mountain. In a moment he was gone, and as the landscape rapidly darkened, I turned again toward the village. As I descended the hill, the howling of wolves and the barking of foxes came up out of the dim woods from far and near. The camp was glowing with a multitude of fires, and alive with dusky naked figures, whose tall shadows flitted among the surroundings crags.

I found a circle of smokers seated in their usual place; that is, on the ground before the lodge of a certain warrior, who seemed to be generally known for his social qualities. I sat down to smoke a parting pipe with my savage friends. That day was the 1st of August, on which I had promised to meet Shaw at Fort Laramie. The Fort was less than two days' journey distant, and that my friend need not suffer anxiety on my account, I resolved to push forward as rapidly as possible to the place of meeting. I went to look after the Hail-Storm, and having found him, I offered him a handful of hawks'-bells and a paper of vermilion, on condition that he would guide me in the morning through the mountains within sight of Laramie Creek.

The Hail-Storm ejaculated "How!" and accepted the gift. Nothing more was said on either side; the matter was settled, and I lay down to sleep in Kongra-Tonga's lodge.

Long before daylight Raymond shook me by the shoulder.

"Everything is ready," he said.

> Soft-hearted philanthropists," thought I, "may sigh long for their peaceful millennium; for from minnows up to men, life is an incessant battle.

I went out. The morning was chill, damp, and dark; and the whole camp seemed asleep. The Hail-Storm sat on horseback before the lodge, and my mare Pauline and the mule which Raymond rode were picketed near it. We saddled and made our other arrangements for the journey, but before these were completed the camp began to stir, and the lodge-coverings fluttered and rustled as the squaws pulled them down in preparation for departure. Just as the light began to appear we left the ground, passing up through a narrow opening among the rocks which led eastward out of the meadow. Gaining the top of this passage, I turned round and sat looking back upon the camp, dimly visible in the gray light of the morning. All was alive with the bustle of preparation. I turned away, half unwilling to take a final leave of my savage associates. We turned to the right, passing among the rocks and pine trees so dark that for a while we could scarcely see our way. The country in front was wild and broken, half hill, half plain, partly open and partly covered with woods of pine and oak. Barriers of lofty mountains encompassed it; the woods were fresh and cool in the early morning; the peaks of the mountains were wreathed with mist, and sluggish vapors were entangled among the forests upon their sides. At length the black pinnacle of the tallest mountain was tipped with gold by the rising sun. About that time the Hail-Storm, who rode in front gave a low exclamation. Some large animal leaped up from among the bushes, and an elk, as I thought, his horns thrown back over his neck, darted past us across the open space, and bounded like a mad thing away among the adjoining pines. Raymond was soon out of his saddle, but before he could fire, the animal was full two hundred yards distant. The ball struck its mark, though much too low for mortal effect. The elk, however, wheeled in its flight, and ran at full speed among the trees, nearly at right angles to his former course.

Illustration of a black-tailed deer (mule deer) by John James Audubon, reproduced as a color lithograph, 1895. Audubon painted himself as the hunter, at right.

I fired and broke his shoulder; still he moved on, limping down into the neighboring woody hollow, whither the young Indian followed and killed him. When we reached the spot we discovered him to be no elk, but a black-tailed deer, an animal nearly twice the size of the common deer, and quite unknown to the East. We began to cut him up; the reports of the rifles had reached the ears of the Indians, and before our task was finished several of them came to the spot. Leaving the hide of the deer to the Hail-Storm, we hung as much of the meat as we wanted behind our saddles, left the rest to the Indians, and resumed our journey. Meanwhile the village was on its way, and had gone so far that to get in advance of it was impossible. Therefore we directed our course so as to strike its line of march at the nearest point. In a short time, through the dark trunks of the pines, we could see the figures of the Indians as they passed. Once more we were among them. They were moving with even more than their usual precipitation, crowded close together in a narrow pass between rocks and old pine trees. We were on the eastern descent of the mountain, and soon came to a rough and difficult defile, leading down a very steep declivity. The whole swarm poured down together, filling the rocky passageway like some turbulent mountain stream. The mountains before us were on fire, and had been so for weeks. The view in front was obscured by a vast dim sea of smoke and vapor, while on either hand the tall cliffs, bearing aloft their crest of pines, thrust their heads boldly through it, and the sharp pinnacles and broken ridges of the mountains beyond them were faintly traceable as through a veil. The scene in itself was most grand and imposing, but with the savage multitude, the armed warriors, the naked children, the gayly appareled girls, pouring impetuously down the heights, it would have formed a noble subject for a painter, and only the pen of a Scott could have done it justice in description.

We passed over a burnt tract where the ground was hot beneath the horses' feet, and between the blazing sides of two mountains. Before long we had descended to a softer region, where we found a succession of little valleys watered by a stream, along the borders of which grew abundance of wild gooseberries and currants, and the children and many of the men straggled from the line of march to gather them as we passed along. Descending still farther, the view changed rapidly. The burning mountains were behind us, and through the open valleys in front we could see the ocean-like prairie, stretching beyond the sight. After passing through a line of trees that skirted the brook, the Indians filed out upon the plains. I was thirsty and knelt down by the little stream to drink. As I mounted again I very carelessly left my rifle among the grass, and my thoughts being otherwise absorbed, I rode for some distance before discovering its absence. As the reader may conceive, I lost no time in turning about and galloping back in search of it. Passing the line of Indians, I watched every warrior as he rode by me at a canter, and at length discovered my rifle in the hands of one of them, who, on my approaching to claim it, immediately

The Snake River Canyon in Idaho, photographed by Timothy O'Sullivan in 1874.

gave it up. Having no other means of acknowledging the obligation, I took off one of my spurs and gave it to him. He was greatly delighted, looking upon it as a distinguished mark of favor, and immediately held out his foot for me to buckle it on. As soon as I had done so, he struck it with force into the side of his horse, who gave a violent leap. The Indian laughed and spurred harder than before. At this the horse shot away like an arrow, amid the screams and laughter of the squaws, and the ejaculations of the men, who exclaimed: "Washtay!—Good!" at the potent effect of my gift. The Indian had no saddle, and nothing in place of a bridle except a leather string tied round the horse's jaw. The animal was of course wholly uncontrollable, and stretched away at full speed over the prairie, till he and his rider vanished behind a distant swell. I never saw the man again, but I presume no harm came to him. An Indian on horseback has more lives than a cat.

The village encamped on a scorching prairie, close to the foot of the mountains. The heat was most intense and penetrating. The coverings of the lodges were raised a foot or

"Sioux Camp Near Fort Laramie," a color engraving from 1884.

The animal was of course wholly uncontrollable, and stretched away at full speed over the prairie, till he and his rider vanished behind a distant swell. I never saw the man again, but I presume no harm came to him. An Indian on horseback has more lives than a cat.

more from the ground, in order to procure some circulation of air; and Reynal thought proper to lay aside his trapper's dress of buckskin and assume the very scanty costume of an Indian. Thus elegantly attired, he stretched himself in his lodge on a buffalo robe, alternately cursing the heat and puffing at the pipe which he and I passed between us. There was present also a select circle of Indian friends and relatives. A small boiled puppy was served up as a parting feast, to which was added, by way of dessert, a wooden bowl of gooseberries, from the mountains.

"Look there," said Reynal, pointing out of the opening of his lodge; "do you see that line of buttes about fifteen miles off? Well, now, do you see that farthest one, with the white speck on the face of it? Do you think you ever saw it before?"

"It looks to me," said I, "like the hill that we were camped under when we were on Laramie Creek, six or eight weeks ago."

"You've hit it," answered Reynal.

"Go and bring in the animals, Raymond," said I: "we'll camp there to-night, and start for the Fort in the morning."

The mare and the mule were soon before the lodge. We saddled them, and in the meantime a number of Indians collected about us. The virtues of Pauline, my strong, fleet, and hardy little mare, were well known in camp, and several of the visitors were mounted upon good horses which they had brought me as presents. I promptly declined their offers, since accepting them would have involved the necessity of transferring poor Pauline into their barbarous hands. We took leave of Reynal, but not of the Indians, who are accustomed to dispense with such superfluous ceremonies. Leaving the camp we rode straight over the prairie toward the white-faced bluff, whose pale ridges swelled gently against the horizon, like a cloud. An Indian went with us, whose name I forget, though the ugliness of his face and the width of his mouth dwell vividly in my recollection. The antelope were numerous, but we did not heed them. We rode directly toward our destination, over the arid plains and barren hills, until, late in the afternoon, half spent with heat, thirst, and fatigue, we saw a gladdening sight; the long line of trees and the deep gulf that mark the course of Laramie Creek. Passing through the growth of huge dilapidated old cottonwood trees that bordered the creek, we rode across to the other side.

The rapid and foaming waters were filled with fish splashing in the shallows. As we gained the farther bank, our horses turned eagerly to drink, and we, kneeling on the sand, followed their example. We had not gone far before the scene began to grow familiar.

"We are getting near home, Raymond," said I.

There stood the Big Tree under which we had encamped so long; there were the white cliffs that used to look down upon our tent when it stood at the bend of the creek; there was the meadow in which our horses had grazed for weeks, and a little farther on, the prairie-dog village where I had beguiled many a languid hour in persecuting the unfortunate inhabitants.

"We are going to catch it now," said Raymond, turning his broad, vacant face up toward the sky.

In truth, the landscape, the cliffs and the meadow, the stream and the groves were darkening fast. Black masses of cloud were swelling up in the south, and the thunder was growling ominously.

"We will camp here," I said, pointing to a dense grove of trees lower down the stream. Raymond and I turned toward it, but the Indian stopped and called earnestly after us. When we demanded what was the matter, he said that the ghosts of two warriors were always among those trees, and that if we slept there, they would scream and throw stones at us all night, and perhaps steal our horses before morning. Thinking it as well to humor him, we left behind us the haunt of these extraordinary ghosts, and passed on toward Chugwater, riding at full gallop, for the big drops began to patter down. Soon we came in sight of the poplar saplings that grew about the mouth of the little stream. We leaped to the ground, threw off our saddles, turned our horses loose, and drawing our knives, began to slash among the bushes to cut twigs and branches for making a shelter against the rain. Bending down the taller saplings as they grew, we piled the young

Laramie Plains, Wyoming, in an engraving from the American School, 1872.

shoots upon them; and thus made a convenient penthouse, but all our labor was useless. The storm scarcely touched us. Half a mile on our right the rain was pouring down like a cataract, and the thunder roared over the prairie like a battery of cannon; while we by good fortune received only a few heavy drops from the skirt of the passing cloud. The weather cleared and the sun set gloriously. Sitting close under our leafy canopy, we proceeded to discuss a substantial meal of wasna which Weah-Washtay had given me. The Indian had brought with him his pipe and a bag of shongsasha; so before lying down to sleep, we sat for some time smoking together. Previously, however, our wide-mouthed friend had taken the precaution of carefully examining the neighborhood. He reported that eight men, counting them on his fingers, had been encamped there not long before. Bisonette, Paul Dorion, Antoine Le Rouge, Richardson, and four others, whose names he could not tell. All this proved strictly correct. By what instinct he had arrived at such accurate conclusions, I am utterly at a loss to divine.

It was still quite dark when I awoke and called Raymond. The Indian was already gone, having chosen to go on before us to the Fort. Setting out after him, we rode for some time in complete darkness, and when the sun at length rose, glowing like a fiery ball of copper, we were ten miles distant from the Fort. At length, from the broken summit of a tall sandy bluff we could see Fort Laramie, miles before us, standing by the side of the stream like a little gray speck in the midst of the bounding desolation. I stopped my horse, and sat for a moment looking down upon it. It seemed to me the very center of comfort and civilization. We were not long in approaching it, for we rode at speed the greater part of the way. Laramie Creek still intervened between us and the friendly walls. Entering the water at the point where we had struck upon the bank, we raised our feet to the saddle behind us, and thus, kneeling as it were on horseback, passed dry-shod through the swift current. As we rode up the bank, a number of men appeared in the gateway. Three of them came forward to meet us. In a moment I distinguished Shaw; Henry Chatillon followed with his face of manly simplicity and frankness, and Delorier came last, with a broad grin of welcome. The meeting was not on either side one of mere ceremony. For my own part, the change was a most agreeable one from the society of savages and men little better than savages, to that of my gallant and high-minded companion and our noble-hearted guide. My appearance was equally gratifying to Shaw, who was beginning to entertain some very uncomfortable surmises concerning me.

Bordeaux greeted me very cordially, and shouted to the cook. This functionary was a new acquisition, having lately come from Fort Pierre with the trading wagons. Whatever skill he might have boasted, he had not the most promising materials to exercise it upon. He set before me, however, a breakfast of biscuit, coffee, and salt pork. It seemed like a new phase of existence, to be seated once more on a bench, with a knife and fork, a plate and teacup, and something resembling a table before me. The coffee seemed delicious, and the bread was a most welcome novelty, since for three weeks I had eaten scarcely anything but meat, and that for the most part without salt. The meal also had the relish of good company, for opposite to me sat Shaw in elegant dishabille. If one is anxious thoroughly to appreciate the value of a congenial companion, he has only to spend a few weeks by himself in an Ogallalla village. And if he can contrive to add to his seclusion a debilitating and somewhat critical illness, his perceptions upon this subject will be rendered considerably more vivid.

Shaw had been upward of two weeks at the Fort. I found him established in his old quarters, a large apartment usually occupied by the absent bourgeois. In one corner was a soft and luxuriant pile of excellent buffalo robes, and here I lay down. Shaw brought me three books.

"Here," said he, "is your Shakespeare and Byron, and here is the Old Testament, which has as much poetry in it as the other two put together."

I chose the worst of the three, and for the greater part of that day lay on the buffalo robes, fairly reveling in the creations of that resplendent genius which has achieved no more signal triumph than that of half beguiling us to forget the pitiful and unmanly character of its possessor.

We leave Francis Parkman here, on his way home via the Sante Fe Trail. The remaining chapters describe the journey back to the settlements, south along the Front Range of the Rockies, first to a building called the Pueblo and then to Bent's Fort, another trading post, nearby. The route is difficult but the trek largely uneventful. There is much killing of rattlesnakes, in which the area abounds. They just miss encountering bands of Arapahoes, pass by Pike's Peak when it is wrapped in the glory of a thunderstorm, the mountain showing itself in glimpses. At Bent's Fort, for safety's sake, they take on several companions for the ride east on the Santa Fe Trail. Along the way they cross paths with a large band of Arapahoes, a group Parkman compares unfavorably with the Sioux. Parkman, his companion, Shaw, and their guide, Henry Chatillon, walk into their camp with gifts, sweet-talk them, and walk out unharmed.

The plains, the mountains, and the buffalo all seemed fresh and boundless in 1846. Now we cross this amazing landscape in a few hours at 35,000 feet. We must thank Parkman for bringing it to us when it was unspoiled, and for doing it so vividly.

FOLLOWING SPREAD:
"Buffalo Trail: The Impending Storm, 1869," also known as "The Last of the Buffalo." Painting by Albert Bierstadt.

"A View on the Columbia River, 1871," an oil painting by Norton Bush.

The End of the Trail

By Ezra Meeker

As we went floating down that wonderful old [Columbia] river, the deep depression of spirits that, for lack of a better name, we call "the blues," seized upon us. Do you wonder why? We were like an army that had burned the bridges behind it. We had scant knowledge of what lay in the track before us. Here we were, more than two thousand miles from home— separated from it by a trackless, uninhabited waste of country. It was impossible for us to retrace our steps. Go ahead we must.

Then, too, we had for months borne the burden of duties that could not be avoided or delayed, until many were on the verge of collapse from strain and overwork. Some were sick, and all were reduced in flesh from the urgent toil at camp duty and from lack of variety of food. Such was the condition of the motley crowd of sixty persons as we slowly neared that wonderful channel through which the great Columbia flows while passing the Cascade range.

For myself, I can truly say that the journey had not drawn on my vitality as it had with so many. True, I had been worked down in flesh … but what weight I had left was the bone and sinew of my system …

In the company was a young couple who excited great sympathy. The husband was so ill that it was plain to be seen he would soon complete the journey to the unknown. All were full of solicitude for these young people, and with a thought to cheer them, the women began in sweet, subdued tones to sing "Home, Sweet Home." Others joined in the song. As the echo died away, at the moment of gliding under the shadow of the high mountain, the second verse was begun, but it was never finished. If an electric shock had struck the entire party, it could not have had a more simultaneous effect than had this line: *O give me my lowly thatched cottage again!*

Instead of song, sobs and outcries of grief burst from all lips. A tumult of sorrow mingled with prayer poured forth without restraint. The rough boatmen rested upon their oars in awe, and gave way in sympathy with the scene before them. No eyes were left dry; there was no aching heart but was relieved. Like the downpour of a summer shower that suddenly clears the atmosphere, this sudden outburst of grief cleared away the despondency. It was succeeded by a feeling of buoyancy and hopefulness. The tears were not dried till mirth took possession. This really hysterical manifestation on the part of the whole company ended all depression for the rest of the trip.

Index

CREDITS

Page 2: J.H. Colton/Library of Congress; **Pages 4-5:** Daniel A. Jenks/Library of Congress; **Pages 6-7:** Thomas Worthington Whittredge/Private Collection/Photo © Christie's Images/Bridgeman Images; **Page 9:** Charles Haight Farnham, A Life of Francis Parkman. Boston: Little, Brown and Co, 1901; **Page 11:** Private Collection/Peter Newark American Pictures/Bridgeman Images; **Pages 12-13:** Daniel A. Jenks/Library of Congress; **Page 14:** Heritage Auctions, Dallas; Pages 16-17: Hagen & Pfau/Anzeiger des Westens/Library of Congress; **Pages 18-19:** Private Collection/Peter Newark American Pictures/Bridgeman Images; **Page 21:** Library of Congress; **Pages 22-23:** William Henry Jackson/Scotts Bluff National Monument, SCBL_275; **Page 24:** Albert Bierstadt/Private Collection/Photo © Christie's Images/Bridgeman Images; **Page 25:** S. G. Goodrich, Illustrated Natural History of the Animal Kingdom, Vol II. Derby, Jackson, New York, 1859; **Pages 26-27:** Daniel A. Jenks/Library of Congress; **Page 29:** John Carbutt/Library of Congress; **Pages 30-31:** Buffalo Bill Center of the West/The Art Archive at Art Resource, NY; **Page 33:** John James Audubon/Heritage Auctions, Dallas; **Page 34:** N.C. Wyeth, Courtesy of the Wells Fargo History Museum, Phoenix, Arizona; **Page 36:** Sherwood T. Grissom/Library of Congress; **Page 37:** Daniel A. Jenks/Library of Congress; **Pages 38-39:** George A. Croufutt/

Library of Congress; **Page 40:** L. Brent Vaughan Hill, Practical Reference Library, Volume II. NewYork, NY: Dixon, Hanson and Company, 1906; **Pages 42-43:** Edward S. Curtis/Library of Congress; **Page 45:** Denver Public Library, X-21915; **Pages 46-47:** Private Collection/Peter Newark American Pictures/Bridgeman Images; **Pages 48-49:** Alfred Jacob Miller/© Walters Art Museum, Baltimore/Bridgeman Images; **Pages 50-51:** Joseph Goldsborough Bruff/Huntington Digital Library, mssHM8044; **Page 53:** Encyclopaedia Britannica/UIG/Bridgeman Images; **Page 54:** Top: Robert Buck Dunton/Heritage Auctions, Dallas; Bottom: H. Alleyne Nicholson, An Introductory Text-book of Zoology, Edinburgh:William Blackwood and Sons, 1971; **Page 57:** Frances Flora Bond Palmer/Yale University Art Gallery, 1946.9.1361; **Pages 58-59:** Daniel A. Jenks/Library of Congress; **Pages 60-61:** William Henry Jackson/Scotts Bluff National Monument, SCBL_43; **Pages 62-63:** Asahel Curtis/University of Washington Libraries, Special Collections, A. Curtis 59418; **Page 65:** Harper's Weekly/Library of Congress; **Pages 66-67:** Edmund Montague Morris/Art Gallery of Ontario, Toronto, Canada/Gift of Ontario College of Art, 1932/Bridgeman Images; **Page 69:** William Henry Jackson/Denver Public Library Western Art Collection, WHJ-10622; **Pages 70-71:** Daniel A. Jenks/Library of Congress; **Pages 72-73:** Karl Bodmer/

Library of Congress; **Page 74:** Werner Forman Archive/Bridgeman Images; **Page 75:** Private Collection/ © Look and Learn/Elgar Collection/Bridgeman Images; **Page 76:** Charles Leonard-Stuart and George J. Hagar, Everybody's Cyclopedia: A Concise and Accurate Compilation of the World's Knowledge, New York: Syndicate Pub. Co, 1912; **Pages 78-79:** Albert Bierstadt/Private Collection/Bridgeman Images; **Page 80:** Harper's Weekly, December 12, 1874; **Pages 82-83:** Daniel A. Jenks/Library of Congress; **Pages 84-85:** Detroit Publishing Company/Library of Congress; **Page 87:** Engraved by Stephane Pannemaker after Eugene Antoine Samuel Lavieille/Private Collection/Ken Welsh/Bridgeman Images; **Page 88:** George Nicholson, The Illustrated Dictionary of Gardening, Div. VI, London, England: L. Upcott Gill, 1884; **Page 89:** Louis Agassiz Fuertes/National Geographic Creative/Bridgeman Images; **Page 91:** David Henry Montgomery, The Beginner's American History, Boston, MA: Ginn & Company, 1899; **Pages 92-93:** Daniel A. Jenks/Library of Congress; **Pages 94-95:** Covered Wagons by N. C. Wyeth, Egg tempera on a gesso board, 26$_{1/8}$ x 24$_{1/2}$ inches, Iowa State University Art Collection, University Museums, Gift of John Morrell Company; **Page 97:** Tallandier/Bridgeman Images; **Page 98:** Joseph Goldsborough Bruff/The Huntington Library,